Instant Pot Cookbook #2019

550 Effortless Recipes

For Beginner & Advanced Users

Carolina Sanders

Copyright © 2018 by Carolina Sanders

All rights reserved worldwide.

ISBN: 978-1791733025

No part of this book may be reproduced or transmitted in any form or by any means, electronic or mechanical, including photocopying, recording or by any information storage and retrieval system, without written permission from the publisher, except for the inclusion of brief quotations in a review.

Warning-Disclaimer

The purpose of this book is to educate and entertain. The author or publisher does not guarantee that anyone following the techniques, suggestions, tips, ideas, or strategies will become successful. The author and publisher shall have neither liability or responsibility to anyone with respect to any loss or damage caused, or alleged to be caused, directly or indirectly by the information contained in this book.

Contents

Introduction

What is an Instant Pot Pressure Cooker?

Meat Recipes

- Holiday Sweet Spare Ribs 19
- Shredded Pork in Sweet BBQ Sauce 19
- Apple Pork Ribs 19
- Pork & Cabbage Soup with Veggies 20
- Brussel Sprout Pork Chops with Onions 20
- Orange & Cinnamon Pork 20
- Rutabaga & Apple Pork 21
- Pineapple Pork Loin 21
- Beans and Pancetta Kale and Chickpeas 22
- Pork Roast with Mushrooms in Beer Sauce 22
- Chili Pork Meatloaf 22
- Ground Pork with Cabbage and Veggies 23
- Pork Butt with Mushrooms and Celery 23
- Tangy Pork in Tomato Sour Cream Sauce 23
- Pork Chops with Brussel Sprouts 24
- Ground Pork and Sauerkraut 24
- Pork with Rutabaga and Granny Smith Apples 24
- Pork Meatballs with Apple Sauce 25
- Pork Cutlets with Baby Carrots 25
- Herby Pork Butt and Yams 25
- Sunday Night Pork Meatloaf 26
- Short Ribs with Red Wine Gravy 26
- Spicy Ground Pork 27
- Pork Steaks with Apple and Prunes 27
- Pork and Green Onion Frittata 27
- Pork Sausage with Bell Peppers and Sweet Onions 28
- Rosemary Dijon-Apple Pork 28
- Gourmet Bacon, Potato, and Endive Casserole 28
- Smothered Cinnamon BBQ Ribs 29
- Braised Red Cabbage and Bacon 29
- Pork Chops in Merlot 29
- BBQ Pork Butt 30
- Pork Chops and Mushrooms in Tomato Sauce 30
- Apple and Cherry Pork Tenderloin 30
- Dinner Pork Roast 31
- Pork Sausage with Cauliflower and Tater Tots 31
- Marinated Flank Steak 31
- Onion & Beef Steaks in Gravy 32
- Pork Chops with Apple Cider 32
- BBQ Pork Rib Chops with Root Vegetables 32
- Braised Chili Pork Chops 33
- Tamari Sauce Pork Belly with Garlic 33
- Pork Fillets with Worcestershire Sauce 33
- Fast Onion-Flavoured Pork Ribs 34

Short Ribs with Mango Sauce	34
Pork Loin Chops with Sauerkraut	34
Pork Ribs in Walnut Sauce	35
Beef Cabbage Rolls	35
Italian Sausage over Muffins	35
Chuck Roast with Potatoes	36
Delicious Pork Shoulder with White Cabbage	36
Pork with Tangy Tomato Sauce	36
Cheesy Rigatoni with Pancetta	37
Ground Beef and Sauerkraut	37
Beef Ribs with ButtonCitrusy Beef	37
Beef Ribs with Mushrooms	38
Beef Medley with Blue Cheese	38
Mustard Rump Roast with Potatoes	38
Steak and Veggies with Ale Sauce	39
Beef with Creamy Sour Sauce	39
Corned Beef with Celery Sauce	39
Beer-Dijon Braised Steak	40
Tender Onion Beef Roast	40
Beef Stew with Quinoa	40
Mexican Brisket	41
Sweet Balsamic Beef	41
Tomato Meatballs	41
Bourbon and Apricot Meatloaf	42
Spicy Shredded Beef	42
Beef Sausage and Spinach Stew	42
Sloppy Joes	43
Savory Fettuccine with Beef Sausage	43
Simple Cheesy Meatballs	44
No-Fuss Beef Chuck Roast	44
Traditional Beef Ragu	44
Short Ribs with Carrots and Potatoes	45
Lamb Shanks Braised Under Pressure	45
Herbed Beef & Yams	46
Beef Pot Roast with Carrots	46
Worcestershire Pork Chops	46
Russet Potatoes Flank Steak	47
Spicy Beef and Pinto Bean Chili	47
Sticky Baby Back Ribs	47
Sloppy Joes and Coleslaw	48
Veggie and Beef Brisket	48
Chuck Roast with Root Vegetables and Herbs	49
Beef Hot Pot	49
Beef and Cheese Taco Pie	49
Beef & Russet Potatoes Soup	50
Fusilli with Beefy Tomato Sauce	50
Ginger-Flavored and Sweet Pork Belly	50
Potted Rump Steak	51
Meatballs in Creamy Sauce	51
Beef with Cabbage, Potatoes, and Carrots	51
Beef Coconut Curry	52
Rib Eye Steak with Vegetables and Herbs	52
Lamb Habanero Chili	52
Pot Roast in Gravy	53

Herbed Lamb Roast with Potatoes 53
Smokey Pork Roast 54
Saucy Beef and Rice 54
Beef and Cabbage with Tomato Sauce 54
Linguine Pasta with Italian Sauce 55
Shredded Beef the Caribbean Way 55
Smoky Beef Brisket Stew 55
Veal Shoulder and Mushrooms 56
Mutton with Potatoes and Tomatoes 56
Lamb Stew with Apricots 56
Port Wine Garlicky Lamb 57

Poultry Recipes

Spicy Rosemary Chicken 58
Creamy Chicken in Beer Sauce 58
Fennel Chicken Breast 58
Black Currant and Lemon Chicken 59
Cajun Chicken and Green Beans 59
Sweet and Gingery Whole Chicken 59
Balsamic Chicken Thighs with Pears 60
Cheesy Drumsticks in Marinara Sauce 60
Delicious BBQ Pulled Turkey 60
Effortless Coq Au Vin 61
Turkey Breasts in Maple and Habanero Sauce 61
Turkey with Tomatoes and Red Beans 61
Orange and Cranberry Turkey Wings 62
Chicken Drumettes in Creamy Tomato Sauce 62
Creamy Chicken with Mushrooms and Carrots 62
Turkey Thighs with Fig Sauce 63
Chicken Thighs with Potatoes and Pesto Sauce 63
Delicious Turkey Meatloaf 63
Thyme and Lemon Drumsticks with Red Sauce 64
Easy and Flavorful Chicken Legs 64
Chicken Stew with Shallots and Carrots 64
Asian-style Sweet Chicken Drumsticks 65
Mexican Cheesy Turkey Breasts 65
Greek-Style Chicken Legs with Herbs 65
Hearty and Hot Turkey Soup 66
Chicken and Beans Casserole with Chorizo 66
Green BBQ Chicken Wings 66
Homemade Cajun Chicken Jambalaya 67
Tasty Turkey with Campanelle and Tomato Sauce 67
Hot and Spicy Shredded Chicken 67
Creamy Turkey Breasts with Mushrooms 68
Hot and Buttery Chicken Wings 68
Simple Pressure Cooked Whole Chicken 68
Chicken Bites Snacks with Chili Sauce 69
Teriyaki Chicken Under Pressure 69
Turkey and Potatoes with Buffalo Sauce 69
Fall-Off-Bone Chicken Drumsticks 70
Salsa and Lime Chicken with Rice 70
Sweet Gingery and Garlicky Chicken Thighs 70
Sweet and Smoked Slow Cooked Turkey 71
Chicken Piccata 71

Cherry Tomato and Basil Chicken Casserole 71
Creamy and Garlicky Chicken 72
Chicken with Mushrooms and Leeks 72
Mexican Chicken 72
Chicken in Roasted Red Pepper Sauce 73
Coconut Chicken with Tomatoes 73
Homemade Whole Chicken 74
Herbed and Garlicky Chicken Wings 74
Duck and Green Pea Soup 74
Sweet Potato & Chicken Curry 75
Chicken with Water Chestnuts 75
Chicken with Red Potatoes & Green Beans 75
Creamy Southern Chicken 76
Easy Chicken Soup 76
Pear and Onion Goose 76
Turkey with Fennel and Celery 77
Stewed Chicken with Kale 77
Lemon-Garlic Chicken with Herby Stuffed 77
Italian-Style Chicken Breasts with Kale Pesto 78
Coconut-Lime Chicken Curry 78
Lemon-Garlic Chicken Thighs 78
Jasmine Rice and Chicken Taco Bowls 79
Hungarian Chicken Thighs in Cherry Tomato Sauce 79
Honey-Ginger Shredded Chicken 80
Tuscany-Style Sun-Dried Tomato Chicken 80
Mediterranean Chicken Meatballs 80
Gorgeous Chicken Fajitas with Guacamole 81
BBQ Sticky Drumettes 81
Feta and Spinach Stuffed Chicken Breasts 82
Herby Balsamic Chicken 82
Buffalo Chicken Chili 83

Side Dish Recipes

Classic Mashed Potatoes 84
Garlic & Herb Potatoes 84
Lime Cabbage with Coconut 84
Turmeric Carrot Mash 85
Simple Steamed Potatoes 85
Creamy Potato and Scallion Salad 85
Cabbage-Onion Side with Pears 86
Cauliflower and Pea Bowl 86
Stewed Yams with Zucchini 86
Potatoes and Green Beans 87
Lemony Rutabaga and Onion Salad 87
Garlicky Sweet Potato Mash 87
Pea and Sweet Potato Bowl 88
Orange Potatoes with Walnuts 88
Paprika Hash Browns 88
Creamy Goat Cheese Cauliflower 89
Garlicky Zucchini and Carrot Noodles 89
Rosemary and Garlic Potatoes 89
Simple Mediterranean Asparagus 90
Orange Broccoli Parmesan 90

Kale and Carrots Side 90
Balsamic Capers Beets 90
Flavorful Bell Peppers 91
Sweet and Mustardy Carrots 91
Zucchini and Cherry Tomato Delight 91
Basil Eggplant Delight 92
Spicy Cauliflower with Peas...92
Spinach with Cottage Cheese 92
Mushroom and Zucchini Platter 93
Cabbage and Pepper Side...93
Gnocchi with Butternut Squash and Tomatoes 93
Frascati and Sage Broccoli 94
Easy Mushroom Pâté 94
Lemony Buckwheat Salad..94
Ricotta Cheese Lasagna with Mushrooms 95
Cajun Potatoes with Brussel Sprouts 95
Turmeric Kale with Shallots 95
Sour Cream Veggies 96
Red Cabbage with Apple 96
Spinach and Tomato Side 96
Smoky Asian-Style Tomato Chutney 97
Vegetable Soup 97
Savoy Cabbage and Beetroot Borscht Soup 97
Hearty Artichokes and Garlic Green Beans 98
Silky Cheese and Cauli Soup 98
Warm Chili Soup 98
Cheesy Soup with Tortillas 99
Power Kale and Chickpea Soup 99
Sicilian Eggplant Delight 100
Miso Sweet Potato Mash 100
Vegetable and Cannellini Beans Pottage 100
Cauliflower Side with Pomegranate and Walnuts 101
Creamy Coconut Squash Soup 101
Creamy Tomato and Basil Soup...101

Vegetarian and Vegan

Mashed Broccoli with Mascarpone..102
Simple Spaghetti Squash with Spinach Dip...102
One-Pot Mushroom and Brown Rice 102
Eggplant and Goat Cheese Homemade Lasagna 103
Sautéed Leafy Greens 103
Celery-Pumpkin Autumn Soup..103
Stuffed Red Peppers with Quinoa and Zucchini...104
Asian-Style Tofu Noddle Soup 104
Hearty Colorful Vegetable Soup 104
Kale and Spinach Cream Soup 105
Spiced Bok Choy Soup with Spiralized Zucchini 105
Fake Mushroom Risotto the Paleo Way 106
Potato Chili 106
White Wine Red Peppers 106
Meatless Shepherd's Pie 107
Mediterranean Steamed Asparagus with Pine Nuts 107
Vegetarian Spaghetti Bolognese 107
Veggie Burger Patties..108

Spicy Moong Beans	108
Sweet Potato and Baby Carrot Medley	108
Tamari Tofu with Sweet Potatoes and Broccoli	109
Tomato Zoodles	109
Leafy Green Risotto	109
Tropical Salsa Mash	110
Roasted Potatoes with Gorgonzola	110
Cheddar and Swiss Chard Relish	110
Cheesy Acorn Squash Relish	111
Pickled Pepperoncini and Parmesan Dip	111
Easy Buttery Corn on the Cob	111
Delicious Eggs de Provence	112
Spicy Tomato Dip	112
Herby Steamed Potatoes	112
Creamy Potato Slices with Chives	113
Sicilian-Style Deviled Eggs	113
Spanish Baked Eggs	113
Hummus Under Pressure	114
Potatoes and Peas Bowl	114
Collard Greens Hummus	114
Saucy BBQ Veggie Meal	115
Vegan Swiss Chard Dip	115
Cheesy Asparagus and Spinach Dip	115
Classic Italian Peperonata	116
Spicy Tomato Sauce	116
Zesty Carrots with Pecans	116
Pressure Cooked Devilled Eggs	117
Lemony and Garlicky Potato and Turnip Dip	117
Easy Street Sweet Corn	117
Cheesy Sour Veggie Casserole	118
Bean and Rice Casserole	118
Vegan Sausage and Pepper Casserole	118
Garlicky and Chili Pomodoro Zoodles	119
Buttery Parsley Corn	119
Eggplant Escalivada Toast	119
Mushroom and Veggie Baguette	120
Root Veggie Casserole	120
Coconut Zucchini Soup	120
Harissa Turnip Stew	121
Pressure Cooked Ratatouille	121
Chipotle Pumpkin Soup	121
Beet Borscht	122
Potato Chili	122
Tofu and Veggie 'Stir Fry'	122
Flavorful Tofu Bowl	123
Veggie Flax Burgers	123
Tempeh Sandwiches	123
Red Lentil Dhal with Butternut Squash	124
Asparagus Dressed in Cheese	124
Spicy Pinto Bean Chili	124
Effortless Cannellini and Black Bean Chili	125
Candied Holiday Yams	125
Walnut & Cinnamon Coconut Potatoes	125
Minty Cauliflower Tabbouleh	126

Navy Beans with Parsley and Garlic 126
Apple and Red Cabbage Vegetarian Dinner 126
Tomato and Kale "Rice" 127
Spicy Cannellini Bean Salad with Dates 127
Potato and Spinach Bowl 127
Pears in Cranberry Sauce 128
Green Minestrone Stew with Parmesan 128
Savory Vegetarian Sandwiches 128
Squash and Sweet Potato Lunch Soup 129
Broccoli and Chickpea Stew 129
Potato & Leek Patties 129
Spicy Tofu Vegan Stew 130
Smoked Tofu Bowl 130
Pearl Barley and Butternut Winter Soup 130
Zucchini Coconut Burgers 131
Chickpea Bell Pepper Soup 131
Basil and Tomato "Pasta" 131
Thyme-Flavored Fries 132
Kale Chips with Garlic and Lime Juice 132
Lime & Mint Zoodles 132
Cabbage, Beet & Apple Stew 132
Blueberry Oatmeal with Walnuts 133
Quick Coconut Moong Dhal 133
Mini Mac and Cheese 133

Beans & Grains Recipes

Kidney Beans with Bacon and Tomatoes 134
Navy Beans with Ground Beef 134
Curried Chickpeas 134
Mixed Bean Italian Sausage Chili 135
Navy Bean Dip 135
Cannellini Beans Chili 135
Ham and Parmesan Grits 136
Black Bean and Mushroom Spread 136
Farmer's Meal 136
Butter Bean and Kale Stew 137
Mushroom and Parmesan Barley 137
Tasty Three-Bean Stew 137
Simple Cornbread 138
Prawns in Moong Dal 138
Herby White Bean and Corn Dip 138
Delicious Yellow Split Lentil Beef Stew 139
Celery and Cheese Chickpea Stew 139
Meatless Lasagna 139
Banana and Fig Millet 140
Parsley Pureed Navy Beans 140
Mexican-Style Black Bean and Avocado Salad 140
Bean and Bacon Dip 141
Apricot and Raisin Oatmeal 141
Cinnamon Bulgur with Pecans 141
Peach Quinoa Pudding 142
Mushroom and Farro Beans 142
Pear and Almond Oatmeal 142
Lemony Oats with Chia Seeds 142

Pearl Barley with Mushrooms 143
Rosemary Goat Cheese Barley 143
Mouth-Watering Lima Beans 143
African Lentil Dip 144
Quinoa Pilaf with Cherries 144
Cheesy Chicken Quinoa 144

Rice & Pasta Recipes

Colorful Risotto 145
Rice Pilaf with Chicken 145
Apple and Apricot Wild Rice 145
Spinach Vermouth Risotto 146
Shrimp Risotto 146
Spring Pearl Barley Salad 146
Fresh Tagliatelle Pasta Bolognese 147
Fennel Jasmine Rice 147
Simple Mushroom Risotto 147
Creamy Coconut Rice Pudding 148
Simple Saucy Jasmine Rice 148
Ziti Pork Meatballs 148
Pizza Pasta 149
Delicious Quinoa Pilaf with Almonds 149
Cheese Tortellini with Broccoli and Turkey 149
Chili and Cheesy Beef Pasta 150
Rice Custard with Hazelnuts 150
Spaghetti with Meatballs 150
Bulgur and Potato Soup 151
Lemony Rice with Veggies 151
Sausage Penne 151
Pineapple and Honey Risotto 152
Buckwheat Breakfast Porridge with Figs 152
Bacon and Cheese Pasta 152
Chicken Enchilada Pasta 153
Noodles with Tuna 153

Soups and Stews

Chicken & Pancetta Noodle Soup 154
Beef Soup with Tacos Topping 154
Ham and Pea Soup 155
Tortellini Minestrone Soup 155
Chicken Enchilada Soup 155
Fall Pumplin and Cauliflower Soup 156
Cream of Broccoli Soup 156
Vegetables and Beef Brisket Stew 156
Smoked Sausage and Seafood Stew 157
Pepperoni and Vegetable Stew 157
Creamy Chicken Stew with Mushrooms & Spinach 158
White Beans and Easy Chicken Chili 158
Spicy Beef Chili with Worcestershire Sauce 158
Chipotle Chile sin Carne 159
Pork Roast Green Chili 159
Mushroom and Beef Stew 160
Pomodoro Soup 160

Skim and Fast Miso and Tofu Soup 160
Navy Bean and Ham Shank Soup 161
Lentil Soup 161
Irish Lamb Stew 161
Pressure Cooked Chili 162
Pumpkin, Corn and Chicken Chowder 162
Spicy Beef and Potato Soup 162
Creamy Curried Cauliflower Soup 163
Spanish-Style Chorizo and Broccoli Soup 163

Fish and Seafood Recipes

Garlicky Mackerel and Vegetables Parcels 164
Sea Bass Stew 164
Power Greens with Lemony Monf Fish 165
Steamed Salmon Filets with Paprika-Lemon Sauce 165
Mediterranean Salmon 165
Alaskan Cod with Fennel and Beans 166
Deliciously Sweet and Spicy Mahi Mahi 166
Party Crab Legs 166
Salmon with Broccoli and Potatoes 167
Veggie Noodle Salmon 167
Crab Cakes 167
Tilapia Chowder 168
Shrimp and Egg Risotto 168
Buttery and Lemony Dill Clams 168
White Wine Steamed Mussels 169
Prawns and Fish Kabobs 169
Almond-Crusted Tilapia 169
Lobster and Gruyere Pasta 170
Clams in White Wine 170
Fancy Shrimp Scampi with Soy Sauce 170
Tuna and Pea Cheesy Noodles 171
Wrapped Fish and Potatoes 171
Lemon Sauce Salmon 171
Creamy Crabmeat 172
Cod in a Tomato Sauce 172
Squid and Peas 172
Glazed Orange Salmon 173
Scallops and Mussels Cauliflower Paella 173

Snacks and Appetizers

Chili Hash Browns 174
Cheese and Prosciutto Eggs 174
Porcini and Sesame Dip 174
Nutty Carrot Sticks 175
Lemony Cippolini Onions 175
Party Duck Bites 175
Pico de Gallo with Carrots 176
Christmas Egg Custard 176
Paprika Potato Slices 176
Buttery Beets 177
Ricotta and Cheddar Veggie Appetizer 177
Appetizer Meatballs 177
Southern Chicken Dip 178

Potato and Bacon Snack 178
Spicy Homemade Peanuts 178
Mini Beefy Cabbage Rolls 179
Buttery Potato Sticks 179
Salmon Bites 179
Agave Carrot Sticks 180
Cheesy Fingerling Potato Rounds 180
Kale Hummus 180
Balsamic Carrots 180
Tahini, Carrot, and Spinach "Hummus" 181
Colby Cheese and Pancetta Frittata 181
Eggs de Provence 181
Pressure Cooked Eggplant Dip 182
Garlicky Pepper and Tomato Appetizer 182
Spicy Sweet Potato Cubes 182
Pea and Avocado Dip 182
Turmeric Potato Sticks 183
Three-Cheese Small Macaroni Cups 183
Turnip and Sultana Dip with Pecans 183
Blue Cheese and Bacon Polenta Squares 184
Barbecue Wings 184
Chili Sriracha Eggs 184
Salty and Peppery Potato Snack 185
Jalapeno and Pineapple Salsa 185

Breakfast & Brunch Recipes

Poached Eggs with Feta and Tomatoes 186
Classic Sunday Big Pancakes 186
Easy Softboiled Eggs 186
Sweet Potato & Carrot Egg Casserole 187
Whole Hog Omelet 187
Onion and Tomato Eggs 187
Cheesy Sausage and Egg Bundt Cake 188
Banana and Cinnamon French Toast 188
Carrot & Pecan Muffins 188
Pear-Coconut Porridge with Walnuts 189
Almond & Gala Apple Porridge 189
Eggs & Smoked Salmon 189
Bell Pepper & Onion Frittata 190
Cheese and Thyme Cremini Oats 190
Kale, Tomato & Carrot Quiche 190
Bacon and Colby Cheese Grits 191
Herby Pork Breakfast Biscuits 191
Cheddar and Eggs Hash Bake 191
Cheesy Eggs in Hollandaise Sauce 192
Egg and Beef Green Casserole 192
Vanilla Quinoa Bowl 192
Crustless Three-Meat Quiche 193
Chorizo and Kale Egg Casserole 193
Cherry and Dark Chocolate Oatmeal 193
Big-Sized Coconut Pancake 194
Crispy Bacon and Egg Burger 194
Zesty and Citrusy French Toast 194
Sweet Potato Tomato Frittata 195
Lemon and Chocolate Bread Pudding 195

Desserts Recipes

Bonfire Lava Cake	196
Strawberry Cottage Cheesecake	196
Tiramisu Cheesecake	197
Chocolate and Banana Squares	197
Coconut Pear Delight	197
Fruity Cheesecake	198
Cinnamon and Lemon Apples	198
Compote with Blueberries and Lemon	198
Full Coconut Cake	199
Very Berry Cream	199
Peanut Butter Bars	199
Milk Dumplings in Sweet Cardamom Sauce	200
Black Currant Poached Peaches	200
Restaurant-Style Crème Brulee	200
Citrus Cheesecake	201
Almond Pear Wedges	201
Creamy Almond and Apple Delight	201
Pressure Cooked Cherry Pie	202
Honeyed Butternut Squash Pie	202
Impossible Oatmeal Chocolate Cookies	202
Easiest Pressure Cooked Raspberry Curd	203
Homemade Chocolate Pudding	203
Tutty Fruity Sauce	203
Chocolate Molten Lava Cake	204
Vanilla and Yogurt Light Cheesecake	204
Buttery Banana Bread	204
Berry-Vanilla Pudding Temptation	205
Peaches with Chocolate Biscuits	205
Hazelnut Chocolate Spread	205
Apricots with Blueberry Sauce	206
Coconut Crème Caramel	206
Hot Milk Chocolate Fondue	206
Delicious Stuffed Apples	207
Homemade Egg Custard	207
Almond Butter Bananas	207
Poached Pears with Orange and Cinnamon	208
Crema Catalana	208
Juicy Apricots with Walnuts and Goat Cheese	208
Apple and Peach Compote	209

Introduction

Hello! Welcome to my book of recipes for the Instant Pot.

My recipes are simply too delicious to keep to myself. And it's the only cookbook you'll need to make the most delicious Instant Pot recipes you've ever tasted!

If there's one kitchen appliance I can't live without, it's my Instant Pot. This gadget has changed my life completely in the kitchen! Gone are the days when I spent hours each week, prepping and then cooking meals. And so many times those meals were tasteless, with leftovers that no one wanted to eat.

Then along came my Instant Pot Pressure Cooker... and now I make delectable meals every day. Quick cooking, tasty recipes - and I have leftovers my family fights and squabbles over! Like the juiciest pork shoulders and spicy rice dishes. In my book, you'll find a collection of mouth watering and flavorsome recipes from every cuisine.

One of the biggest appealing features of the Instant Pot is that it makes fresh and fast homey meals in no time. Whether you're vegetarian or love your meat and chicken, my book has the best recipes for making amazing, healthy meals. And make sure you make an extravagant cheat recipe on those days when you're not counting calories and fat! Those are the best recipes of all.

In this book, I share my favorite recipes with you, and I'll help you get familiar with the Instant Pot, so you know exactly how to use one. Breakfasts, appetizers, Sunday dinners, and delightfully sweet desserts! I have just the recipe for you.

So now, let's learn all about the Instant Pot so you can start cooking!

What is an Instant Pot Pressure Cooker?

Now that you know how much I love my Instant Pot, you'll want to know just what an electric pressure cooker is. The Instant Pot is an appliance that's a combination of pressure cooker, slow cooker, rice cooker, and yogurt maker – all in one handy kitchen device.

What parts makes up the Instant Cooker? There's an outer pot, which is the base and heat source of the pressure cooker. Inside of this outer pot goes the inner pot, which is made from durable stainless steel. This inner pot is where all the cooking happens. There's a lid that goes on top of the inner pot, which has a Silicone ring that seals tightly to keep food, liquids, and pressure securely in the pot.

On top of the lid are the pressure release and the float valve. The pressure release does just that – it releases pressure from inside the Instant Pot. The float valve on the lid pops up when the Instant Pot is pressurized and lowers back down when it's not. You'll know it's safe to open the lid when the float valve is down.

The Instant Pot has a condensation collector on the side of the base unit that can be removed. Its purpose is to collect condensation, usually when the Instant Pot is being used as a slow cooker.

Depending on the model of Instant Pot you have, it may come with some useful accessories – a steaming rack, measuring cup, and a set of spoons.

Not a complex appliance at all, right?

Get to know your brand of Instant Pot by taking a few minutes to read the instruction manual. Even though all electric pressure cookers have pretty much the same functions and settings, every brand comes with some unique features.

BENEFITS OF COOKING WITH THE INSTANT POT

Nutritious meals
Pressure cooking, slow cooking, and steaming foods keep in flavor and nutrients and create delicious and moist dishes. The recipes in my book use all of these functions.

Save time and energy
Using the Instant Pot saves you a lot of time. You can eat healthy at home, without spending the time you don't have, prepping and then cooking your meals. And fast cooking = energy saving. Cooking with your Instant pot is fast and efficient, cutting down your electricity bill by cooking in less time than you would on the stovetop or in the oven.

Pick your size
Most Instant Pots models come in three convenient sizes: 3, 6, and 8-quart. For most families, the 6-quart is the right size. The 3-quart mini Instant Pot is perfect for when you want to cook a small meal or a small amount of pasta or rice. And the 8-quart works for large families, or if you just like to make extra meals for another time. I've included recipes in my book that you can double so you can freeze mouth watering meals for lunches and dinner.

No more mad-rush cooking
How often have you had no time at all to even think about what you're making for dinner? Those days of panic are over. Your Instant Pot is there for you! There are some fast and easy meals included in the recipe book that in just minutes help you get a fantastic dinner on the table.

Hot breakfast!

Tired of waking up to cold cereal as your only breakfast option? Your Instant Pot can make hot oatmeal in minutes. Or make breakfast in your Instant Pot the night before and just heat up in the morning.

Cook perfect rice every time!

Make rice in your electric pressure cooker, and you'll never go back to making it stove-top again. White, brown, or basmati – some people would say the Instant Pot was made for rice.

Even heating

Heat is evenly distributed in the Instant Pot. This means everything is cooked at the same time and is done to the same perfection.

Time your meals

Because of the Instant Pot cooks so fast, use the Delay Start function to time your meals, so they're ready when you get home. Many of my recipes let you prep your food the night before and then put them in the Instant Pot on the timer, cooking them to perfection every time.

The handy "Keep Warm" function

Most Instant Pot models will have a Keep Warm function. When cooking is done, Keep Warm will turn on, so your meal is ready, warm, and waiting for whenever you're ready to sit down and eat.

USING THE INSTANT POT

When you first get your Instant Pot don't be intimidated by all the buttons, functions, and programs. That's what my recipe book is for – to guide you through the steps of using an electric pressure cooker with no confusion. Here are some basic things about your Instant Pot that can make it easy for you to start cooking.

Just what is pressure cooking?

Let's get some of the technical information out of the way so you can get to the good stuff… the recipes! The Instant Pot uses a cooking method that seals ingredients and liquids inside a sealed pot. It uses heat to create steam, which then builds up the pressure in the pot. This steam is released or trapped in the pot to control the amount of pressure. The more pressure there is, the higher the temperature – and the faster food cooks. Sound complex? All you really need to know is that your Instant Pot cooks food fast, fast, fast!

Water test before first use

I know you'll be anxious to find a recipe and start cooking right away but take a few minutes to set up your Instant Pot and do a water pressure test. This is a great way to get familiar with how an electric pressure cooker works. Just pour 2 to 3 cups of water into the Instant Pot. Lock the lid and seal. Choose a setting with a short time or use the Manual button and set for 5 minutes. Then watch the magic happen. The water will first heat until pressure is built up. When high pressure is reached cooking begins, and the time on the Instant Pot will start counting down.

Instant Pot settings

Those buttons may look complicated, with a different button for each different program. Don't worry; it won't take you long to understand which ones to press. To simplify it – depending on your brand of Instant Pot, each button refers to its methods of cooking, such as the Rice function or the Poultry function.

Releasing pressure

Releasing pressure is easy. When you want to lower the temperature, or stop cooking altogether, use either the Natural Release or the Quick Release. The easy way is to use the Natural Release, where you don't do anything at all. When the cooking cycle is complete just wait until the pressure drops on its own before opening the pot. This can take between 10 to 30 minutes depending on the amount of food and liquid in the pot.

Use the Quick Release when you want to release steam quickly to stop cooking, so food isn't overcooked. This method of pressure release is great for foods such as fish and vegetables. To do a quick release turn the valve on the lid of the instant pot from the "sealing" position to "venting".

Cleaning the Instant Pot

Ah... clean up is nice and easy with an electric pressure cooker. For daily cleaning, just wipe the outside of the outer pot and clean the rim as well. I recommend using a soft foam brush for the rim. Clean the inside pot, either by hand ,or you can toss it in the dishwasher with the rest of your dinner dishes. Some of the little parts, such as the pressure release on the lid, can get sticky so remember to wipe them down.

Safety tips

Your Instant Pot is completely safe to use, but as with any kitchen appliance there are a few safety tips to keep in mind:

- **Always** follow instructions for releasing pressure from the pot. For fatty cuts of meat use the Natural Release method to avoid a burn from splattering hot fat.
- **Never** use force to take off the lid.
- **Avoid** using more than ¼ cup of oil or other fat in a recipe.

MY TOP 5 INSTANT POT TIPS AND TRICKS TO MAKE PERFECTLY AMAZING FOOD!

1. The Friendly, Dried Bean

Using canned beans can get pricey if you're using a lot of them in soups and stews. The Instant Pot can cook dried beans in less than an hour, much faster than the 3 to 4 hours it takes to cook them on the stove. Using your electric pressure cooker, you can buy a variety of dried beans and have them on hand to make many of the delicious meals in my cookbook.

2. Creamy, Rich Yogurt

Eat a lot of yogurts? The Instant Pot is perfect for making low fat or creamy, rich yogurt. You'll save a lot of money by making your own. It's much tastier than store bought yogurt! And you can use it in my recipes.

3. Don't Forget the Sauté Function!

An often-over-looked function of your electric pressure cooker is the Sauté Function. Use this setting to brown, sauté, and simmer meat and other ingredients, such as onions. Sautéing gives recipes a richness that infuses your meals with flavor.

4. Avoid Messy Clean sup

Use the Natural Release, or as I call it the "do nothing release", to avoid messy clean up in your kitchen. Dishes that have a lot of liquid, such as soups, can move around a lot in the pot if you use the Quick Release, resulting in spills. Using the Natural Release means there less movement of liquid in the pot, so less clean up. And more time for you to read through my book for your next recipe!

5. Buy a Second Instant Pot!

Buy an Instant Pot for yourself... and an extra one as a gift. Because when your family and friends taste the great meals that come out of your kitchen, they're going to want to know how you're doing it. And when you share with them that it's my recipe book behind your delicious dinners, they'll want an Instant Pot of their own.

MY INSTANT POT RECIPES

Ready to use your Instant Pot? I've created some great recipes for my Instant Pot, and now I'm sharing them with you. These recipes are easy to follow… and the result is delicious!

Before you start cooking, let's take a look at some of the basics for using my recipes for the Instant Pot, basics that will make it easier for you to jump right in and make some great meals.

What can you cook in your Instant Pot?

Any foods that you usually cook in liquid can be cooked in the Instant Pot, such as beans, rice, risotto, soups, and stews. Chicken and meats are great cooked in an electric pressure cooker, so long as you don't want them to be crispy. And don't forget your vegetables. Steam broccoli, green beans, and cauliflower. Harder vegetables such as carrots, onions, and potatoes cook nicely in the pressure cooker.

Basic functions you need to know

There are a few basic functions that your Instant Pot can perform, all of which are used in my recipes:

- **Pressure Cook/Manual:** Foods that take a long time for the flavors to blend are best cooked using the Pressure Cooker method. Roasts cooked this way are great – juicy, tender, and full of flavor.

- **Sauté:** This function lets the bottom of the pot sauté and sear foods first. Then you can pressure cook them. This gives foods a nice deep flavor.

- **Slow Cook:** Use the Slow Cook function for tough cuts of meat that need to cook for a long time as well as for meals that you want to simmer for a few hours, such as beef stew.

- **Steam:** You can steam foods using the steamer rack that comes with your Instant Pot. This is good for foods such as vegetables when you don't want to cook them in a liquid where they become soggy.

Use enough liquid

The Instant Pot uses steam to build up the pressure so food cooks. My recipes will let you know how much liquid to use, but as a rule, most recipes for the electric pressure cooker will need 1 to 2 cups of liquid. If you're cooking meat that is juicy, you can lower the liquid amount to a ½ cup.

Filling the Instant Pot

When you're using your Instant Pot for pressure cooking, never fill it more than halfway. If there are too much liquid and food in the pot, hot liquid can come spraying out of the release valve and cause burns.

Using frozen is okay

You don't need to remember to take food out of the freezer to use for your evening meal. The Instant Pot cooks frozen foods with no problems. I use frozen fruit and vegetables in many of my recipes – they defrost and then cook perfectly.

Dessert, dessert, and more dessert

If you don't use your Instant Pot to make desserts and other sweets, you'll be missing out! In my house, dessert is a big deal. Cakes, pies, even apple crisp. All types of yummy desserts are possible in your Instant Pot! I've included some of my favorite dessert recipes in this book.

People all over the world have fallen for the Instant Pot, and now you can too! My tips, tricks, and recipes for using your Instant Pot are all you need to make delicious meals that you and your family won't be able to get enough of.

The recipes in this book are the ones I make over and over again. Not only are these recipes easy to make, they're also delicious and full of flavor. Look through my recipes and find one that catches your eye. Then send out the invitations to your first Instant Pot dinner!

Meat Recipes

Holiday Sweet Spare Ribs

Ready in about: 35 minutes | **Serves:** 6 | **Per serving:** Calories 634; Carbs 43g; Fat 41g; Protein 47g

INGREDIENTS

3 pounds Spare Ribs, cut into 3-inch pieces
18 ounces canned Pineapple, undrained
1 cup Onions, sliced
½ tsp Garlic Salt
¼ cup Tamari Sauce

2 tbsp Apple Cider Vinegar
½ cup Tomato Paste
3 tsp Olive Oil
¼ tsp Ginger Powder
¼ tsp Pepper

DIRECTIONS

Heat oil and brown spare ribs on all sides, 4-5 minutes per side on SAUTÉ mode. Remove to a plate. Sauté onion in hot oil for 3-4 minutes until translucent.

Add the remaining ingredients, return the spareribs to the cooker, and seal the lid. Cook for 20 minutes on MEAT/STEW at High. Use a natural release, for 10 minutes and serve.

Shredded Pork in Sweet BBQ Sauce

Ready in about: 70 minutes | **Serves:** 8 | **Per serving:** Calories 420; Carbs 47g; Fat 12g; Protein 33g

INGREDIENTS

4 pounds Pork Shoulder
1 tbsp Onion Powder
1 tbsp Garlic Powder
1 tbsp Pepper
1 tbsp Chili Powder

2 cups Chicken Stock
For BBQ Sauce:
6 Dates, soaked
¼ cup Tomato Paste
½ cup Coconut Aminos

DIRECTIONS

In a small bowl combine onion powder, garlic powder, pepper, and chili powder. Rub the mixture onto the pork. Place the pork inside your pressure cooker.

Pour the broth around the meat, not over it, and then seal the lid. Select PRESSURE COOK mode and set the timer to 60 minutes, at High pressure.

Meanwhile, place all sauce ingredients in a food processor and pulse until smooth. Release the pressure quickly. Grab two forks and shred the meat inside the pot. Pour the sauce over and stir to combine.

Apple Pork Ribs

Ready in about: 40 minutes | **Serves:** 4 | **Per serving:** Calories 432; Carbs 28g; Fat 3g; Protein 47g

INGREDIENTS

½ cup Apple Cider Vinegar
2 pounds Pork Ribs

3 ½ cups Apple Juice

DIRECTIONS

Pour apple juice and apple cider vinegar into the pressure cooker and lower the trivet. Place the pork ribs on top of the trivet and seal the lid. Cook at High pressure for 30 minutes.

Once it goes off, let the valve drop on its own for a natural release, for about 10 minutes.

Pork & Cabbage Soup with Veggies

Ready in about: 25 minutes | **Serves:** 6 | **Per serving:** Calories 351; Carbs 20g; Fat 18g; Protein 26g

INGREDIENTS

1 pound Ground Pork
1 Onion, diced
2 pounds Napa Cabbage, chopped
1 Potato, diced
6 Button Mushrooms, sliced

3 Scallions, sliced
2 Carrots, chopped
1 tbsp Butter
4 cups Chicken Broth
Salt and Pepper, to taste

DIRECTIONS

Melt butter on SAUTÉ, and add the pork. Cook until it browned, breaking it with a spatula. Once browned, add onions and mushrooms, and cook for another 4-5 minutes.

Season with salt and pepper. Pour in chicken broth and stir in the remaining ingredients. Seal the lid, cook on PRESSURE COOK for 6 minutes at High. Do a quick release. Ladle into serving bowls and serve.

Brussel Sprout Pork Chops with Onions

Ready in about: 40 minutes | **Serves:** 4 | **Per serving:** Calories 434; Carbs 13g; Fat 29g; Protein 31g

INGREDIENTS

1 pound Pork Chops
1 cup Onions, sliced
1 cup Carrots, sliced
1 tbsp Butter
2 cups Brussel Sprouts

1 tbsp Arrowroot
1 tsp Garlic, minced
1 cup Chicken Stock
½ tsp dried Thyme

DIRECTIONS

Melt butter on SAUTÉ mode. Add the pork chops, and cook on all sides until golden in color. Transfer to a plate. Add the onions, and cook for 3 minutes, then add the garlic.

Saute for one more minute. Return the pork chops to the pot and pour the broth over. Seal the lid and cook at High pressure for 15 minutes.

When the timer goes off, do a quick pressure release. Stir in carrots and brussel sprouts. Seal the lid again, and cook for 3 minutes at High pressure. Do a quick pressure release.

Transfer the chops and veggies to a serving platter. Whisk the arrowroot into the pot and cook on SAUTÉ until it thickens. Pour the sauce over the chops and veggies. Serve immediately.

Orange & Cinnamon Pork

Ready in about: 60 minutes | **Serves:** 10 | **Per serving:** Calories 635; Carbs 14g; Fat 47g; Protein 61g

INGREDIENTS

2 tbsp Olive Oil
5 pounds Pork Shoulder
1 Cinnamon Stick
2 cups Fresh Orange Juice
1 tbsp Cumin
½ tsp Garlic Powder
¼ tsp Onion Powder

1 Onion, chopped
1 Jalapeno Pepper, diced
2 tsp Thyme
½ tsp Oregano
½ tsp Pepper

DIRECTIONS

Place half of the oil in a small bowl. Add all of the spices and stir well to combine the mixture. Rub it all over the meat, making sure that the pork is well-coated.

Heat the remaining oil on SAUTÉ. Add the pork and sear it on all sides until browned. Transfer to a plate. Pour the orange juice into the pan and deglaze the bottom with a spatula.

Add the rest of the ingredients and stir to combine well. Return the pork to the pot. Seal the lid, select the PRESSURE COOK cooking mode for 40 minutes, at High pressure.

When ready, allow for a natural pressure release, for about 10 minutes. Grab two forks and shred the pork inside the pot. Stir to combine with the juices, and serve.

Rutabaga & Apple Pork

Ready in about: 40 minutes | **Serves:** 4 | **Per serving:** Calories 421; Carbs 2g; Fat 23g; Protein 44g

INGREDIENTS

1 tbsp Olive Oil
1 pound Pork Loin, cut into cubes
2 Apples, peeled and chopped
2 Rutabaga, peeled and chopped
1 Onion, diced
1 Celery Stalk, diced

1 tbsp Parsley, chopped
½ cup Leeks, sliced
1 ½ cups Beef Broth
½ tsp Cumin
½ tsp Thyme

DIRECTIONS

Heat half of the olive oil on SAUTÉ. Add the beef and cook until it browned on all sides. Remove to a plate. Add leeks, onions, celery, and drizzle with the remaining oil.

Stir to combine and cook for 3 minutes. Add the beef back to the cooker, pour the broth over, and stir in all of the herbs and spices. Seal the lid, and cook at High pressure for 10 minutes.

After the beep, do a quick pressure release. Stir in the rutabaga and apples. Seal the lid again and cook for 5 minutes at High. Do a quick pressure release, and serve right away.

Pineapple Pork Loin

Ready in about: 30 minutes | **Serves:** 6 | **Per serving:** Calories 546; Carbs 42g; Fat 21g; Protein 41g

INGREDIENTS

2 pounds Pork Loin, cut into 6 equal pieces
16 ounces canned Pineapple
1 cup Vegetable Broth
1 tbsp Brown Sugar
3 tbsp Olive Oil
½ cup Tomato Paste
1 cup sliced Onions

½ tsp Ginger, grated
½ tsp Garlic Salt
½ tsp Pepper
¼ cup Tamari
¼ cup Rice Wine Vinegar
½ tbsp. Cornstarch
1 tbsp. Water

DIRECTIONS

Heat the 2 tbsp oil on SAUTÉ. Cook the onions a few minutes, until translucent. Add the pork and stir in the rest of the ingredients, except for water and cornstarch.

Seal the lid and cook for 20 minutes on SOUP/BROTH mode at High. Release the pressure quickly.

In a bowl, mix cornstarch and water, with a fork, until slurry. Stir in the cornstarch slurry in the pressure cooker, and cook for 2 more minutes, or until thickened, on SAUTÉ. Serve hot to enjoy!

Beans and Pancetta Kale and Chickpeas

Ready in about: 30 minutes | **Serves:** 8 | **Per serving:** Calories 486; Carbs 49g; Fat 21g; Protein 31g

INGREDIENTS

5 cups Water, divided
1 pack (2 oz) Onion soup mix
¼ cup Olive Oil
1 tbsp Garlic, minced
1 ½ pounds canned Chickpeas, soaked overnight

2 tsp Mustard
½ pound Pancetta slices, chopped
1 Onion, chopped
1 cup Kale, chopped

DIRECTIONS

Heat the oil and cook the onions, garlic, and pancetta for 5 minutes on SAUTÉ mode. Add 1 cup of water and the soup mix, and cook for 5 more minutes. Then, add the chickpeas and 4 cups of water.

Add in the kale and mustard. Seal the lid and cook for 15 minutes on PRESSURE COOK at High Pressure. Once cooking is completed, perform a quick pressure release and serve immediately.

Pork Roast with Mushrooms in Beer Sauce

Ready in about: 50 minutes | **Serves:** 8 | **Per serving:** Calories 379; Carbs 10g; Fat 16g; Protein 47g

INGREDIENTS

3 pounds Pork Roast
8 ounces Mushrooms, sliced
12 ounces Root Beer

10 ounces Cream of Mushroom Soup
1 package Dry Onion Soup

DIRECTIONS

In the pressure cooker, whisk together mushroom soup, dry onion soup mix, and root beer. Add the mushrooms and pork. Seal the lid, and set to MEAT/STEW mode for 40 minutes at High.

When ready, let sit for 5 minutes before doing a quick pressure release.

Chili Pork Meatloaf

Ready in about: 70 minutes | **Serves:** 6 | **Per serving:** Calories 529; Carbs 29g; Fat 29g; Protein 42g

INGREDIENTS

1 pound ground Sausage
1 pound Ground Pork
1 cup cooked Rice
1 cup Milk
½ tsp Cayenne Powder

½ tsp Marjoram
2 Eggs, beaten
2 Garlic Cloves, minced
1 Onion, diced
Cooking spray, to grease

TOPPING:

2 tbsp Brown Sugar

1 cup Ketchup

DIRECTIONS

In a bowl, crack the eggs and whisk them with milk. Stir in the meat, cayenne, marjoram, rice, onion and garlic. With hands, mix in the ingredients to combine and form meatloaf mixture.

Grease a baking dish with cooking spray. Add and shape the meatloaf mixture inside. Whisk together the ketchup and sugar and pour over the meatloaf. Place the trivet inside the pressure cooker, and pour 1 cup of water. Lay the dish on top, seal the lid and cook on SOUP/BROTH for 50 minutes at High. When ready, do a quick release.

Ground Pork with Cabbage and Veggies

Ready in about: 25 minutes | **Serves:** 6 | **Per serving:** Calories 352; Carbs 13g; Fat 21g; Protein 27g

INGREDIENTS

1 ¼ pounds Ground Pork
1 cup Cabbage, shredded
½ cup chopped Celery
2 Red Onions, chopped
2 large Tomatoes, chopped
1 Carrot, shredded
2 cups Water
1 Red Bell Pepper, chopped

1 Green Bell Pepper, chopped
1 Yellow Bell Pepper, chopped
¼ tsp Cumin
1 tsp Red Pepper Flakes
Salt and Black Pepper, to taste
Cooking spray, to grease
Freshly chopped Coriander leaves, for garnish

DIRECTIONS

Coat with cooking spray. Add the pork and cook them until browned on SAUTÉ. Stir in the remaining ingredients, and pour the water. Seal the lid and set to PRESSURE COOK for 15 minutes at High. Do a quick pressure release. Sprinkle with freshly chopped coriander, to serve.

Pork Butt with Mushrooms and Celery

Ready in about: 354 minutes | **Serves:** 8 | **Per serving:** Calories 318; Carbs 2g; Fat 20g; Protein 29g

INGREDIENTS

1 pound Pork Butt, sliced
2 cups Mushrooms, sliced
1 ½ cups Celery Stalk, chopped
½ cup White Wine
1 tsp Garlic, minced

½ cup Chicken Broth
½ tsp Salt
¼ tsp Black Pepper
Cooking spray, to grease

DIRECTIONS

Grease with cooking spray and heat on SAUTÉ mode. Brown the pork slices and for a few minutes. Stir in the remaining ingredients. Season with salt and pepper.

Seal the lid and cook for 20 minutes on MEAT/STEW at High. When done, do a quick release.

Tangy Pork in Tomato Sour Cream Sauce

Ready in about: 45 minutes | **Serves:** 6 | **Per serving:** Calories 416; Carbs 12g; Fat 26g; Protein 32g

INGREDIENTS

1 ½ pounds Pork Shoulder, cut into pieces
2 Onions, chopped
1 ½ cups Sour Cream
1 cup Tomato Puree
½ tbsp Coriander

¼ tsp Cumin
¼ tsp Cayenne Pepper
1 tsp Garlic, minced
Salt and Pepper, to taste
Cooking spray, to grease

DIRECTIONS

Coat with cooking spray and add the pork. Cook for a few minutes on SAUTÉ mode, until lightly browned. Add onions and garlic and cook for 1 minute, until fragrant.

Stir in the remaining ingredients and turn the vent clockwise to seal. Set to 30 minutes on SOUP/BROTH at High. When it beeps, let sit for 5 minutes before quick release the pressure.

Pork Chops with Brussel Sprouts

Ready in about: 30 minutes | **Serves:** 4 | **Per serving:** Calories 406; Carbs 7g; Fat 22g; Protein 44g

INGREDIENTS

4 Pork Chops
½ pound Brussel Sprouts
¼ cup Sparkling Wine
1 ½ cups Beef Stock
2 Shallots, chopped

1 tbsp Olive Oil
1 cup Celery Stalk, chopped
1 tbsp Coriander
¼ tsp Salt
¼ tsp Black Pepper

DIRECTIONS

Heat olive oil on SAUTÉ. Add the pork chops and cook until browned on all sides.

Stir in the remaining ingredients. Seal the lid and cook for 20 minutes on MEAT/STEW at High. Release the pressure quickly.

Ground Pork and Sauerkraut

Ready in about: 25 minutes | **Serves:** 4 | **Per serving:** Calories 415; Carbs 16g; Fat 9g; Protein 33g

INGREDIENTS

1 pound Ground Pork
4 cups Sauerkraut, shredded
1 cup Tomato Puree
1 cup Chicken Stock

1 Red Onion, chopped
2 Garlic Cloves, minced
2 Bay Leaves
Salt and Pepper, to taste

DIRECTIONS

Add onions, garlic, and cook until soft and fragrant, on SAUTÉ. Add the pork and cook it until lightly browned. Stir in the remaining ingredients, and season with salt, and black pepper.

Seal the lid and cook for 20 minutes on MEAT/STEW mode at High. When done, press CANCEL and release the pressure quickly. Discard the bay leaves, serve and enjoy.

Pork with Rutabaga and Granny Smith Apples

Ready in about: 40 minutes | **Serves:** 4 | **Per serving:** Calories 418; Carbs 33g; Fat 17g; Protein 33g

INGREDIENTS

1 pound Pork Loin, cut into cubes
1 Onion, diced
2 Rutabagas, peeled and diced
1 cup Chicken Broth
½ cup White Wine
2 Granny Smith apples, peeled and diced
½ cup sliced Leeks

1 tbsp Vegetable Oil
1 Celery Stalk, diced
2 tbsp dried Parsley
¼ tsp Thyme
½ tsp Cumin
¼ tsp Lemon Zest
Salt and Black Pepper, to taste

DIRECTIONS

Season the pork with salt and pepper. Heat oil on SAUTÉ mode. Add pork and cook for a few minutes, until browned. Add the onions and cook for 2 more minutes, until soft.

Stir in the remaining ingredients, except for the apples. Seal the lid and cook for 15 minutes on PRESSURE COOK mode at High. When ready, release the pressure quickly. Stir in apples, seal the lid again, and cook at High for another 5 minutes. Do a quick release.

Pork Meatballs with Apple Sauce

Ready in about: 30 minutes | **Serves:** 8 | **Per serving:** Calories 454; Carbs 7g; Fat 30g; Protein 38g

INGREDIENTS

2 ½ pounds Ground Pork
¼ cup Tamari Sauce
3 Garlic Cloves, minced
½ tbsp dried Thyme
½ cup diced Onions

2 tsp Honey
¼ cup Apple Juice
1 ½ cups Water
1 cup Breadcrumbs
Salt and Pepper, to taste

DIRECTIONS

Whisk together honey, tamari, apple juice, water, and thyme in the pressure cooker. Season with salt and pepper. Set on SAUTÉ mode and cook for 15 minutes, lid off.

Meanwhile, combine all the remaining ingredients in a bowl. Shape meatballs out of the mixture. Drop the meatballs into the sauce, and press CANCEL.

Seal the lid, and set on PRESSURE COOK mode for 15 minutes at High. When done, release the pressure naturally, for 10 minutes. Serve immediately.

Pork Cutlets with Baby Carrots

Ready in about: 30 minutes | **Serves:** 4 | **Per serving:** Calories 213; Carbs 13g; Fat 9g; Protein 22g

INGREDIENTS

1 pound Pork Cutlets
1 pound Baby Carrots
1 Onion, sliced
1 tbsp Butter

1 cup Vegetable Broth
1 tsp Garlic Powder
Salt and Black Pepper, to taste

DIRECTIONS

Season the pork with salt and pepper. Melt butter on SAUTÉ, and brown the pork on all sides. Stir in carrots and onions and cook for 2 more minutes, until soft.

Pour in the broth, and add garlic powder. Season with salt and pepper. Seal the lid and cook for 20 minutes on MEAT/STEW mode at High. When ready, release the pressure quickly.

Herby Pork Butt and Yams

Ready in about: 20 minutes | **Serves:** 4 | **Per serving:** Calories 488; Carbs 41g; Fat 22g; Protein 31g

INGREDIENTS

1 pound Pork Butt, cut into 4 equal pieces
1 pound Yams, diced
2 tsp Butter
¼ tsp Thyme

¼ tsp Oregano
1 ½ tsp Sage
1 ½ cups Beef Broth
Salt and Black Pepper, to taste

DIRECTIONS

Season the pork with thyme, sage, oregano, salt, and pepper. Melt butter on SAUTÉ mode.

Add pork and cook until brown, for a few minutes. Add the yams and pour the broth. Seal the lid and cook for 20 minutes on MEAT/STEW at High. Do a quick release and serve hot.

Sunday Night Pork Meatloaf

Ready in about: 30 minutes | **Serves:** 4 | **Per serving:** Calories 290; Carbs 29g; Fat 11g; Protein 21g

FOR THE MEATLOAF:

2 pounds Ground Pork
2 Garlic Cloves, minced
1 cup Breadcrumbs
1 large-sized Egg
1 cup Milk

2 small Onions, finely chopped
Salt and cracked Black Pepper, to taste
½ tsp Turmeric powder
½ tsp dried Oregano
Nonstick Cooking Spray, for greasing

FOR THE TOPPING:

1 cup Ketchup
2 tbsp Brown Sugar
¼ cup Tomato Paste

1 tsp Garlic powder
½ tsp Onion powder
½ tsp Cayenne Pepper

DIRECTIONS

Place the trivet at the bottom of your pressure cooker and pour 1 cup of water. Lightly grease a round sheet pan, that fits in your pressure cooker.

Mix ground pork, bread crumbs, milk, onion, egg, salt, black pepper, oregano, and thyme in a mixing bowl. Use your hands to combine thoroughly. Shape into a loaf and place onto the prepared sheet pan.

In another bowl, mix the ingredients for the topping. Spread the topping over the meatloaf and lower the sheet pan onto the trivet. Seal the lid, select PRESSURE COOK and cook for 24 minutes at High.

Once ready, do a quick pressure release. Remove to a cutting board and slice before serving.

Short Ribs with Red Wine Gravy

Ready in about: 70 minutes | **Serves:** 4 | **Per serving:** Calories 479; Carbs 4g; Fat 31g; Protein 46

INGREDIENTS

2 pounds boneless Beef Short Ribs, cut into 3-inch pieces
1 tsp Kosher Salt
½ tsp ground Black Pepper
½ Onion, chopped

½ cup Red Wine
3 tbsp Oil
½ tbsp Tomato paste
2 Carrots, sliced

DIRECTIONS

Rub the ribs on all sides with salt, and black pepper. Heat the oil on SAUTÉ, and brown short ribs on all sides, 3-5 minutes per side, working in batches. Remove ribs to a plate.

Add onions and cook for 3-5 minutes, until tender. Pour in wine and tomato paste to deglaze by scraping any browned bits from the bottom of the cooker.

Cook for 2 minutes until wine has reduced slightly. Return ribs to pot and cover with carrots, garlic, parsley, rosemary, and oregano. Pour beef broth over ribs and vegetables.

Hit Cancel to stop Sauté mode. Seal the lid, and select MEAT/STEW at High Pressure for 35 minutes. When ready, let pressure release naturally for 10 minutes. Transfer ribs to a plate.

Remove and discard vegetables and herbs. Stir in mushrooms. Press Sauté and cook until mushrooms are soft, 2-4 minutes. In a bowl, add water and cornstarch and mix until smooth.

Pour this slurry into broth, stirring constantly, until it thickens slightly, 2 minutes. Season gravy with salt and pepper to taste. Pour over the ribs and garnish with minced parsley to serve.

Spicy Ground Pork

Ready in about: 55 minutes | **Serves:** 6 | **Per serving:** Calories 510; Carbs 4g; Fat 34g; Protein 41g

INGREDIENTS

2 pounds Ground Pork
1 Onion, diced
1 can diced Tomatoes
1 can Peas
5 Garlic Cloves, crushed
3 tbsp Butter
1 Serrano Pepper, chopped
1 cup Beef Broth

1 tsp ground Ginger
2 tsp ground Coriander
1 tsp Salt
¾ tsp Cumin
¼ tsp Cayenne Pepper
½ tsp Turmeric
½ tsp Black Pepper

DIRECTIONS

Melt butter on SAUTÉ mode. Add onions and cook for 3 minutes, until soft. Stir in the spices and garlic and cook for 2 more minutes. Add pork and cook until browned.

Pour broth and add serrano pepper, peas, and tomatoes. Seal the lid and cook for 30 minutes on MEAT/STEW mode at High. When ready, release the pressure naturally for 10 minutes.

Pork Steaks with Apple and Prunes

Ready in about: 30 minutes | **Serves:** 4 | **Per serving:** Calories 587; Carbs 24g; Fat 31g; Protein 43g

INGREDIENTS

4 Pork Steaks
¼ cup Milk
8 Prunes, pitted
½ cup White Wine
2 Apples, peeled and sliced

¼ cup Heavy Cream
1 tbsp Fruit Jelly
½ tsp ground Ginger
Salt and Pepper, to taste

DIRECTIONS

Place all ingredients, except the jelly, in your pressure cooker. Stir to combine well, and season with salt and pepper. Seal the lid and cook at High pressure for 15 minutes. Once done, wait 5 minutes and do a quick pressure release. Stir in the jelly, serve, and enjoy.

Pork and Green Onion Frittata

Ready in about: 30 minutes | **Serves:** 5 | **Per serving:** Calories 275; Carbs 3g; Fat 19g; Protein 15g

INGREDIENTS

1 tbsp Butter, melted
1 cup Green Onions, chopped
1 pound Ground Pork, chopped

6 Eggs
Salt and ground Black Pepper, to taste
1 cup Water

DIRECTIONS

In a deep bowl, break the eggs and whisk until frothy. Mix in the onions and ground meat, and season with the salt and pepper. Grease a casserole dish with 1 tablespoon of melted butter. Pour the egg mixture into the dish.

Place a metal trivet in the pressure cooker and add 1 cup of water. Select RICE mode and cook for 25 minutes at High. Do a quick pressure release and serve immediately.

Pork Sausage with Bell Peppers and Sweet Onions

Ready in about: 20 minutes | **Serves:** 8 | **Per serving:** Calories 278; Carbs 11g; Fat 19g; Protein 14g

INGREDIENTS

8 Pork Sausages
2 large Sweet Onions, sliced
4 Red Bell Peppers, cut into strips
1 tbsp Olive Oil
½ cup Beef Broth
¼ cup White Wine
1 tsp Garlic, minced

DIRECTIONS

On SAUTÉ, add the sausages, and brown them for a few minutes. Remove to a plate and discard the liquid. Press CANCEL. Wipe clean the cooker and heat the oil on SAUTÉ mode.

Stir in onions and peppers. Stir-fry them for 5 minutes, until soft. Add garlic and cook for a minute. Add the sausages and pour in broth and wine. Seal the lid and cook for 5 minutes at High pressure. Once done, do a quick pressure release.

Rosemary Dijon-Apple Pork

Ready in about: 60 minutes | **Serves:** 6 | **Per serving:** Calories 513; Carbs 14g; Fat 23g; Protein 61g

INGREDIENTS

3 pounds Pork Roast
2 Apples, peeled and slices
3 tbsp Dijon Mustard
1 tbsp dried Rosemary
½ cup White Wine
1 cup Water
1 tbsp Garlic, minced
1 tbsp Olive Oil
Salt and Pepper, to taste

DIRECTIONS

Brush the pork with mustard. Heat oil on SAUTÉ, and sear the pork on all sides, for a few minutes. Add apples and stir in the remaining ingredients.

Seal the lid and cook for 40 minutes on MEAT/STEW at High pressure. When ready, release the pressure naturally, for 10 minutes. The internal temperature should be at least 160 F.

Gourmet Bacon, Potato, and Endive Casserole

Ready in about: 30 minutes | **Serves:** 4 | **Per serving:** Calories 489; Carbs 74g; Fat 17g; Protein 17g

INGREDIENTS

½ pound Smoked Bacon, chopped
½ cup Carrots, sliced
2 cups Water
1 cup Chicken Stock
¾ cup Half and Half
4 Golden Potatoes, peeled and chopped
4 Endives, halved lengthwise
Salt and Pepper, to taste

DIRECTIONS

Set on SAUTÉ mode and add the bacon. Cook for 2 minutes until slightly crispy. Add the potatoes, carrots, and chicken stock. Seal the lid and cook for 10 minutes at High pressure.

Press CANCEL and release the pressure quickly. Add the endives and cook for 5 more minutes at High pressure. Press CANCEL again and quick-release the pressure.

Strain the bacon and veggies and return them to the pressure cooker. Add the half and half and season with salt and pepper. Cook on SAUTÉ mode, for 3 more minutes, lid off.

Smothered Cinnamon BBQ Ribs

Ready in about: 75 minutes | **Serves:** 6 | **Per serving:** Calories 422; Carbs 25g; Fat 13g; Protein 47g

INGREDIENTS

3 pounds Pork Ribs
½ cup Apple Jelly
1 cup Barbecue Sauce
1 Onion, diced
2 tbsp ground Cloves

½ cup Water
1 tbsp Brown Sugar
1 tsp Worcestershire Sauce
1 tsp ground Cinnamon

DIRECTIONS

Whisk together all ingredients in your pressure cooker, except the ribs. Place the ribs inside and seal the lid. Set the cooker to MEAT/STEW mode and cook for 45-55 minutes at High.

When ready, release the pressure naturally, for 10 minutes.

Braised Red Cabbage and Bacon

Ready in about: 20 minutes | **Serves:** 8 | **Per serving:** Calories 149; Carbs 5g; Fat 12g; Protein 5g

INGREDIENTS

1 pound Red Cabbage, chopped
8 Bacon Slices, chopped
1 ½ cups Beef Broth

2 tbsp Butter
1 tsp Salt
½ tsp Black Pepper

DIRECTIONS

Add the bacon slices in your pressure cooker, and cook for 5 minutes, until crispy, on SAUTÉ.

Stir in the cabbage, salt, pepper, and butter. Seal the lid, select STEAM mode for 10 minutes at High pressure. When ready, release the pressure naturally, for 10 minutes.

Pork Chops in Merlot

Ready in about: 30 minutes | **Serves:** 4 | **Per serving:** Calories 455; Carbs 13g; Fat 24g; Protein 43g

INGREDIENTS

4 Pork Chops
3 Carrots, chopped
1 Tomato, chopped
1 Onion, chopped
2 Garlic Cloves, minced
¼ cup Merlot Red Wine
½ cup Beef Broth
1 tsp dried Oregano

2 tbsp Olive Oil
2 tbsp Flour
2 tbsp Water
2 tbsp Tomato Paste
1 Beef Bouillon Cube
¼ tsp Black Pepper
¼ tsp Salt

DIRECTIONS

Heat the oil on SAUTÉ mode. In a bowl, mix in flour, pepper, and salt. Coat the pork chops. Place them in the pressure cooker and cook for a few minutes, until browned on all sides.

Add the carrots, onion, garlic, and oregano. Cook for 2 more minutes. Stir in the remaining ingredients and seal the lid. Cook on SOUP/BROTH mode and cook for 25 minutes at High. When ready, do a natural pressure release, for 10 minutes, and serve immediately.

BBQ Pork Butt

Ready in about: 55 minutes | **Serves:** 6 | **Per serving:** Calories 488; Carbs 20g; Fat 26g; Protein 38g

INGREDIENTS

2 pounds Pork Butt
¼ tsp Garlic Powder
¼ tsp Salt
¼ tsp Pepper
1 cup Barbecue Sauce

¼ tsp Cumin Powder
½ tsp Onion Powder
1 ½ cups Beef Broth
Cooking oil, to grease

DIRECTIONS

In a bowl, combine the barbecue sauce and all of the spices. Brush the pork with the mixture. On SAUTÉ, coat with cooking oil. Add the pork, and sear on all sides, for a few minutes.

Pour the beef broth around the meat. Seal the lid and cook for 40 minutes on MEAT/STEW at High. When ready, press CANCEL and wait 5 minutes before releasing the pressure quickly.

Pork Chops and Mushrooms in Tomato Sauce

Ready in about: 35 minutes | **Serves:** 4 | **Per serving:** Calories 446; Carbs 18g; Fat 21g; Protein 42g

INGREDIENTS

4 large Bone-In Pork Chops
1 cup Tomato Sauce
1 ½ cups White Button Mushrooms, sliced
1 Onion, chopped

1 tsp Garlic, minced
½ cup Water
1 tbsp Oil
Salt and Black Pepper, to taste

DIRECTIONS

Heat oil on SAUTÉ. Add garlic, onion and cook for 2 minutes, until soft and fragrant. Add pork and cook until browned on all sides. Stir in the remaining ingredients and seal the lid.

Cook for 20 minutes on MEAT/STEW mode at High. When ready, do a quick pressure release.

Apple and Cherry Pork Tenderloin

Ready in about: 55 minutes | **Serves:** 4 | **Per serving:** Calories 349; Carbs 18g; Fat 12g; Protein 40g

INGREDIENTS

1 ¼ pounds Pork Tenderloin
1 chopped Celery Stalk
2 cups Apples, peeled and chopped
1 cup Cherries, pitted
½ cup Apple Juice

½ cup Water
¼ cup Onions, chopped
Salt and Pepper, to taste
2 tbsp Olive Oil

DIRECTIONS

Heat oil on SAUTÉ mode, and cook the onion and celery for 5 minutes until softened. Season the pork with salt and pepper, and add to the cooker. Brown for 2-3 minutes per side.

Then, top with apples and cherries, and pour the water and apple juice. Seal the lid and cook on MEAT/STEW mode for 40 minutes, at High pressure.

Once ready, do a quick pressure release. Slice the pork tenderloin and arrange on a serving platter. Spoon the apple-cheery sauce over the pork slices, to serve.

Dinner Pork Roast

Ready in about: 45 minutes | **Serves:** 6 | **Per serving:** Calories 290; Carbs 4g; Fat 6g; Protein 52g

INGREDIENTS

3 pounds Sirloin Pork Roast
1 tbsp Honey
1 tsp Chili Powder
1 tbsp Rosemary

1 tbsp Olive Oil
1 ¼ cups Water
2 tbsp Lemon Juice

DIRECTIONS

Combine the spices, in a bowl, and rub them onto the pork. Heat oil on SAUTÉ mode and sear the pork on all sides. Stir in the remaining ingredients and seal the lid.

Cook for 30 minutes, on MEAT/STEW at High. Do a natural pressure release, for 15 minutes.

Pork Sausage with Cauliflower and Tater Tots

Ready in about: 20 minutes | **Serves:** 6 | **Per serving:** Calories 431; Carbs 66g; Fat 12g; Protein 23g

INGREDIENTS

1 pound Pork Sausage, sliced
1 pound Tater Tots
1 pound Cauliflower Florets, frozen and thawed
10 ounces canned Mushroom Soup

10 ounces canned Cauliflower Soup
10 ounces Evaporated Milk
Salt and Pepper, to taste

DIRECTIONS

Place roughly ¼ of the sausage slices in your pressure cooker. In a bowl, whisk together the soups and milk. Pour some of the mixtures over the sausages.

Top the sausage slices with ¼ of the cauliflower florets followed by ¼ of the tater tots. Pour some of the soup mixtures again. Repeat the layers until you use up all ingredients.

Seal the lid, and cook on PRESSURE COOK for 10 minutes, at High. When ready, do a quick release.

Marinated Flank Steak

Ready in about: 80 minutes | **Serves:** 4 | **Per serving:** Calories 589; Carbs 43g; Fat 21g; Protein 55g

INGREDIENTS

2 pounds Flank Steak
1 cup Beef Broth
1 Onion, diced

2 tbsp Potato Starch
1 Carrot, chopped
Cooking Spray, to grease

MARINADE:

2 tbsp Fish Sauce
½ tsp Cajun Seasoning
2 tsp Garlic, minced

½ cup Soy Sauce
1 tbsp Sesame Oil

DIRECTIONS

Combine marinade ingredients in a bowl. Add in the beef and let marinate for 30 minutes.

Coat the pressure cooker with cooking spray. Add onions and carrots and cook until soft on SAUTÉ. Add the beef along with the marinade. Whisk in the broth and starch.

Seal the lid and cook for 40 minutes on MEAT/STEW at High. Do a quick release and serve.

Onion & Beef Steaks in Gravy

Ready in about: 30 minutes | **Serves:** 4 | **Per serving:** Calories 445; Carbs 6g; Fat 21g; Protein 53g

INGREDIENTS

4 Round Beef Steaks
2 Onions, sliced
1 ½ cups Beef Broth
1 tsp Garlic, minced
1 tbsp dried Parsley
½ tsp Rosemary

1 tbsp Oil
½ tsp Red Pepper Flakes
¼ cup Half and Half
2 tbsp Flour
¼ tsp Salt
¼ tsp Black Pepper

DIRECTIONS

Heat the oil on SAUTÉ mode. Add the beef and brown the steaks on all sides. Remove to a plate. Sauté the onions and garlic for 2 minutes, until translucent and fragrant.

Return the steaks to the pressure cooker. Stir in the salt, pepper, pepper flakes, rosemary, parsley, and pour in broth. Seal the lid and cook for 20 minutes on MEAT/STEW at High.

When ready, do a quick pressure release, and stir in the flour and half and half. Cook for 3 more minutes, until thickened, with the lid off, on SAUTÉ mode. Serve immediately.

Pork Chops with Apple Cider

Ready in about: 35 minutes | **Serves:** 4 | **Per serving:** Calories 402; Carbs 20g; Fat 21g; Protein 28g

INGREDIENTS

1 lb Pork Fillets
½ lb Granny Smith apples, cored and cut into wedges
2 Leeks, white part only, cut into rings
2 tbsp Olive Oil
1 ¼ cups Apple Cider

1 tsp Chilli Pepper
Kosher Salt and ground Black Pepper, to taste
1 tsp dry Rosemary
1 tsp dry Thyme

DIRECTIONS

On SAUTÉ mode, heat 1 tbsp of olive oil. Season the pork with salt, black and cayenne pepper. Brown the fillets for about 4 minutes per side. Set aside. Heat the remaining oil in the pressure cooker.

Add in leeks and sauté until soft, for about 4 minutes. Add in apples, rosemary, thyme and pour in cider. Place the pork loin among the apples and leeks. Seal the lid and cook for 20 minutes on MEAT/STEW mode at High.

Once cooking is complete, perform a quick pressure release and remove the lid. To serve, arrange the pork on a plate and pour the apple leeks mixture over the pork tenderloins.

BBQ Pork Rib Chops with Root Vegetables

Ready in about: 25 minutes | **Serves:** 4 | **Per serving:** Calories 332; Carbs 42g; Fat 7g; Protein 29g

INGREDIENTS

4 Pork Rib Chops
1 cup Carrots, thinly sliced
1 cup Turnips, thinly sliced

1 cup Onions, slice into rings
1 ½ cups BBQ sauce
2 cups Water

DIRECTIONS

Add the pork cutlets in your cooker. Pour in half cup of BBQ sauce and 2 cups of water. Select Meat/Stew mode. Stir in the onions, turnip, and carrots. Lock the lid and cook for 20 minutes at High. Once ready, release the pressure quickly. Open the lid, drizzle with the remaining BBQ sauce and serve.

Braised Chili Pork Chops

Ready in about: 30 minutes | **Serves:** 4 | **Per serving:** Calories 437; Carbs 11g; Fat 24g; Protein 44g

INGREDIENTS

4 Pork Chops
1 Onion, chopped
2 tbsp Chili Powder
14 ounces canned Tomatoes with Green Chilies
1 Garlic Clove, minced

½ cup Beer
½ cup Vegetable Stock
1 tsp Olive Oil
Salt and Pepper, to taste

DIRECTIONS

Heat oil on SAUTÉ mode. Add onion, garlic, and chili powder and cook for 2 minutes. Add the pork chops and cook until browned on all sides.

Stir in the tomatoes, broth, and beer. Season with salt and pepper. Seal the lid and cook for 20 minutes on MEAT/STEW at High. When ready, quick release the pressure and serve hot.

Tamari Sauce Pork Belly with Garlic

Ready in about: 40 minutes | **Serves:** 6 | **Per serving:** Calories 520; Carbs 5g; Fat 28g; Protein 49g

INGREDIENTS

4 Garlic Cloves, sliced
½ tsp ground Cloves
1 tsp grated fresh Ginger
1 ½ pounds Pork Belly, sliced
2 ¼ cups Water

¼ cup White Wine
½ cup Yellow Onions, peeled and chopped
¼ cup Tamari Sauce
1 tsp Maple Syrup
4 cups short-grain White Rice, cooked, warm

DIRECTIONS

Brown pork belly, for about 6 minutes per side, on SAUTÉ mode. Add the remaining ingredients. Seal the lid and cook for 25 minutes on PRESSURE COOK at High Pressure. Cook until the meat is tender.

Once ready, switch the pressure release valve to open, and do a quick pressure release. Serve with rice.

Pork Fillets with Worcestershire Sauce

Ready in about: 30 minutes | **Serves:** 6 | **Per serving:** Calories 587; Carbs 39g; Fat 29g; Protein 48g

INGREDIENTS

1 lb Pork Loin Filets
16 ounces canned peach
½ tsp Black Pepper
½ tsp Cilantro, ground
½ tsp Ginger, finely chopped
½ cup Worcestershire sauce
¼ cup Apple Cider Vinegar

½ tsp Garlic, minced
1 tsp Salt
1 cup Onions, sliced
1 tbsp Brown Sugar
2 tbsp Olive Oil
1 cup Tomato Sauce
1 tbsp Arrowroot slurry

DIRECTIONS

On SAUTÉ mode, heat oil. Cook onions until tender, for about 4 minutes. Stir in the remaining ingredients, except for the arrowroot. Seal the lid, Select MEAT/STEW and cook for 20 minutes at High.

Do a quick pressure release. Stir in the arrowroot slurry and cook on SAUTÉ, until the sauce thickens.

Fast Onion-Flavoured Pork Ribs

Ready in about: 35 minutes | **Serves:** 4 | **Per serving:** Calories 355; Carbs 8g; Fat 19g; Protein 28g

INGREDIENTS

1 ½ cups Tomato Puree
1 tbsp Garlic, minced
1 ½ cups Water
½ tsp Black Pepper
1 tsp Salt

½ tsp dried Sage
1 ¼ cups Sweet Onions
½ cup Carrots, thinly sliced
1 lb cut Pork Spare Ribs

DIRECTIONS

Brown the ribs on SAUTÉ. Pour in water and tomato puree. Add the remaining ingredients. Seal the lid and cook for 30 minutes on PRESSURE COOK at High. Once ready, do a quick pressure release and serve.

Short Ribs with Mango Sauce

Ready in about: 35 minutes | **Serves:** 6 | **Per serving:** Calories 625; Carbs 41g; Fat 31g; Protein 62g

INGREDIENTS

1 lb Short Ribs, cut into 3-inch pieces
18 ounces canned Mango, undrained
½ tsp Black Pepper, to taste
½ tsp ground Parsley
1 tsp Salt
1 cup Onions, sliced
1-inch piece Ginger, finely chopped

½ tsp Garlic, minced
½ cup Tomato Paste
3 tsp Olive Oil
½ cup Soy sauce
2 tbsp Vinegar
¼ cup prepared Arrowroot slurry

DIRECTIONS

On SAUTÉ, heat olive oil and cook the onions until tender, about 4 minutes. Stir in the remaining ingredients, except the arrowroot. Seal the lid, select Meat/Stew and cook for 20 minutes at High Pressure.

Once ready, do a quick release Stir in the arrowroot slurry and cook on SAUTÉ until the sauce thickens.

Pork Loin Chops with Sauerkraut

Ready in about: 35 minutes | **Serves:** 4 | **Per serving:** Calories 383; Carbs 11g; Fat 18g; Protein 22g

INGREDIENTS

4 Pork Loin Chops, boneless
4 cups Sauerkraut, shredded
1 cup dry White Wine
cloves Garlic, peeled and crushed
1 cup Carrots, coarsely chopped
½ cup Celery, coarsely chopped
2 Onions, sliced

2 cups Vegetable Stock
2 tsp Mustard
1 tsp Salt
½ tsp Chili powder
½ cup Tomato Paste
½ tsp ground Black Pepper

DIRECTIONS

Place the pork on the bottom of the pressure cooker. Add the shredded cabbage on top of the pork.

Add in the remaining ingredients and seal the lid. Select PRESSURE COOK and cook for 30 minutes at High Pressure. Once cooking is done, do a quick pressure release. Serve immediately.

Pork Ribs in Walnut Sauce

Ready in about: 30 minutes | **Serves:** 4 | **Per serving:** Calories 273; Carbs 4g; Fat 16g; Protein 27g

INGREDIENTS

1 pound Pork Ribs
¼ cup Roasted Walnuts, chopped
4 Garlic Cloves, minced
1 ½ cups Beef Broth
2 tbsp Apple Cider Vinegar

3 tbsp Butter
½ tsp Red Pepper Flakes
1 tsp Sage
Salt and Black Pepper, to taste

DIRECTIONS

Melt butter on SAUTÉ. Season the ribs with salt, pepper, sage, and pepper flakes. Place them in the pressure cooker and brown, for about 5 minutes. Stir in the remaining ingredients.

Seal the lid and cook for 20 minutes on MEAT/STEW mode at High pressure. Once ready, release the pressure quickly. Serve the ribs drizzled with the sauce.

Beef Cabbage Rolls

Ready in about: 25 minutes | **Serves:** 10 | **Per serving:** Calories 467; Carbs 36g; Fat 17g; Protein 36g

INGREDIENTS

10 Cabbage Leaves, blanched
1 ½ pounds Ground Beef
2 cups Rice
22 ounces canned, diced, Tomatoes
1 tbsp Garlic, minced

15 ounces Tomato Sauce
½ Cup Water
1 Onion, chopped
½ tsp Cayenne Pepper
Salt and Pepper, to taste

DIRECTIONS

In a bowl, combine the beef, rice, cayenne pepper, garlic, diced tomatoes, and onions. Spoon mixture between the cabbage rolls and roll them up. Arrange the rolls in the cooker.

Pour the tomato sauce on top, and add the water. Seal the lid, select SOUP/BROTH mode and adjust to 20 minutes at High. Once done, wait 5 minutes before doing a quick release.

Italian Sausage over Muffins

Ready in about: 20 minutes | **Serves:** 8 | **Per serving:** Calories 478; Carbs 29g; Fat 31g; Protein 28g

INGREDIENTS

8 toasted English Muffins, split
1 ½ pounds Italian Sausage
1 ¼ cups Milk
¼ cup Flour
1 cup Eggplants, sliced

1 cup Bone Broth
1 tsp Salt
½ tsp Black Pepper, freshly cracked
2 sprigs dry Thyme
2 sprigs dry Rosemary

DIRECTIONS

Select SAUTÉ and add in the eggplants and sausage. Cook for 5 minutes. Sprinkle with rosemary and thyme, and pour in the broth. Seal the lid, select Meat/Stew mode and cook for 5 minutes at High.

Do quick pressure release. In a measuring cup, whisk the flour and milk, and season with salt and pepper. Add this mixture to the pressure cooker. Select Sauté, and let simmer for 3 minutes, lid off.

To serve, spoon the gravy over the toasted split muffins and enjoy.

Chuck Roast with Potatoes

Ready in about: 50 minutes | **Serves:** 6 | **Per serving:** Calories 441; Carbs 20g; Fat 17g; Protein 53g

INGREDIENTS

2 ½ pounds Chuck Roast
1 pound Red Potatoes, chopped
2 Carrots, chopped
½ cup Parsnip, chopped
1 cup Onions, sliced
½ cup Red Wine
½ Celery Stalk, sliced

1 tbsp Rosemary
1 tsp Thyme
½ tsp Pepper
½ tsp Salt
2 tbsp Tomato Paste
1 tbsp Garlic, minced
1 cup Beef Broth

DIRECTIONS

Coat the cooker with cooking spray. In a bowl, combine the thyme, rosemary, salt, and pepper and rub the mixture onto the meat. Place the meat inside the cooker and sear on all sides.

Add the remaining ingredients and seal the lid. Set to MEAT/STEW for 40 minutes at High. Once the cooking is over, do a quick pressure release. Serve and enjoy!

Delicious Pork Shoulder with White Cabbage

Ready in about: 25 minutes | **Serves:** 6 | **Per serving:** Calories 203; Carbs 13g; Fat 2g; Protein 25g

INGREDIENTS

1 head Cabbage, shredded
½ cup Vegetable Stock
4 Cloves Garlic, finely minced
2 Red Onions, chopped
1 cup Tomato Puree

3 Tomatoes, chopped
1 ¼ pounds Pork Shoulder, boneless, cut into cubes
1 Bay Leaf
½ tsp Paprika, crushed
Salt and Black Pepper, to taste

DIRECTIONS

Select SAUTÉ and add the pork, onions and garlic. Cook the pork until lightly browned. Remove any fat.

Add in the remaining ingredients. Seal the lid, press MEAT/STEW and cook for 15 minutes at High Pressure. Once cooking is complete, do a quick pressure release. Discard the bay leaf and serve.

Pork with Tangy Tomato Sauce

Ready in about: 35 minutes | **Serves:** 6 | **Per serving:** Calories 503; Carbs 11g; Fat 41g; Protein 32g

INGREDIENTS

1 ½ pounds Pork Shoulder, cubed
1 cup Tomato Sauce
½ cups Buttermilk
1 cup Green Onions, chopped
2 tsp Butter, melted

¼ tsp Chili Pepper
3 Garlic Cloves, minced
½ tbsp Cilantro
Salt and Black Pepper, to taste

DIRECTIONS

Select SAUTÉ and melt butter. Cook onions and minced garlic until soft, 2-3 minutes. Add the remaining ingredients, except for the buttermilk. Sea the lid and cook for 25 minutes on MEAT/STEW at High.

Once cooking is complete, do a quick pressure release. Stir in the sour cream until well incorporated.

Cheesy Rigatoni with Pancetta

Ready in about: 30 minutes | **Serves:** 6 | **Per serving:** Calories 481; Carbs 2g; Fat 32g; Protein 19g

INGREDIENTS

1 ½ box Penne Pasta
6 slices Pancetta, fried and crumbled
½ cup Grana Padano cheese, grated
1 cup Cottage cheese
3 tsp Olive Oil
1 cup Yellow Onions, finely chopped

3 Garlic Cloves, finely minced
3 ½ cups Vegetable Broth
1 ½ cups Water
2 sprigs dry Rosemary
Salt and freshly ground Black Pepper, to taste

DIRECTIONS

Add rigatoni, broth, water, salt, black pepper, and rosemary to your pressure cooker. Seal the lid, select PRESSURE COOK for 12 minutes at High Pressure. Once ready, do a quick pressure release. Set aside.

Select SAUTÉ and melt the butter. Cook onions and garlic, until fragrant, about 2-3 minutes. Add pancetta, cottage cheese, and rigatoni mixture back to the cooker, and toss until everything is well mixed. Serve immediately topped with freshly grated Grana Padano cheese.

Ground Beef and Sauerkraut

Ready in about: 25 minutes | **Serves:** 6 | **Per serving:** Calories 337; Carbs 8g; Fat 20g; Protein 30g

INGREDIENTS

1 ½ pounds Ground Beef
10 ounces canned Tomato Soup
½ cup Beef Broth
3 cups Sauerkraut

1 cup sliced Leeks
1 tbsp Butter
1 tsp Mustard Powder
Salt and Pepper, to taste

DIRECTIONS

Melt butter on SAUTÉ. Add leeks and cook for a few minutes. Add beef and brown, for a few minutes.

Stir in the sauerkraut, broth and mustard powder and season with salt and pepper. Seal the lid and cook for 20 minutes on SOUP/BROTH mode at High. When ready, do a quick pressure release.

Beef Ribs with ButtonCitrusy Beef

Ready in about: 90 minutes | **Serves:** 6 | **Per serving:** Calories 477; Carbs 8g; Fat 36g; Protein 35g

INGREDIENTS

Juice of 1 Lemon
Juice of 2 Oranges
2 pounds Beef, cut into chunks

1 tbsp Butter
1 tbsp Italian Seasoning
½ tsp Sea Salt

DIRECTIONS

Place the beef in the pressure cooker and sprinkle with salt, pepper, and seasoning. Massage the meat with hands to season it well. Pour the lemon and orange juice over and seal the lid.

Select PRESSURE COOK for 50 minutes, at High pressure. When the timer goes off, do a quick pressure release. Shred the meat inside the pot with two forks.

Set to SAUTÉ mode, lid off. Stir to combine well and cook for about 20 minutes, or until the liquid is absorbed. Add butter, give it a good stir, and cook for an additional 5 minutes.

Beef Ribs with Mushrooms

Ready in about: 30 minutes | **Serves:** 6 | **Per serving:** Calories 509; Carbs 9g; Fat 43g; Protein 22g

INGREDIENTS

1 ½ pounds Beef Ribs
2 cups White Button Mushrooms, quartered
1 Onion, chopped
¼ cup Ketchup
2 cups Veggie Stock
1 cup chopped Carrots
¼ cup Olive Oil
1 tsp Garlic, minced
Salt and Pepper, to taste

DIRECTIONS

Heat the oil on SAUTÉ mode. Season the ribs with salt and pepper, and brown them on all sides. Then, set aside. Add the onion, garlic, carrots, and mushrooms and cook for 5 minutes.

Add the ribs back to the cooker and stir in the remaining ingredients. Seal the lid and cook for 35 minutes on MEAT/STEW at High pressure. When cooking is over, do a quick release.

Beef Medley with Blue Cheese

Ready in about: 50 minutes | **Serves:** 6 | **Per serving:** Calories 267; Carbs 6g; Fat 13g; Protein 30

INGREDIENTS

1 pound Sirloin Steak, cut into cubes
6 ounces Blue Cheese, crumbled
½ Cabbage, diced
1 cup Parsnip, chopped
2 Red Bell Peppers, chopped
1 cup Beef Broth
2 cups canned Tomatoes, undrained
1 Onion, diced
1 tsp Garlic, minced
Salt and Black Pepper, to taste
Cooking spray, for greasing

DIRECTIONS

Coat the cooker with cooking spray and add the meat. On SAUTÉ, brown it on all sides, for a few minutes. Then, add the remaining ingredients, except for the cheese.

Seal the lid and cook for 40 minutes on MEAT/STEW mode at High. Once cooking is complete, release the pressure quickly. Top with blue cheese, to serve.

Mustard Rump Roast with Potatoes

Ready in about: 65 minutes | **Serves:** 6 | **Per serving:** Calories 559; Carbs 63g; Fat 11g; Protein 51g

INGREDIENTS

3-pound Rump Roast
6 medium Red Potatoes, quartered
1 Onion, diced
1 Celery Stalk, chopped
1 ½ tbsp Dijon Mustard
2 cups Beef Broth
1 tbsp Butter
2 Garlic Cloves, minced
Salt and Pepper, to taste

DIRECTIONS

Heat the oil on SAUTÉ mode. Add onion and celery, and cook for a few minutes, until soft. Brush the mustard over the beef and season with salt and pepper.

Place in the cooker and sear on all sides, for a few minutes. Stir in the remaining ingredients and seal the lid. Cook for 45 minutes on MEAT at High. Do a natural release, for 10 minutes.

Steak and Veggies with Ale Sauce

Ready in about: 50 minutes | **Serves:** 6 | **Per serving:** Calories 370; Carbs 32g; Fat 11g; Protein 36g

INGREDIENTS

2 pounds Beef Steak, cut into 6 or 8 equal pieces
1 Sweet Onion, chopped
1 cup Celery, chopped
1 pound Sweet Potatoes, diced
2 Carrots, chopped
3 Garlic Cloves, minced

2 Bell Peppers, chopped
1 ½ cups Tomato Puree
1 cup Ale
1 Chicken Bouillon Cube
Salt and Pepper, to taste
1 tbsp Olive Oil

DIRECTIONS

Heat oil on SAUTÉ and sear the steaks, for a few minutes. Then, set aside. Press CANCEL. Arrange the veggies in the pressure cooker and top with the steaks.

In a bowl, whisk together bouillon cube, ale, and tomato puree. Pour over the steaks. Season with salt and pepper, and seal the lid. Cook for 30 minutes on MEAT/STEW at High. Quick-release the pressure.

Beef with Creamy Sour Sauce

Ready in about: 35 minutes | **Serves:** 6 | **Per serving:** Calories 340; Carbs 10g; Fat 19g; Protein 33g

INGREDIENTS

1 ½ pounds Beef Roast, cubed
1 cup Onion, diced
1 can Cream of Mushroom Soup
1 ½ cups Sour Cream
½ cups Water
½ tbsp Cumin

½ tbsp Coriander
1 tbsp Garlic, minced
1 tbsp Butter
½ tsp Chili Powder
Salt and Pepper, to taste

DIRECTIONS

Melt butter on SAUTÉ and stir in the onion. Stir-fry until soft, for about 3 minutes. Add garlic and cook for one more minute. Add beef and cook until browned, for about 3 – 5 minutes.

Combine the remaining ingredients in a bowl and pour this mixture over the beef. Seal the lid and cook for 20 minutes on MEAT/STEW mode at High. Once done, do a quick release.

Corned Beef with Celery Sauce

Ready in about: 50 minutes | **Serves:** 6 | **Per serving:** Calories 287; Carbs 8g; Fat 20g; Protein 18g

INGREDIENTS

1 ½ pounds Corned Beef Brisket
2 cups Cream of Celery Soup
1 tsp Garlic, minced
1 Onion, diced

1 cup Water
2 Tomatoes, diced
2 tsp Olive Oil
Salt and Black Pepper, to taste

DIRECTIONS

Season the beef with salt, and black pepper. Heat oil on SAUTÉ, and stir onions. Cook for 2 minutes, until translucent. Add garlic and cook for 1 minute.

Add beef and sear on all sides, for a few minutes. Pour in the soup and water. Seal the lid, cook for 40 minutes on MEAT/STEW at High. When ready, do a quick pressure release.

Beer-Dijon Braised Steak

Ready in about: 40 minutes | **Serves:** 4 | **Per serving:** Calories 525; Carbs 12g; Fat 21g; Protein 69g

INGREDIENTS

4 Beef Steaks
12 ounces Dark Beer
2 tbsp Dijon Mustard
2 Carrots, chopped
1 tbsp Tomato Paste
1 Onion, chopped
1 tsp Paprika
2 tbsp Flour
1 cup Beef Broth
Salt and Pepper, to taste
Olive oil, to grease

DIRECTIONS

Brush the meat with the mustard and season with paprika, salt, and pepper. Coat the pressure cooker with cooking spray and sear the steak on SAUTÉ mode. Remove steaks to a plate.

Press CANCEL. Pour ¼ cup water and scrape the bottom of the cooker. Wipe clean. Whisk in the tomato paste and flour. Gradually stir in the remaining ingredients, except for the beer.

Return the steak to the cooker, pour in beer and seal the lid. Cook for 20 minutes on MEAT/STEW mode at High. When ready, release the pressure quickly and serve hot.

Tender Onion Beef Roast

Ready in about: 55 minutes | **Serves:** 8 | **Per serving:** Calories 369; Carbs 9g; Fat 16g; Protein 47g

INGREDIENTS

3 pounds Beef Roast
2 Large Sweet Onions, sliced
1 envelope Onion Mix
1 cup Beef Broth
1 cup Tomato Juice
1 tsp Garlic, minced
2 tbsp Worcestershire Sauce
1 tbsp Olive Oil
Salt and Pepper, to taste

DIRECTIONS

Warm the oil on SAUTÉ mode. Season the beef with salt and pepper, and sear on all sides. Transfer to a plate. Add onions, and cook for 3 minutes. Stir in garlic and cook for 1 minute.

Add the beef and stir in the remaining ingredients. Seal the lid and cook for 40 minutes on MEAT/STEW at High. Release the pressure naturally, for 10 minutes.

Beef Stew with Quinoa

Ready in about: 50 minutes | **Serves:** 8 | **Per serving:** Calories 285; Carbs 49g; Fat 8g; Protein 31g

INGREDIENTS

2 pounds Lean Beef Stew Meat, cut into cubes
2 tbsp Cayenne Pepper
2 tsp Fish Sauce
2 (14.5 oz) cans Tomatoes
2 cups Quinoa, rinsed
½ tsp Red Pepper flakes, crushed
Salt and freshly ground Black Pepper, to taste
4 cups Water

DIRECTIONS

Select SAUTÉ mode and add the beef; brown it for 5 minutes, stirring occasionally. Add the rest of the ingredients. Seal the lid, press MEAT/STEW button and cook for 30 minutes at High Pressure.

When ready, do a quick release. Taste and adjust the seasoning. Fluff quinoa with a fork and serve.

Mexican Brisket

Ready in about: 55 minutes | **Serves:** 6 | **Per serving:** Calories 407; Carbs 3g; Fat 30g; Protein 30g

INGREDIENTS

2 ½ pounds Beef Brisket
1 tbsp Chili Powder
1 tbsp Tomato Paste
½ cup Salsa
1 cup Beef Broth
1 tbsp Butter
1 Spanish Onion, sliced
2 Garlic Cloves, minced

DIRECTIONS

Season the beef with chili powder. Coat the pressure cooker with cooking spray and cook the beef until browned on all sides, for about 4 – 6 minutes.

Add onion and cook for 2 more minutes, until soft. Stir in the remaining ingredients. Seal the lid and cook for 35 minutes on MEAT/STEW at High. Do a natural release, for 10 minutes.

Sweet Balsamic Beef

Ready in about: 55 minutes | **Serves:** 8 | **Per serving:** Calories 401; Carbs 30g; Fat 15g; Protein 37g

INGREDIENTS

3 pounds Chuck Steak, sliced
1 cup Maple Syrup
½ cup Balsamic Vinegar
2 cups Bone Broth
1 tsp Garlic, minced
1 tsp Salt
2 tbsp Olive Oil
1 tsp ground Ginger

DIRECTIONS

Heat oil on SAUTÉ. Season the beef with salt and ginger. Brown on all sides for a few minutes. Stir in the remaining ingredients. Seal the lid and cook for 45 minutes on MEAT/STEW at High. Do a quick release.

Tomato Meatballs

Ready in about: 30 minutes | **Serves:** 4 | **Per serving:** Calories 329; Carbs 12g; Fat 16g; Protein 34g

INGREDIENTS

1 pound Ground Beef
½ cup Breadcrumbs
½ Onion, diced
1 tsp Garlic, minced
1 Egg
1 tsp dried Parsley
1 tsp dried Thyme
¼ tsp Salt
¼ tsp Black Pepper
1 ½ cups Tomato Juice
1 cup canned Diced Tomatoes
1 tbsp Brown Sugar
¼ tsp Garlic Powder
¼ tsp Oregano
Cooking Spray, to grease

DIRECTIONS

Combine the first 9 ingredients in a bowl. Mix well with hands. Shape the mixture into meatballs, about 4. Coat the Pressure cooker with cooking spray.

Place meatballs in the cooker and brown them for a few minutes, on SAUTÉ mode. Stir in the remaining ingredients. Seal the lid and cook for 20 minutes on MEAT/STEW at High.

When ready, release the pressure quickly and serve hot.

Bourbon and Apricot Meatloaf

Ready in about: 30 minutes | **Serves:** 4 | **Per serving:** Calories 523; Carbs 58g; Fat 13g; Protein 34g

INGREDIENTS

1 ½ cups Water

MEATLOAF:

1 pound Ground Beef	Glaze:
1 Egg White	1 cup Apricot Jam
⅔ cup Breadcrumbs	½ cup Bourbon
2 tbsp Ketchup	½ cup Barbecue Sauce
⅔ cup Onion, diced	¼ cup Honey
½ tsp Basil	½ cup Water
1 tsp Garlic, minced	1 tbsp Hot Sauce

DIRECTIONS

Combine all of the meatloaf ingredients in a bowl. Mix well with hands and shape into a meatloaf. Place on a greased pan that can fit in your pressure cooker.

Whisk the glaze ingredients in another bowl. Brush this mixture over the meatloaf. Place a trivet and pour in the water. Place the baking dish on top of the trivet, and seal the lid.

Cook for 50 minutes on MEAT/STEW mode at High. When ready, do a quick pressure release.

Spicy Shredded Beef

Ready in about: 55 minutes | **Serves:** 8 | **Per serving:** Calories 346; Carbs 7g; Fat 15g; Protein 46g

INGREDIENTS

3 pounds Beef Roast	2 tsp Mustard Powder
½ cup Ketchup	1 tsp Chili Powder
½ cup Red Wine	1 tsp Garlic, minced
1 cup Water	¼ tsp Nutmeg
2 tsp Soy Sauce	½ tsp Cinnamon ground
1 tbsp Brown Sugar	1 tsp Black Pepper
1 tbsp Balsamic Vinegar	¼ tsp Salt
2 tbsp Onions, minced	¼ tsp Ginger powder

DIRECTIONS

Place the beef in your pressure cooker. Whisk together the remaining ingredients in a bowl. Pour this mixture over the beef. Seal the lid and cook for 40 minutes on MEAT/STEW mode at High. When ready, release the pressure naturally, for 10 minutes.

Beef Sausage and Spinach Stew

Ready in about: 25 minutes | **Serves:** 4 | **Per serving:** Calories 388; Carbs 49g; Fat 13g; Protein 15g

INGREDIENTS

1 pound Spinach, shredded	1 cup Onion, chopped
1 pound Beef Sausage, crumbled	1 tsp Salt
2 Cloves Garlic, minced	¼ tsp ground Black Pepper
1 ½ cups Tomatoes, chopped	½ cup fresh Parsley, chopped
1 cup Brown rice, cooked	1 cup Beef Broth

DIRECTIONS

In a mixing bowl, stir in spinach and fennel seeds. Take half of this mixture to make a bed at the bottom of the cooker. In another bowl, mix in rice, sausage, fresh cilantro, scallions, garlic, salt, and pepper.

Ladle half of this mixture over the spinach mixture and then, top with another layer of the remaining spinach mixture. Finally, top with the remaining part of the meat mixture.

In a large-sized mixing bowl, whisk the tomato puree, cider vinegar, and water. Pour over the mixture.

Select MEAT/STEW, seal the lid and cook for 15 minutes at High Pressure. Once the cooking is complete, do a quick pressure release. Serve immediately in individual serving bowls.

Sloppy Joes

Ready in about: 50 minutes | **Serves:** 8 | **Per serving:** Calories 458; Carbs 44g; Fat 18g; Protein 29g

INGREDIENTS

1 ½ pounds Ground Beef
2 Tomatoes, diced
8 Kaiser Rolls
½ cup Barley
1 tsp Chili Powder
3 tsp Canola Oil
¼ cup Worcestershire Sauce
¼ cup Tomato Ketchup
2 tbsp Brown Sugar
1 cup chopped Scallions
½ tbsp Cayenne Pepper
3 cups Water

DIRECTIONS

Combine all ingredients, except the rolls, in your pressure cooker. Seal the lid, Set it to MEAT/STEW mode and cook for 25 minutes at High. When ready, do a quick pressure release.

Divide the mixture between the rolls and serve immediately.

Savory Fettuccine with Beef Sausage

Ready in about: 40 minutes | **Serves:** 6 | **Per serving:** Calories 512; Carbs 58g; Fat 10g; Protein 23g

INGREDIENTS

1 pound Beef Sausage, chopped
1 pound dried Fettuccine Pasta
½ cup dry White Wine
1 clove Garlic, minced
½ cups Green Peas, frozen
½ Chipotle Pepper, seeded and chopped
1 cup Black Beans, soaked overnight
2 Yellow Bell Peppers, seeded and chopped
2 tsp Olive Oil
2 cups Water
1 cup Scallions, chopped
1 (28 ounce) can whole plum Tomatoes
¼ tsp crushed Red Pepper flakes
1 cup Parmesan cheese, shredded
½ tsp dried Basil
½ tsp dried Oregano
1 tsp Salt
¼ tsp ground Black Pepper
Fresh Parsley, for garnish

DIRECTIONS

Heat the oil, and sauté the scallions, peppers, and garlic for 3 minutes on SAUTÉ mode. Stir in the beef sausage. Sear until lightly browned, for about 3-4 minutes.

Add the remaining ingredients, except for the parsley and parmesan cheese. Add more water if needed. Seal the lid, Select PRESSURE COOK mode and cook for 10 more minutes at High Pressure.

Once ready, do a quick release. Stir in parmesan cheese until melted. Serve sprinkled with parsley.

Simple Cheesy Meatballs

Ready in about: 30 minutes | **Serves:** 4 | **Per serving:** Calories 460; Carbs 9g; Fat 28g; Protein 40g

INGREDIENTS

1 pound Ground Beef
½ cup Onion, diced
1 Egg
½ tsp Garlic Powder
½ cup Feta Cheese, crumbled
1 tbsp mixed dried Herbs
½ cup Breadcrumbs
¼ tsp Black Pepper
1 cup canned Cream of Mushroom Soup
½ cup Water
½ cup Cheddar Cheese, grated
Cooking Spray, to grease

DIRECTIONS

In a bowl, combine the first 8 ingredients. Mix well with hands, and shape into meatballs, about 4. Coat the pressure cooker with spray. Add meatballs and brown on all sides, for a few minutes, on SAUTÉ.

Pour in water and soup, seal the lid, and cook for 20 minutes on MEAT/STEW mode at High. Do a quick pressure release. Stir in the freshly grated cheddar cheese. Cook for an additional 3 minutes, until the cheese melts, lid off, on SAUTÉ mode. Serve immediately.

No-Fuss Beef Chuck Roast

Ready in about: 1 hour | **Serves:** 6 | **Per serving:** Calories 485; Carbs 29g; Fat 15g; Protein 48g

INGREDIENTS

2 pounds boneless Beef Chuck Roast, trimmed
½ pound Carrots, peeled and chopped
2 pounds Yukon Gold Potatoes, chopped
1 (14.5 ounce) can Beef Broth
4 Cloves Garlic, minced
3 tsp Olive Oil
½ pound Celery, chopped
2 Bell Peppers, sliced
1 cup Tomato Paste
2 Yellow Onions, chopped
¼ cup dry White Wine
1 ½ cups Water
3 tsp Flour
½ tsp dried Basil
2 sprigs dried Thyme
Kosher Salt and ground Black Pepper, to taste

DIRECTIONS

Heat the oil on SAUTÉ mode. Brown the beef for 3-4 minutes. Dissolve the cooker with a little bit of beef broth. Stir in the onions and garlic, and sauté for another 3 minutes.

Stir in the rest of the ingredients, except the flour. Seal the lid and switch the pressure release valve to close. Select Pressure Cook mode and cook for 50 minutes at High Pressure.

Once the cooking is complete, do a quick pressure release. Make the slurry by whisking the flour with 1 tbsp. of water. Add to the cooker and place the lid on. Let simmer for about 5 minutes before serving.

Traditional Beef Ragu

Ready in about: 60 minutes | **Serves:** 6 | **Per serving:** Calories 276; Carbs 18g; Fat 11g; Protein 31g

INGREDIENTS

18 ounces Beef Stew Meat, cubed
2 Bay Leaves
5 Garlic Cloves, crushed
7 ounces jarred Roasted Red Peppers, chopped
28 ounces canned crushed Tomatoes, undrained
1 tbsp Parsley, chopped
½ cup Beef Broth
½ tbsp Olive Oil
1 tsp Sea Salt
½ tsp Black Pepper

DIRECTIONS

Season the beef with salt and pepper. Heat the oil on SAUTÉ, and place the beef inside. Cook until the meat is browned on all sides. Add the rest of the ingredients and stir to combine.

Seal the lid, select PRESSURE COOK mode for 45 minutes at High pressure. When ready, wait for the valve to drop on its own for a natural pressure release, for about 10 minutes.

Short Ribs with Carrots and Potatoes

Ready in about: 55 minutes | **Serves:** 6 | **Per serving:** Calories 412; Carbs 28g; Fat 13g; Protein 51g

INGREDIENTS

- 1 ½ cups Beef Broth
- ½ pounds small Potatoes
- 3 tsp Butter
- 2 medium-sized Red Onions, chopped
- 2 Bay Leaves
- 1 14.5-ounce can diced Tomatoes
- 2 sprigs Rosemary
- 2 pounds short Ribs, excess fat trimmed
- ½ pound Carrots, peeled and thinly sliced
- ½ cup Water
- ½ tsp freshly ground Black Pepper
- ½ tsp Salt
- 2 Cloves Garlic, peeled and finely minced

DIRECTIONS

Rub the ribs with salt, and black pepper. Heat the oil on SAUTÉ mode and sear the spare ribs on all sides. Set aside. Add the carrots, garlic, and onion; stir-fry for another 4-5 minutes.

Return the browned ribs to the Pressure cooker and stir in the remaining ingredients. Seal the lid and switch the pressure release valve to close. Cook for 45 minutes on MEAT/STEW mode at High.

Once cooking is complete, perform a quick pressure release and remove the lid. Serve immediately.

Lamb Shanks Braised Under Pressure

Ready in about: 50 minutes | **Serves:** 4 | **Per serving:** Calories 612; Carbs 19g; Fat 43g; Protein 63g

INGREDIENTS

- 4 Lamb Shanks
- 3 Carrots, sliced
- 2 Tomatoes, peeled and quartered
- 1 Garlic Clove, crushed
- 1 tbsp chopped Fresh Oregano
- ¼ cup plus 4 tsp Flour
- 8 tsp Olive Oil
- 1 Onion, chopped
- ¾ cup Red Wine
- ¼ cup Beef Broth
- 8 tsp Cold Water

DIRECTIONS

In a plastic bag, place the lamb shanks and ¼ cup of the flour. Shake until you coat the shanks well. Discard excess flour. Heat 4 tbsp oil on SAUTÉ, and brown shanks on both sides.

Remove to a covered plate. Add the remaining olive oil and sauté the onions, garlic, and carrots for 3-4 minutes. Stir in tomatoes, wine, broth, and oregano. Return the shanks to the cooker. Seal the lid.

Select MEAT/STEW mode at High, and set the timer to 40 minutes. When it beeps, do a quick pressure release. Whisk together the remaining flour and water. Stir this mixture into the lamb sauce and cook with the lid off until it thickens, on SAUTÉ mode. Serve immediately.

Herbed Beef & Yams

Ready in about: 50 minutes | **Serves:** 6 | **Per serving:** Calories 391; Carbs 22g; Fat 27g; Protein 43g

INGREDIENTS

1 Onion, diced
2 Yams, peeled and cubed
1 tbsp Basil, chopped
1 tbsp Parsley, chopped
1 tbsp Coriander, chopped
2 pounds Beef, cubed

1 tsp Garlic, minced
1 ½ cups Bone Broth
3 tbsp Tomato Paste
1 Bell Pepper, chopped
1 tbsp Olive Oil

DIRECTIONS

Heat oil on SAUTÉ mode. Add the peppers and onions and cook for about 3 minutes. Stir in the garlic and sauté for another minute. Add the beef and cook until browned on all sides. Add the rest of the ingredients.

Stir to combine. Seal the lid and cook on PRESSURE COOK mode, at High pressure for 30 minutes. When it goes off, do a quick pressure release.

Beef Pot Roast with Carrots

Ready in about: 65 minutes | **Serves:** 6 | **Per serving:** Calories 532; Carbs 14g; Fat 45g; Protein 55g

INGREDIENTS

1 tbsp Italian Seasoning
5 Carrots, peeled and chopped
2 ½ pounds Beef Roast
2 cups Chicken Stock
2 tbsp Olive Oil

1 Onion, diced
1 tsp Garlic, minced
½ tsp Pepper
½ tsp Sea Salt

DIRECTIONS

Melt the oil on SAUTÉ, add the onions and cook for 4 minutes. Add the garlic and cook for another minute. Season the beef with pepper and salt, and place it on top of the onions.

Pour in stock and seal the lid. Hit PRESSURE COOK mode, and set to 40 minutes at High. When done, do a quick pressure release. Stir in the carrots, and seal the lid again.

Cook on PRESSURE COOK mode at High pressure for 10 more minutes. Release the pressure quickly.

Worcestershire Pork Chops

Ready in about: 35 minutes | **Serves:** 6 | **Per serving:** Calories 613; Carbs 26g; Fat 42g; Protein 62g

INGREDIENTS

1 Onion, diced
8 Pork Chops
¼ cup Olive Oil
3 tbsp Worcestershire Sauce

1 cup Water
4 Potatoes, diced
Salt and Pepper, to taste

DIRECTIONS

Season pork chop with salt and pepper. Heat half of the oil on SAUTÉ, and brown the pork chops on all sides for about 5-6 minutes. Set aside. Add the rest of the oil, stir in onions and sauté for 2-3 minutes.

Add in potatoes and stir in the water and Worcestershire sauce. Return the pork chops to the cooker. Seal the lid, set to MEAT/STEW for 25 minutes at High. When ready, do a quick release.

Russet Potatoes Flank Steak

Ready in about: 50 minutes | **Serves:** 8 | **Per serving:** Calories 402; Carbs 38g; Fat 9g; Protein 41g

INGREDIENTS

1 pound Beef Flank Steak, cut into serving portions
2 Red Onions, peeled and sliced
1 pound Russet Potatoes, peeled and diced
½ Jalapeño Pepper, deveined and thinly sliced
2 Bell Peppers, deveined and thinly sliced
1 cup Celery with leaves, chopped
3 Cloves Garlic, peeled and minced
2 cups Water
2 Carrots, diced
1 6-ounce can Tomato Paste
Salt and ground Black Pepper, to taste

DIRECTIONS

Place the meat in the cooker. Set on SAUTÉ and brown the meat on all sides, for about 7-8 minutes. Set aside. Lay the vegetables at the bottom of your pressure cooker and place on top of the steak.

In a deep bowl, mix in the remaining ingredients; give it a good stir, and pour over the meat. Seal the lid, select MEAT/STEW and cook for 30 minutes at High. Do a quick pressure release, and serve.

Spicy Beef and Pinto Bean Chili

Ready in about: 25 minutes | **Serves:** 6 | **Per serving:** Calories 255; Carbs 12g; Fat 11g; Protein 35g

INGREDIENTS

1 ½ pounds Ground Beef
1 tbsp Chili powder
2 Green Bell Peppers, stemmed, seeded, and chopped
1 tsp Garlic, minced
2 Tomatoes, chopped
2 (14 oz) cans Pinto Beans, drained and rinsed
1 cup Red Onion, chopped
1 cup Beef Broth
2 tsp Grapeseed Oil
½ tsp dried Oregano
½ tsp dried Basil

DIRECTIONS

Heat oil on SAUTÉ, and add onions and green peppers. Stir-fry for about 3-4 minutes, until translucent.

Add in garlic and cook for about 30 seconds. Add the rest of the ingredients. Seal and switch the pressure release valve to close. Select PRESSURE COOK, and cook for 15 minutes at High pressure. Once the cooking is complete, perform a quick pressure release. Serve immediately.

Sticky Baby Back Ribs

Ready in about: 55 minutes | **Serves:** 4 | **Per serving:** Calories 228; Carbs 36g; Fat 7g; Protein 8g

INGREDIENTS

3 pounds Baby Beef Racks, cut into individual bones
2 tsp Olive Oil
1 cup Beer
Salt and Black Pepper to taste
12 ounces Barbecue Sauce
½ tsp Onion Powder
¼ tsp Paprika
¼ tsp Garlic Powder

DIRECTIONS

Mix all spices in a small bowl. Pour the mixture over meat; turn ribs to coat. Heat oil on SAUTÉ, and sear the meat for 3 minutes per side, until browned. Insert the rack, arrange the ribs on top, and pour the beer over.

Seal the lid, set to MEAT/STEW for 35 minutes, at High. Do a quick release. Pour barbecue sauce over the ribs. Simmer for 5 minutes until sticky, on SAUTÉ.

Sloppy Joes and Coleslaw

Ready in about: 30 minutes | **Serves:** 6 | **Per serving:** Calories 313; Carbs 18g; Fat 22g; Protein 24g

INGREDIENTS

1 cup Tomatoes, chopped
1 Onion, chopped
1 Carrot, chopped
1 pound Ground Beef
1 Bell Pepper, chopped
½ cup Rolled Oats
4 tbsp Apple Cider Vinegar

1 tbsp Olive Oil
4 tbsp Tomato Paste
1 cup Water
2 tsp Garlic Powder
1 tbsp Worcestershire Sauce
1 ½ tsp Salt

COLESLAW:

½ Red Onion, chopped
1 tbsp Honey
½ head Cabbage, sliced

2 Carrots, grated
2 tbsp Apple Cider Vinegar
1 tbsp Dijon Mustard

DIRECTIONS

Warm olive oil on SAUTÉ, and brown the meat for 3-4 minutes. Sauté onions, carrots, pepper, garlic, and salt, until soft. Stir in tomatoes, vinegar, Worcestershire sauce, water, and paste.

When starting to boil, stir in the oats. Seal the lid, select PRESSURE COOK for 25 minutes at High. Do a quick pressure release. Mix all slaw ingredients in a large bowl. Serve the sloppy joes with the slaw.

Veggie and Beef Brisket

Ready in about: 1 hour 30 minutes | **Serves:** 4 | **Per serving:** Calories 389; Carbs 10g; Fat 18g; Protein 28g

INGREDIENTS

2 pounds Beef Brisket
6 Red Potatoes, chopped
1 Onion, chopped
4 Bay Leaves
2 tbsp Olive Oil
2 cups Carrots, chopped

3 tbsp Garlic, chopped
3 tbsp Worcestershire Sauce
2 Celery Stalks, chopped
Black Pepper, to taste
1 tbsp Knorr Demi-Glace Sauce
1 cup Vegetable Broth

DIRECTIONS

Season the meat with black pepper. Heat 1 tbsp oil and sauté the onion until caramelized, on SAUTÉ mode. Transfer to a bowl. Heat the remaining oil and cook the meat until browned on all sides. Pour in broth and Worcestershire sauce over the meat.

Seal the lid, Set to MEAT/STEW mode and adjust the timer to 45 minutes at High. When ready, do a quick pressure release. Add in the veggies and bay leaves.

Seal the lid. Set the time to 12 minutes on PRESSURE COOK mode at High. Do a quick pressure release. Discard bay leaves. Transfer the meat and veggies to a serving platter. Whisk in the Knorr sauce and simmer for 5 minutes until thickened. Slice the brisket and pour gravy over the meat to serve.

Chuck Roast with Root Vegetables and Herbs

Ready in about: 50 minutes | **Serves:** 8 | **Per serving:** Calories 403; Carbs 13g; Fat 11g; Protein 52g

INGREDIENTS

1 pound Sweet Potatoes
½ cup White Wine
1 tbsp Garlic, minced
½ cup Celery Root, peeled and thinly sliced
1 tsp Salt
¼ tsp ground Black Pepper, to taste
2 ½ pounds Chuck Roast

4 tbsp Tomato Puree
1 ½ cups Vegetable Broth
2 sprigs Thyme
1 tsp Rosemary
3 tsp oil
1 cup Onions, thinly sliced
2 Carrots, peeled and thinly sliced

DIRECTIONS

Season the roast with salt, and black pepper. Heat the oil on SAUTÉ mode and brown the beef on all sides. Set aside. Add the veggies to the cooker and cook for about 6 minutes, until lightly browned.

Return the beef to the cooker, along with the remaining ingredients. Lock the lid and, select Meat/Stew and cook for 40 minutes at High Pressure. Once ready, do a quick pressure release and serve.

Beef Hot Pot

Ready in about: 40 minutes | **Serves:** 4 | **Per serving:** Calories 542; Carbs 78g; Fat 19g; Protein 11g

INGREDIENTS

1 ½ pounds Beef Stew Meat, cubed
2 Carrots, chopped
2 Celery Stalks, chopped
4 Potatoes, diced
1 Onion, chopped
2 cups Water

2 tbsp Red Wine
2 tbsp Olive Oil
4 tbsp Flour
1 tsp Thyme
Salt and Pepper, to taste

DIRECTIONS

In a bowl, mix in flour, salt, and pepper. Toss the beef. Heat oil on SAUTÉ mode. Add the beef and cook until browned, for a few minutes. Add onion and cook until soft, for 2 minutes.

Stir in the remaining ingredients. Seal the lid and cook for 25 minutes on MEAT/STEW mode at High pressure. When ready, release the pressure naturally, for 10 minutes.

Beef and Cheese Taco Pie

Ready in about: 20 minutes | **Serves:** 4 | **Per serving:** Calories 363; Carbs 29g; Fat 19g; Protein 25g

INGREDIENTS

1 package Corn Tortillas
1 packet of Taco Seasoning
1 pound Ground Beef

12 ounces Mexican Cheese Blend
¼ cup Refried Beans
1 cup Water

DIRECTIONS

Combine the meat with the seasoning. Pour water in your cooker. Place 1 tortilla at the bottom of a pan and lay in the cooker on the trivet. Top with beans, beef, and cheese.

Top with another tortilla. Repeat until you use up all ingredients. The final layer should be a tortilla. Seal the lid, set the time to 12 minutes on MEAT/STEW mode at High pressure. When ready, do a quick pressure release. Remove the pan and serve immediately.

Beef & Russet Potatoes Soup

Ready in about: 35 minutes | **Serves:** 6 | **Per serving:** Calories 273; Carbs 18g; Fat 8g; Protein 29g

INGREDIENTS

1 pound Beef Stew Meat, cut into cubes
1 ½ Russet Potatoes, diced
2 Tomatoes, chopped
1 cup stalk Celery, chopped
1 cup Carrots, diced

1 cup Spring Onion, chopped
5 cups Beef Broth
Sea Salt and ground Black Pepper, to taste
½ cup fresh Cilantro, chopped

DIRECTIONS

In your pressure cooker mix in all ingredients, except for the fresh cilantro. Select SOUP/BROTH mode and adjust the cooking time for to 30 minutes at High pressure.

Seal the lid and switch the pressure release valve to close. Once the cooking is complete, allow for natural pressure release, for 10 minutes. Open the lid and stir in fresh cilantro. Serve warm and enjoy!

Fusilli with Beefy Tomato Sauce

Ready in about: 25 minutes | **Serves:** 6 | **Per serving:** Calories 99; Carbs 4g; Fat 5g; Protein 13g

INGREDIENTS

½ lb. pound Ground Beef
2 Cloves Garlic, sliced
3 tbsp Tomato paste
¼ tsp ground Black Pepper, to taste
1 tsp dried Thyme
1 tsp dried Oregano
½ tsp Salt

2 shallots, chopped
½ tsp Red Pepper flakes
2 tbsp Vegetable Oil
1 tsp Chipotle Peppers, minced
1 tbsp fresh Basil, chopped
3 cups Fusilli Pasta, cooked

DIRECTIONS

Heat oil on SAUTÉ, and cook the shallots and garlic for about 3 minutes. Add in ground meat and season with black pepper. Cook until browned, for around 5 minutes. Stir in tomato paste, flakes and salt.

Lock the lid, select MEAT/STEW and cook for 15 minutes at High Pressure. Once ready, allow for natural pressure release, for 10 minutes. Serve immediately over cooked fusilli garnished with fresh basil.

Ginger-Flavored and Sweet Pork Belly

Ready in about: 1 hour | **Serves:** 4 | **Per serving:** Calories 525; Carbs 11g; Fat 55g; Protein 64g

INGREDIENTS

2 pounds Pork Belly, cut into pieces
1 tbsp Blackstrap Molasses
2 tbsp Coconut Aminos
3 tbsp Sherry

3 cups Water
2 tbsp Maple Syrup
1-inch Piece of Ginger, smashed
A pinch of Sea Salt

DIRECTIONS

Bring 2 cups of water to a boil, on SAUTÉ. Add the pork belly and let boil for 3 minutes. Drain and rinse with cold water. Return the pork to the cooker, and stir in the maple syrup.

Stir in the remaining ingredients, and 1 cup of water. Seal the lid, select the MEAT/STEW mode, and set the timer to 30 minutes at High. When ready, do a quick pressure release.

Potted Rump Steak

Ready in about: 35 minutes | **Serves:** 15 | **Per serving:** Calories 616; Carbs 11g; Fat 34g; Protein 59g

INGREDIENTS

3 tbsp Olive Oil
3 Bay Leaves
9 pounds Rump Steak
2 cups Celery, diced
1 tsp Salt

3 Onions, chopped
2 cups Mushrooms, sliced
18 ounces canned Tomato Paste
10 ½ ounces Beef Broth
1 ½ cups Dry Red Wine

DIRECTIONS

Warm the oil on SAUTÉ, and brown the steak on all sides. Add the vegetables and stir in all of the seasonings. Combine the paste with the wine and broth. Add this mixture to the cooker.

Seal the lid, set on MEAT/STEW for 35 minutes at High. When ready, do a quick release.

Meatballs in Creamy Sauce

Ready in about: 25 minutes | **Serves:** 4 | **Per serving:** Calories 532; Carbs 17g; Fat 43g; Protein 41g

INGREDIENTS

½ cup Milk
1 Onion, minced
1 ½ tbsp dried Thyme
1 pound Ground Beef
1 tbsp dried Oregano
8 ounces Ground Pork
¼ cup Flour

½ tsp Salt
1 slice Bread
14 ounces Chicken Stock mixed with 14 ounces Water
1 Egg
¼ cup Butter
½ cup Whipping Cream

DIRECTIONS

Start by soaking the bread in the milk. Add beef and pork and mix with your hands. Stir in onion, thyme, oregano, egg, and salt. Form ¾-inch balls out of the mixture.

Melt the butter on SAUTÉ. Whisk in the flour and gradually add the diluted chicken broth. When the mixture begins to simmer, add the meatballs. Lock the lid, Set on PRESSURE COOK mode for 10 minutes at High.

Once it goes off, do a quick pressure release. Stir in cream and simmer, lid off, until the sauce thickens, on SAUTÉ.

Beef with Cabbage, Potatoes, and Carrots

Ready in about: 1 hour 5 minutes | **Serves:** 6 | **Per serving:** Calories 531; Carbs 55g; Fat 36g; Protein 36g

INGREDIENTS

6 Potatoes, peeled and quartered
4 Carrots, cut into pieces
2 ½ pounds Beef Brisket
1 Cabbage Head, shredded and stems removed

3 Garlic Cloves, quartered
3 Turnips, chopped
2 Bay Leaves
4 cups of Water

DIRECTIONS

Put garlic, beef, and bay leaves into your pressure cooker and pour water in. Seal the lid and adjust the time to 45 minutes on MEAT/STEW mode at High.

When cooking is over, do a quick pressure release. Stir in the veggies and seal the lid, set the timer to 6 minutes at High. Do a quick pressure release. Discard bay leaves and serve.

Beef Coconut Curry

Ready in about: 45 minutes | **Serves:** 4 | **Per serving:** Calories 541; Carbs 47g; Fat 21g; Protein 41g

INGREDIENTS

1 Onion, diced
1 cup Milk
4 Carrots, sliced
4 Potatoes, peeled and chopped
1 cup Beef Broth
1 pound Beef, cubed
2 tsp Garlic, minced

2 tbsp Curry Powder
½ tsp Black Pepper
½ tsp Paprika
½ tsp Sea Salt
½ tsp dried Parsley
2 tbsp Olive Oil

DIRECTIONS

Heat olive oil on SAUTÉ. Add garlic and onions, and cook for 2 minutes. Stir in beef and cook until the browned, for a few minutes. Add the remaining ingredients and stir to combine.

Seal the lid, press PRESSURE COOK, and set the timer to 30 minutes at High pressure. When it goes off, do a quick pressure release. Ladle into serving bowls immediately.

Rib Eye Steak with Vegetables and Herbs

Ready in about: 50 minutes | **Serves:** 4 | **Per serving:** Calories 315; Carbs 14g; Fat 9g; Protein 38g

INGREDIENTS

2 Rib Eye Steaks
1 cup Leeks, chopped
¼ cup Tomato Sauce
1 tsp Garlic, minced
1 Turnip, chopped
½ pound Carrots, chopped
2 ½ cups Beef Broth

2 tsp Butter
2 tsp Flour
2 oz dry Italian salad dressing mix
1 tsp Ginger, grated
½ tsp Celery seeds
¼ tsp Black Pepper
½ tsp Cayenne Pepper

DIRECTIONS

Melt butter on SAUTÉ. Add in the meat and brown it for 4 minutes, stirring occasionally. Add the rest of the ingredients and give it a good stir. Seal the lid and set on MEAT/STEW for 35 minutes at High.

Once the cooking is complete, perform a quick pressure release. To prepare the slurry, take a mixing bowl and whisk together the flour with one-fourth cup of the cooking liquid.

Add to the pressure cooker. Give it a good stir until everything is well combined.

Lamb Habanero Chili

Ready in about: 50 minutes | **Serves:** 4 | **Per serving:** Calories 332; Carbs 21g; Fat 13g; Protein 41g

INGREDIENTS

1 pound Ground Beef
3 Carrots, chopped
3 Celery Stalks, chopped
1 Bell Pepper, chopped
1 Onion, diced
1 Habanero, minced
1 tsp Garlic, minced
14 ounces canned diced Tomatoes

1 tbsp Chili Powder
1 tsp Cumin
2 cups Chicken Broth
½ tsp Paprika
½ tsp Sea Salt
½ tsp Pepper
1 tbsp Olive Oil

DIRECTIONS

Add the onions and cook for 3 minutes, on SAUTÉ mode. Add garlic and cook for 1 minute. Stir in the ground beef and cook until lightly browned, for a few minutes.

Add the remaining ingredients, and give it a good stir. Seal the lid, select the MEAT/STEW mode, and set the timer to 35 minutes at High pressure. Do a natural pressure release, for about 10 minutes.

Pot Roast in Gravy

Ready in about: 1 hour 10 minutes | **Serves:** 8 | **Per serving:** Calories 324; Carbs 21g; Fat 10g; Protein 37g

INGREDIENTS

3-4 pounds Beef Roast
1 Onion, peeled and quartered
3 ½ tbsp Cornstarch
1 ½ quarts Peach Juice
1 cup Beef Broth

3 ounces Cold Water
2 Garlic Cloves, minced
2 tbsp Olive Oil
Salt and Pepper, to taste

DIRECTIONS

Generously season the beef with salt and pepper. Warm olive oil and add the pot roast; brown on all sides, for about 5-6 minutes per side, on SAUTÉ. Remove to a plate.

Add onions and garlic and cook for 1-2 minutes. Pour beef broth to deglaze the bottom of your cooker's pot. Return the beef, seal the lid, select MEAT/STEW for 50 minutes at High.

Do a quick pressure release, remove the roast to a plate and leave to rest. Whisk the water and cornstarch together and stir into the juice in the cooker. Simmer, lid off, until the gravy thickens.

Slice the meat and pour the gravy over.

Herbed Lamb Roast with Potatoes

Ready in about: 60 minutes | **Serves:** 4 | **Per serving:** Calories 562; Carbs 2g; Fat 51g; Protein 56g

INGREDIENTS

6 pounds Leg of Lamb
1 tsp dried Sage
1 tsp dried Marjoram
1 Bay Leaf, crushed
1 tsp dried Thyme
3 Garlic Cloves, minced

3 pounds Potatoes, cut into pieces
2 tbsp Olive Oil
3 tbsp Arrowroot Powder
½ cup Water
2 cups Chicken Broth
Salt and Pepper, to taste

DIRECTIONS

Combine the herbs with salt and pepper and rub the mixture onto the meat. Melt the butter and brown the lamb on all sides, about 3-4 minutes, on SAUTÉ. Pour the broth around the meat, seal the lid, and cook for 45 minutes on MEAT/STEW mode at High pressure.

When cooking is over, release the pressure quickly, and add the potatoes. Seal the lid and turn the pressure valve to close. Set on PRESSURE COOK mode at High for 10 minutes.

Once cooking is complete wait 5 minutes before releasing the pressure quickly. Transfer the meat and potatoes to a plate. Combine the water and arrowroot and stir the mixture into the pot sauce. Pour the gravy over the meat and potatoes and enjoy.

Smokey Pork Roast

Ready in about: 1 hour 15 minutes | **Serves:** 4 | **Per serving:** Calories 561; Carbs 2g; Fat 41g; Protein 69g

INGREDIENTS

2 pounds Pork Meat
1 tsp Oregano
1 tsp Cumin
1 tsp Liquid Smoke
1 tsp Coconut Sugar

1 tbsp Coconut Oil
1 tsp ground Ginger
½ cup Beef Broth
1 tsp Paprika
½ tsp Pepper

DIRECTIONS

Mix all spices in a bowl and stir to combine. Rub the meat with the spice mixture, covering it completely. Melt the coconut oil and add the pork; cook until browned on all sides, on SAUTÉ.

Combine the liquid smoke and broth, and pour over the pork. Seal the lid, select MEAT/STEW mode, and set to 60 minutes at High. Once it goes off, do a quick pressure release.

Saucy Beef and Rice

Ready in about: 30 minutes | **Serves:** 4 | **Per serving:** Calories 358; Carbs 64g; Fat 7g; Protein 8g

INGREDIENTS

2 tsp Salt
2 pounds Sirloin Steaks, cut into pieces
2 tbsp Vegetable Oil
2 Onions, chopped
½ tsp Paprika
¼ tsp Mustard Powder

½ tsp Black Pepper
3 tbsp Flour
2 Garlic Cloves, minced
4 cups cooked Rice
10 ½ ounces Beef Consommé

DIRECTIONS

In a plastic bag, mix flour, mustard powder, salt, pepper, and paprika. Add beef and shake the bag to coat well. Heat oil and sear the meat on all sides, until browned, about 5-6 minutes, on SAUTÉ.

Add the onions and garlic and cook until translucent. Stir in the beef consommé. Seal the lid press MEAT/STEW and adjust the time to 25 minutes at High. Do a quick pressure release. Let simmer, lid off, for a few minutes until desired consistency.

Beef and Cabbage with Tomato Sauce

Ready in about: 50 minutes | **Serves:** 5 | **Per serving:** Calories 293; Carbs 10g; Fat 11g; Protein 32g

INGREDIENTS

1 ½ pound Ground Beef
3 cups Cabbage, shredded and stems removed
1 cup Leeks, chopped
1 (10.75 oz) can Tomato Soup
1 tbsp Garlic, pressed

1 tbsp Olive Oil
1 tsp Mustard powder
1 Bay Leaf
Sea Salt and ground Black Pepper, to taste

DIRECTIONS

Heat olive oil on SAUTÉ mode. Cook leeks and garlic in hot oil for about 5 minutes. Stir in ground beef, mustard, cabbage, tomato soup, and bay leaf and cook for about 10 minutes, stirring frequently.

Season with salt and pepper. Seal the lid, select PRESSURE COOK mode and cook for 30 minutes at High pressure. Once the cooking is complete, do a quick pressure release, and serve.

Linguine Pasta with Italian Sauce

Ready in about: 20 minutes | **Serves:** 6 | **Per serving:** Calories 415; Carbs 39g; Fat 11g; Protein 38g

INGREDIENTS

1 ½ 12 ounces Linguine Pasta
1 ½ pounds Ground Beef
1 (14.5 oz) can diced Tomatoes, drained
1 Onion, finely minced
1 Garlic Cloves, minced
1 cup Ketchup
2 tsp Olive Oil
½ tsp Sea Salt
½ tsp freshly ground Black Pepper
½ tsp Red Chili flakes Pepper
1 tsp Italian Seasoning
3 cups Water
2 tsp Parmesan cheese

DIRECTIONS

Heat the oil on SAUTÉ mode. Cook the garlic, scallions, and beef for 4 minutes. Add in the rest of the ingredients and give it a good stir. Make sure the linguine pasta is submerged into the sauce.

Seal the lid, press PRESSURE COOK button and cook for 9 minutes at High Pressure. Once the cooking is complete, do a quick pressure release. Sprinkle with Parmesan cheese and serve immediately.

Shredded Beef the Caribbean Way

Ready in about: 1 hour | **Serves:** 4 | **Per serving:** Calories 562; Carbs 3g; Fat 57g; Protein 57g

INGREDIENTS

2 pounds Beef Roast
½ tsp Turmeric
1 tsp grated Ginger
1 cup Water
4 Whole Cloves
1 tsp dried Thyme
1 tsp Garlic Powder
1 tbsp Olive Oil

DIRECTIONS

Rub olive oil onto the roast to coat. Mix the turmeric, garlic, thyme, and ginger in a small bowl, and rub the mixture into the meat. Stick the cloves into the beef roast. Place the beef inside your pressure cooker and pour the water around it.

Seal the lid, and set to 50 minutes on MEAT/STEW mode, at High pressure. When cooking is over, do a quick pressure release. Shred the meat to serve.

Smoky Beef Brisket Stew

Ready in about: 40 minutes | **Serves:** 4 | **Per serving:** Calories 385; Carbs 25g; Fat 9g; Protein 37g

INGREDIENTS

1 ½ pounds Beef Brisket, cubed
2 slices Bacon, diced
2 tsp Paprika
2 Garlic Cloves, smashed
2 Red Bell Peppers, finely minced
3 Potatoes, peeled and diced
1 tbsp Butter, softened
2 cups Shallots, peeled and chopped
2 tbsp Red wine
2 cups Beef stock
2 Tomatoes, finely chopped
1 tsp Chili Pepper, minced

DIRECTIONS

Melt butter on SAUTÉ. Place the bacon and beef, and brown them for 3 minutes, stirring occasionally. Add in the remaining ingredients. Seal the lid, and cook for 30 minutes on PRESSURE COOK mode at High. Once the cooking is complete, do a quick pressure release. Serve hot.

Veal Shoulder and Mushrooms

Ready in about: 45 minutes | **Serves:** 4 | **Per serving:** Calories 521; Carbs 42g; Fat 17g; Protein 53g

INGREDIENTS

2 pounds Veal Shoulder, cut into chunks
16 ounces Shallots, chopped
16 ounces Potatoes, chopped
10 ounces Beef Stock
8 ounces Mushrooms, sliced
3 ½ tbsp Olive Oil

2 tbsp Chives, chopped
2 ounces White Wine
1 tsp Garlic, minced
1 tbsp Flour
1 tsp Sage

DIRECTIONS

Heat 1 ½ tbsp oil on SAUTÉ, add veal and coat with flour. Cook until browned.

Stir 2 tbsp of the oil and cook the mushrooms for 3 minutes. Add onions and garlic, and cook for 2 minutes, until soft and translucent. Pour in the wine, stock, and sage, and stir.

Seal the lid and cook on SOUP/BROTH mode for 20 minutes at High pressure. When cooking is over, release the pressure quickly. Serve and enjoy!

Mutton with Potatoes and Tomatoes

Ready in about: 45 minutes | **Serves:** 4 | **Per serving:** Calories 389; Carbs 37g; Fat 13g; Protein 32g

INGREDIENTS

1 pound Mutton, cubed
3 Potatoes, peeled and chopped
1 cup Carrots, chopped
½ cup Turnip, chopped
2 cups canned diced Tomatoes
1 Onion, diced

2 Garlic Cloves, minced
½ cup Chicken Broth
½ tsp Salt
¼ tsp Black Pepper
1 tbsp Olive Oil

DIRECTIONS

Heat the oil on SAUTÉ, add the mutton pieces and cook until browned on all sides. Remove to a plate. Add onions and cook until soft, for 3 minutes. Stir in garlic and cook for a minute.

Return the cooked mutton to the cooker, and add the remaining ingredients. Stir well to combine and seal the lid. Select PRESSURE COOK mode for 25 minutes at High pressure.

When done, let the valve to drop on its own for a natural pressure release, for 5-10 minutes.

Lamb Stew with Apricots

Ready in about: 40 minutes | **Serves:** 4 | **Per serving:** Calories 422; Carbs 14g; Fat 19g; Protein 43g

INGREDIENTS

1 pound Lamb, cubed
4 dried Apricots, diced
1 tsp Garlic, minced
1 Onion, diced
2 Potatoes, peeled and chopped
2 Carrots, peeled and chopped
2 ½ cups Chicken Broth
3 cups chopped Kale

28 ounces diced canned Tomatoes
½ tsp Cinnamon
1 tsp Cumin
½ tsp Ginger Powder
¼ tsp Allspice
¼ tsp Pepper
½ tsp Sea Salt
1 tbsp Olive Oil

DIRECTIONS

Heat oil on SAUTÉ, add the lamb and cook until browned on all sides. Add onions and cook for 3 more minutes. When softened a bit, stir in the garlic, and sauté only for a minute.

Stir in all remaining ingredients, and seal the lid. Press the PRESSURE COOK button, and set the timer to 20 minutes at High pressure. When it goes off, do a quick pressure release.

Port Wine Garlicky Lamb

Ready in about: 30 minutes | **Serves:** 4 | **Per serving:** Calories 587; Carbs 9g; Fat 35g; Protein 60g

INGREDIENTS

2 pounds Lamb Shanks
1 tbsp Olive Oil
½ cup Port Wine
1 tbsp Tomato Paste
10 Whole Garlic Cloves, peeled

½ cup Chicken Broth
1 tsp Balsamic Vinegar
½ tsp dried Rosemary
1 tbsp Butter

DIRECTIONS

Season lamb shanks with salt and pepper. Warm the oil and brown the lamb shanks on all sides, about 2-3 minutes, on SAUTÉ. Add the garlic and cook until fragrant. Stir in the rest of the ingredients, except for the butter and vinegar.

Lock and seal the lid, set on MEAT/STEW and adjust the timer to 35 minutes at High pressure. Do a quick pressure release. Remove lamb shanks and let the sauce boil for 5 minutes. lid off on SAUTÉ mode. Stir in vinegar and butter. Serve the gravy poured over the shanks.

Poultry Recipes

Spicy Rosemary Chicken

Ready in about: 55 minutes | **Serves:** 4 | **Per serving:** Calories 294; Carbs 4g; Fat 7g; Protein 50g

INGREDIENTS

1 Whole Chicken
1 tbsp Cayenne Pepper
2 Rosemary Sprigs
2 Garlic Cloves, crushed

¼ Onion, halved, or sliced
1 tsp dried Rosemary
Salt and Pepper, to taste
1 ½ cups Chicken Broth

DIRECTIONS

Wash and pat dry the chicken. Season with salt, pepper, rosemary, and cayenne pepper. Rub the spices onto the meat. Stir in onion, garlic, and rosemary sprig inside the chicken's cavity.

Place the chicken in the cooker, and pour in broth around the chicken, not over. Seal the lid and cook for 30 minutes on MEAT/STEW, at High. When done, let pressure drop naturally, for about 10 minutes.

Creamy Chicken in Beer Sauce

Ready in about: 40 minutes | **Serves:** 4 | **Per serving:** Calories 534; Carbs 9g; Fat 33g; Protein 46g

INGREDIENTS

1 ½ pounds Chicken Breasts
10 ounces Beer
1 cup Green Onions, chopped
1 ¼ cups Greek Yogurt
¼ cup Arrowroot

½ tsp Sage
2 tsp dried Thyme
2 tsp dried Rosemary
2 tbsp Olive Oil

DIRECTIONS

Heat the oil on SAUTÉ mode. Add onions and cook for 2 minutes. Coat the chicken with the arrowroot. Add the chicken to the cooker and cook until browned on all sides.

Pour the beer over and bring the mixture to a boil. Stir in the herbs and cook on SOUP/BROTH for 30 minutes at High pressure. Do a quick release, and stir in yogurt before serving.

Fennel Chicken Breast

Ready in about: 25 minutes | **Serves:** 8 | **Per serving:** Calories 422; Carbs 3g; Fat 22g; Protein 51g

INGREDIENTS

2 pounds Chicken Breasts, boneless and skinless
1 cup Celery, chopped
1 cup Fennel, chopped

2 ¼ cups Chicken Stock
Salt and Pepper, to taste

DIRECTIONS

Chop the chicken into small pieces and place in your pressure cooker. Add the remaining ingredients and stir well to combine. Seal the lid, and set to PRESSURE COOK for 15 minutes at High.

When ready, release the pressure naturally, for 10 minutes. Season with salt and pepper, to taste.

Black Currant and Lemon Chicken

Ready in about: 20 minutes | **Serves:** 6 | **Per serving:** Calories 286; Carbs 8g; Fat 18g; Protein 25g

INGREDIENTS

1 ½ pound Chicken Breasts
¼ cup Red Currants
2 Garlic Cloves, minced
6 Lemon Slices
1 cup Scallions, chopped
1 cup Black Olives, pitted

2 tbsp Canola Oil
¼ tsp Pepper
1 tsp Coriander Seeds
1 tsp Cumin
¼ tsp Salt
2 ¼ cups Water

DIRECTIONS

Heat the oil on SAUTÉ. Add scallions, coriander, and garlic and cook for 30 seconds. Add the chicken and top with olives and red currants. Season with salt and pepper.

Arrange the lemon slices on top, and pour the water over. Seal the lid and cook on POULTRY for 15 minutes at High pressure. When ready, release the pressure naturally, for 10 minutes.

Cajun Chicken and Green Beans

Ready in about: 35 minutes | **Serves:** 4 | **Per serving:** Calories 449; Carbs 13g; Fat 12g; Protein 68g

INGREDIENTS

4 boneless and skinless Chicken Breasts, frozen
2 cups Green Beans, frozen
14 ounces Cornbread Stuffing

1 tsp Cajun Seasoning
1 cup Chicken Broth

DIRECTIONS

Combine the chicken and broth in the pressure cooker, seal the lid, and cook on MEAT/STEW for 20 minutes at High. When ready, do a quick pressure release. Add the green beans, seal the lid again, and cook for 2 more minutes on PRESSURE COOK at High.

Do a quick release, stir in the cornbread stuffing and Cajun seasoning and cook for another 5 minutes, on SAUTÉ, lid off. When ready, release the pressure quickly.

Sweet and Gingery Whole Chicken

Ready in about: 60 minutes | **Serves:** 6 | **Per serving:** Calories 234; Carbs 5g; Fat 8g; Protein 33g

INGREDIENTS

1 medium Whole Chicken
1 Green Onion, minced
2 tbsp Sugar
1 tbsp Ginger, grated
2 tsp Soy Sauce

¼ cup White Wine
½ cup Chicken Broth
1 ½ tbsp Olive Oil
1 tsp Salt
¼ tsp Pepper

DIRECTIONS

Heat oil on SAUTÉ mode. Season the chicken with sugar and half the salt and pepper, and brown on all sides, for a few minutes. Remove from the cooker and set aside.

Whisk in together wine, broth, soy sauce, and salt. Add the chicken and seal the lid. Cook for 35 minutes on MEAT/STEW mode at High. When ready, release the pressure quickly.

Balsamic Chicken Thighs with Pears

Ready in about: 30 minutes | **Serves:** 6 | **Per serving:** Calories 488; Carbs 11g; Fat 34g; Protein 33g

INGREDIENTS

6 large Chicken Thighs
½ cup Sweet Onions, chopped
3 small Pears, peeled and sliced
2 tbsp Balsamic Vinegar

3 tsp Butter
1 cup Chicken Broth
1 tsp Cayenne Pepper
Salt and Pepper, to taste

DIRECTIONS

Melt the butter on SAUTÉ mode. Add chicken and sprinkle with the spices. Brown on all sides. Stir in the remaining ingredients. Seal the lid and cook for 20 minutes at High pressure.

When ready, release the pressure naturally, for 10 minutes, and serve immediately.

Cheesy Drumsticks in Marinara Sauce

Ready in about: 35 minutes | **Serves:** 4 | **Per serving:** Calories 588; Carbs 15g; Fat 43g; Protein 36g

INGREDIENTS

4 Chicken Drumsticks
1 cup Sour Cream
1 ¾ cups Marinara Sauce
1 cup grated Cheddar Cheese

½ Butter Stick
1 tsp Chipotle Powder
½ tsp Rosemary
Salt and Pepper, to taste

DIRECTIONS

Melt the butter on SAUTÉ. Add marinara, chipotle, rosemary, and chicken. Season with salt and pepper. Seal the lid and cook for 20 minutes at High pressure. When ready, release the pressure naturally, for 10 minutes. Stir in the cheese and sour cream, and serve.

Delicious BBQ Pulled Turkey

Ready in about: 100 minutes | **Serves:** 6 | **Per serving:** Calories 456; Carbs 19g; Fat 26g; Protein 37g

INGREDIENTS

2 pounds Turkey Breasts, boneless and skinless
1 cup Beer

1 ½ tbsp Oil

SAUCE:

2 tbsp Honey
½ cup Apple Cider Vinegar
1 tsp Liquid Smoke
2 tsp Sriracha
1 tsp Garlic Powder
1 tsp Onion Powder

½ cup Mustard
1 tbsp Worcestershire Sauce
2 tbsp Honey
1 tsp Mustard Powder
2 tbsp Olive Oil

DIRECTIONS

Heat the oil on SAUTÉ mode. Add turkey and brown on all sides. Whisk together all the sauce ingredients in a small bowl. Add beef and sauce to the Pressure cooker. Stir to combine.

Seal the lid and cook for 45 minutes on MEAT/STEW mode at High. When ready, release the pressure quickly. Remove the turkey to a plate and shred with two forks. Set to SAUTÉ, and cook until the sauce is reduced and thickened, lid off. Return the turkey and stir to coat well.

Effortless Coq Au Vin

Ready in about: 60 minutes | **Serves:** 8 | **Per serving:** Calories 538; Carbs 40g; Fat 30g; Protein 26g

INGREDIENTS

2 pounds Chicken Thighs
4 ounces Bacon, chopped
14 ounces Red Wine
1 cup Parsley, chopped
2 Onions, chopped
4 small Potatoes, halved
7 ounces White Mushrooms, sliced

1 tsp Garlic Paste
2 tbsp Flour
¼ cup Olive Oil
2 tbsp Cognac
Salt and Black Pepper, to taste
Water, as needed

DIRECTIONS

Heat oil on SAUTÉ mode, and brown the chicken on all sides. Then, set aside. Add in onion, garlic, and bacon and cook for 2 minutes, until soft. Whisk in the flour and cognac.

Stir in the remaining ingredients, except for the mushrooms. Add enough water to cover everything. Seal the lid, press SOUP/BROTH mode and cook for 20 minutes at High.

When cooking is over, release the pressure quickly. Stir in the mushrooms, seal the lid again and cook for 5 more minutes at High pressure. When ready, do a quick pressure release

Turkey Breasts in Maple and Habanero Sauce

Ready in about: 30 minutes | **Serves:** 4 | **Per serving:** Calories 446; Carbs 23g; Fat 16g; Protein 51g

INGREDIENTS

2 pounds Turkey Breasts
6 tbsp Habanero Sauce
½ cup Tomato Puree
¼ cup Maple Syrup

1 ½ cups Water
½ tsp Cumin
1 tsp Smoked Paprika
Salt and Black Pepper, to taste

DIRECTIONS

Pour the water in your pressure cooker and place the turkey inside. Season with salt and black pepper. Seal the lid, press POULTRY, for 15 minutes at High pressure.

Release the pressure naturally, for 10 minutes. Discard cooking liquid. Shred turkey inside the cooker and add the remaining ingredients. Cook on SAUTÉ mode, lid off, for a few minutes, until thickened.

Turkey with Tomatoes and Red Beans

Ready in about: 20 minutes | **Serves:** 6 | **Per serving:** Calories 212; Carbs 12g; Fat 8g; Protein 23g

INGREDIENTS

1-pound Turkey Breast, cut into bite-sized cubes
1 (16 oz) can Stewed Tomatoes
1 (16 oz) can Red Kidney Beans, drained
2 cups Chicken Stock

½ cup Sour Cream
Salt and Black Pepper, to taste
2 tbsp Parsley, chopped

DIRECTIONS

Place beans, tomatoes, turkey, stock, and sour cream in your pressure cooker. Season with salt and pepper. Seal the lid, set on SOUP/BROTH, and cook for 20 minutes at High.

When ready, release the pressure quickly. Sprinkle with freshly chopped parsley to serve.

Orange and Cranberry Turkey Wings

Ready in about: 40 minutes | **Serves:** 4 | **Per serving:** Calories 525; Carbs 20g; Fat 38g; Protein 26g

INGREDIENTS

1 pound Turkey Wings
¼ cup Orange Juice
1 stick Butter, softened
2 cups Cranberries

2 Onions, sliced
2 cups Vegetable Stock
½ tsp Cayenne Pepper
Salt and Pepper, to taste

DIRECTIONS

Melt the butter on SAUTÉ. Add the turkey wings, season with salt, pepper, and cayenne pepper, and cook until browned, for a few minutes. Stir in the remaining ingredients. Seal the lid.

Cook for 25 minutes on MEAT/STEW at High. Release the pressure naturally, for 10 minutes, and serve.

Chicken Drumettes in Creamy Tomato Sauce

Ready in about: 25 minutes | **Serves:** 2 | **Per serving:** Calories 525; Carbs 21g; Fat 41g; Protein 28g

INGREDIENTS

2 Chicken Drumsticks, trimmed of fat
2 cups Tomato Sauce
1 cup Heavy Cream
1 cup sharp Parmesan cheese, grated
4 tbsp Butter

1 tsp Garlic paste
1 tsp Chipotle powder
1 tbsp fresh Basil leaves, chopped
Salt and ground Black Pepper, to taste
½ tsp fresh Rosemary, chopped

DIRECTIONS

Melt butter on SAUTÉ mode. Add garlic paste, chipotle powder, tomato sauce, rosemary, and basil leaves. Sprinkle the chicken drumsticks with salt and ground black pepper. Place the chicken down into the sauce, so it resembles a nestle.

Seal the lid, select PRESSURE COOK and cook at High pressure for 20 minutes. Once it goes off, release the pressure naturally, for 10 minutes. Stir in the cheese and sour cream and serve right away.

Creamy Chicken with Mushrooms and Carrots

Ready in about: 30 minutes | **Serves:** 6 | **Per serving:** Calories 603; Carbs 14g; Fat 31g; Protein 59g

INGREDIENTS

6 Chicken Breasts, boneless and skinless
1 Sweet Onion, diced
1 cup Water
8 ounces Mushrooms, sliced
1 can Cream of Mushroom Soup

1 pound Baby Carrots
1 tbsp Butter
1 tbsp Olive Oil
2 tbsp Heavy Cream

DIRECTIONS

Heat oil and butter on SAUTÉ mode, until melted. Add onions and mushrooms, and cook for 3 minutes, until soft. Stir in the carrots, add chicken, and pour mushroom soup, and water.

Seal the lid and cook for 8 minutes on RICE mode at High. When ready, do a quick pressure release and remove the mushrooms, chicken, and carrots to a plate.

In the pressure cooker, stir in the heavy cream and cook the sauce until it thickens, on SAUTÉ, for a few minutes. Serve the chicken and veggies drizzled with the sauce.

Turkey Thighs with Fig Sauce

Ready in about: 35 minutes | **Serves:** 6 | **Per serving:** Calories 455; Carbs 62g; Fat 8g; Protein 34g

INGREDIENTS

2 pounds Turkey Thighs, skinless
1 cup Carrots, sliced
1 Onion, chopped
4 Potatoes, cubed
¼ cup Balsamic Vinegar

12 dried Figs, halved
2 cups Chicken Broth
½ Celery Stalk, diced
Salt and Black Pepper, to taste

DIRECTIONS

Place carrots, onion, potatoes, celery and turkey inside the pressure cooker. Whisk together the remaining ingredients, except the figs, in a bowl and pour the mixture over the turkey.

Season with salt and pepper, and stir in the figs, and 1 cup of water. Seal the lid, and cook for 15 minutes on POULTRY, at High. When done, do a natural release, for 10 minutes.

Remove the figs, turkey, and veggies to serving plates. To serve, strain the sauce that's left in the cooker, and pour over the turkey and veggies.

Chicken Thighs with Potatoes and Pesto Sauce

Ready in about: 25 minutes | **Serves:** 8 | **Per serving:** Calories 537; Carbs 52g; Fat 25g; Protein 26g

INGREDIENTS

2 pounds Chicken Thighs, boneless and skinless
6 medium Potatoes, cut into wedges
1 tsp Lemon Juice

¼ cup Pesto Sauce
1 Sweet Onion, sliced
1 cup Chicken Broth

DIRECTIONS

In a bowl, mix in the pesto sauce and lemon juice. Add the chicken and coat well. Meanwhile, place the remaining ingredients in the pressure cooker. Add in the coated chicken.

Seal the lid, set on PRESSURE COOK for 10 minutes at High. Do a natural release, for 10 minutes.

Delicious Turkey Meatloaf

Ready in about: 30 minutes | **Serves:** 4 | **Per serving:** Calories 317; Carbs 7g; Fat 16g; Protein 37g

INGREDIENTS

1 ½ pounds ground Turkey
1 Carrot, grated
1 Onion, diced
1 Celery Stalk, diced
½ cup Breadcrumbs
1 Egg, cracked in the bowl
1 tsp Garlic, minced

½ tsp Thyme
¼ tsp Oregano
¼ tsp Salt
¼ tsp Black Pepper
1 tsp Worcestershire Sauce
1 ½ cups Water
Cooking spray, to grease

DIRECTIONS

Pour the water in your pressure cooker. Combine the remaining ingredients in a large bowl. Grease a baking pan with cooking spray and add in the mixture, pressing it tightly.

Lay the trivet and lower the pan on top of the trivet, inside your Pressure cooker. Seal the lid and cook on POULTRY mode for 15 minutes at High. Do a natural release, for 10 minutes.

Thyme and Lemon Drumsticks with Red Sauce

Ready in about: 35 minutes | **Serves:** 4 | **Per serving:** Calories 268; Carbs 2g; Fat 16g; Protein 26g

INGREDIENTS

4 Chicken Drumsticks, fresh
1 Onion, sliced
½ cup canned, diced, Tomatoes
2 tsp dried Thyme
1 tsp Lemon Zest

½ cup Water
2 tbsp Lemon Juice
1 tbsp Olive Oil
Salt and Black Pepper, to taste

DIRECTIONS

Heat oil on SAUTÉ. Add drumsticks and cook them for a few minutes, until lightly browned. Stir in the remaining ingredients. Seal the lid and cook for 15 minutes on POULTRY at High.

Once cooking is complete, release the pressure naturally, for 10 minutes. Serve immediately.

Easy and Flavorful Chicken Legs

Ready in about: 30 minutes | **Serves:** 4 | **Per serving:** Calories 418; Carbs 7g; Fat 18g; Protein 53g

INGREDIENTS

4 Chicken Legs about 8-ounce each
1 Onion, chopped
1 Tomato, chopped
½ cup Sour Cream
1 cup Chicken Broth

1 tbsp Olive Oil
2 tsp Smoked Paprika
½ tsp Garlic Powder
¼ tsp Salt
¼ tsp Black Pepper

DIRECTIONS

Season the chicken with salt, black pepper, garlic powder, and smoked paprika, in a big bowl. Heat the oil on SAUTÉ, and add the seasoned chicken legs.

Cook until browned on all sides. Stir in the remaining ingredients and seal the lid. Cook for 15 minutes on POULTRY at High. When ready, release the pressure naturally, for 15 minutes.

Chicken Stew with Shallots and Carrots

Ready in about: 25 minutes | **Serves:** 6 | **Per serving:** Calories 305; Carbs 15g; Fat 5g; Protein 39g

INGREDIENTS

1 cup Chicken Stock
3 tsp Vegetable Oil
3 Carrots, peeled, cored, and sliced
6 Shallots, halved and thinly sliced
½ tsp ground Black Pepper
1 tsp Cayenne Pepper

1 tsp Salt
10 boneless, skinless Chicken Thighs, trimmed bone-in, skin-on
2 tbsp Balsamic Vinegar
1 tbsp chopped fresh Parsley, for garnish

DIRECTIONS

Sprinkle the chicken with the salt, cayenne pepper, and black pepper. Select SAUTÉ and heat the oil. Add in the thighs and brown lightly on both sides, turning once or twice. Set it aside.

Add the remaining ingredients. Dip the browned chicken in the mixture. Seal the lid and cook for 20 minutes on PRESSURE COOK mode at Hgh Pressure.

When ready, allow for a natural pressure release, for 10 minutes, sprinkle with parsley and serve.

Asian-style Sweet Chicken Drumsticks

Ready in about: 25 minutes | **Serves:** 4 | **Per serving:** Calories 384; Carbs 26g; Fat 19g; Protein 25g

INGREDIENTS

4 Chicken Drumsticks
1 cup Pineapples, chopped
½ cup Coconut Milk
½ cup Tomato Sauce
2 tbsp Brown Sugar

2 tbsp Apple Cider Vinegar
1 tbsp Lime Juice
4 tbsp Water
Salt and Pepper, to taste

DIRECTIONS

In a bowl, whisk together all ingredients, except for the chicken and pineapples. Place the chicken drumsticks and pineapples in the pressure cooker and pour the sauce over.

Seal the lid, set to POULTRY, and adjust the cooking time to 15 minutes at High. Once the cooking is complete, do a quick pressure release. Give it a good stir before serving hot!

Mexican Cheesy Turkey Breasts

Ready in about: 25 minutes | **Serves:** 4 | **Per serving:** Calories 404; Carbs 20g; Fat 12g; Protein 50g

INGREDIENTS

24 ounces Turkey Breasts, frozen
1 cup shredded Mozzarella Cheese
1 cup mild Salsa
½ cup Chicken Broth

1 cup Tomato Sauce
3 tbsp Lime Juice
Salt and Pepper, to taste

DIRECTIONS

Place the tomato sauce, salsa, broth, lime juice, and turkey in your pressure cooker. Seal the lid, and cook on POULTRY for 15 minutes at High. Do a natural pressure release, for 10 minutes.

Shred the turkey inside the cooker, and stir in the cheese. Cook for 1 minute on SAUTÉ, to melt cheese.

Greek-Style Chicken Legs with Herbs

Ready in about: 35 minutes | **Serves:** 4 | **Per serving:** Calories 317; Carbs 15g; Fat 16g; Protein 28g

INGREDIENTS

4 Chicken Legs, skinless
1 cup Onions, thinly sliced
2 ripe Tomatoes, chopped
1 tsp Garlic, minced
2 tbsp corn Flour
1 ½ cups Chicken broth

3 tsp Olive Oil
1 tsp ground Cumin
2 tsp dried Rosemary
Salt and ground Black Pepper
½ cup Feta Cheese, cubes for garnish
10 Black Olives for garnish

DIRECTIONS

Season the chicken with salt, black pepper, rosemary, and cumin. Heat oil on SAUTÉ mode. Brown the chicken legs, for 3 minutes per side. Stir in the onions and cook for another 4 minutes.

Add the garlic and cook for another minute. In a measuring cup, stir the cornflour into the stock to make a slurry. When mixed, add the stock to the chicken. Add the tomatoes and give it a good stir.

Seal the lid and switch the pressure release valve to close. Hit PRESSURE COOK and set to 20 minutes at High. Once it goes off, release the pressure quickly. Serve with a side of feta cheese and black olives.

Hearty and Hot Turkey Soup

Ready in about: 40 minutes | **Serves:** 6 | **Per serving:** Calories 398; Carbs 40g; Fat 11g; Protein 51g

INGREDIENTS

1 ½ pounds Turkey thighs, boneless, skinless and diced
1 cup Carrots, trimmed and diced
2 (8 oz) cans White Beans
2 Tomatoes, chopped
1 potato, chopped
1 cup Green Onions, chopped
2 Cloves Garlic, minced
6 cups Vegetable Stock
¼ tsp ground Black Pepper
¼ tsp Salt
½ tsp Cayenne Pepper
½ cup Celery head, peeled and chopped

DIRECTIONS

Place all ingredients, except the beans, into the pressure cooker, and select SOUP/BROTH mode. Seal the lid and cook for 20 minutes at High Pressure. Release the pressure quickly.

Remove the lid and stir in the beans. Cover the cooker and let it stand for 10 minutes before serving.

Chicken and Beans Casserole with Chorizo

Ready in about: 35 minutes | **Serves:** 5 | **Per serving:** Calories 587; Carbs 52g; Fat 29g; Protein 29g

INGREDIENTS

1 tsp Garlic, minced
1 cup Onions, chopped
1 pound Chorizo Sausage, cut into pieces
4 Chicken Thighs, boneless, skinless
3 tbsp Olive Oil
2 cups Chicken Stock
11 ounces Asparagus, quartered
1 tsp Paprika
½ tsp ground Black Pepper
1 tsp Salt
2 Jalapeno Peppers, stemmed, cored, and chopped
26 oz canned whole Tomatoes, roughly chopped
1 ½ cups Kidney Beans

DIRECTIONS

On SAUTÉ, heat the oil and brown the sausage, for about 5 minutes per side. Transfer to a large bowl. In the same oil, add the thighs and brown them for 5 minutes. Remove to the same bowl as the sausage.

In the cooker, stir in onions and peppers. Cook for 3 minutes. Add in garlic and cook for 1 minute. Stir in the tomatoes, beans, stock, asparagus, paprika, salt, and black pepper.

Return the reserved sausage and thighs to the cooker. Stir well. Seal the lid and cook for 10 minutes on PRESSURE COOK mode at High Pressure. When ready, do a quick release and serve hot.

Green BBQ Chicken Wings

Ready in about: 20 minutes | **Serves:** 4 | **Per serving:** Calories 311; Carbs 1g; Fat 10g; Protein 51g

INGREDIENTS

2 pounds Chicken Wings
5 tbsp Butter
1 cup Barbeque Sauce
5 Green Onions, minced

DIRECTIONS

Add the butter, ¾ parts of the sauce and chicken in the pressure cooker.

Select PRESSURE COOK, seal the lid and cook for 15 minutes at High.

Do a quick release. Garnish wings with onions and top with the remaining sauce.

Homemade Cajun Chicken Jambalaya

Ready in about: 30 minutes | **Serves:** 6 | **Per serving:** Calories 299; Carbs 31g; Fat 8g; Protein 41g

INGREDIENTS

1 ½ pounds, Chicken Breast, skinless
3 cups Chicken Stock
1 tbsp Garlic, minced
1 tsp Cajun Seasoning

1 Celery stalk, diced
1 ½ cups chopped Leeks, white part
1 ½ cups dry White Rice
2 tbsp Tomato Paste

DIRECTIONS

Select SAUTÉ and brown the chicken for 5 minutes. Add the garlic and celery, and fry for 2 minutes until fragrant. Deglaze with broth. Add the remaining ingredients to the cooker. Seal the lid.

Select PRESSURE COOK, and cook for 15 minutes at High. Do a quick pressure release and serve

Tasty Turkey with Campanelle and Tomato Sauce

Ready in about: 20 minutes | **Serves:** 4 | **Per serving:** Calories 588; Carbs 71g; Fat 11g; Protein 60g

INGREDIENTS

3 cups Tomato Sauce
½ tsp Salt
½ tbsp Marjoram
1 tsp dried Thyme
½ tbsp fresh Basil, chopped
¼ tsp ground Black Pepper, or more to taste

1 ½ pounds Turkey Breasts, chopped
1 tsp Garlic, minced
1 ½ cup spring Onions, chopped
1 package dry Campanelle Pasta
2 tbsp Olive Oil
½ cup Grana Padano cheese, grated

DIRECTIONS

Select SAUTÉ and heat the oil in the cooker. Place the turkey, spring onions and garlic. Cook until cooked, about 6-7 minutes. Add the remaining ingredients, except the cheese.

Seal the lid and press PRESSURE COOK button. Cook for 5 minutes at High Pressure. Once cooking has completed, quick release the pressure. To serve, top with freshly grated Grana Padano cheese.

Hot and Spicy Shredded Chicken

Ready in about: 1 hour | **Serves:** 4 | **Per serving:** Calories 307; Carbs 12g; Fat 10g; Protein 38g

INGREDIENTS

1 ½ pounds boneless and skinless Chicken Breasts
2 cups diced Tomatoes
½ tsp Oregano
2 Green Chilies, seeded and chopped
½ tsp Paprika

2 tbsp Coconut Sugar
½ cup Salsa
1 tsp Cumin
2 tbsp Olive Oil

DIRECTIONS

In a small mixing dish, combine the oil with all spices. Rub the chicken breast with the spicy marinade. Lay the meat into your pressure cooker. Pour the diced tomatoes. Seal the lid, and adjust the time to 20 minutes on POULTRY mode at High pressure.

Once ready, press CANCEL and do a quick pressure release, by turning the valve to "open" position. Remove chicken to a cutting board; shred it. Return the shredded chicken to the cooker.

Set to SAUTÉ mode, and let simmer for about 15 minutes.

Creamy Turkey Breasts with Mushrooms

Ready in about: 35 minutes | **Serves:** 4 | **Per serving:** Calories 192; Carbs 5g; Fat 12g; Protein 15g

INGREDIENTS

20 ounces Turkey Breasts, boneless and skinless
6 ounces White Button Mushrooms, sliced
3 tbsp Shallots, chopped
½ tsp dried Thyme
¼ cup dry White Wine
⅔ cup Chicken Stock

1 Garlic Clove, minced
2 tbsp Olive Oil
3 tbsp Heavy Cream
1 ½ tbsp Cornstarch
Salt and Pepper, to taste

DIRECTIONS

Warm half of the olive oil on SAUTÉ mode.

Meanwhile, tie turkey breast with a kitchen string horizontally, leaving approximately 2 inches apart. Season the meat with salt and pepper. Add the turkey to the pressure cooker and cook for about 3 minutes on each side.

Transfer to a plate. Heat the remaining oil and cook shallots, thyme, garlic, and mushrooms until soft. Add white wine and scrape up the brown bits from the bottom.

When the alcohol evaporates, return the turkey to the pressure cooker. Seal the lid, and cook on POULTRY for 30 minutes at High.

Meanwhile, combine heavy cream and cornstarch in a small bowl. Do a quick pressure release. Open the lid and stir in the mixture. Bring the sauce to a boil, then turn the cooker off. Slice the turkey in half and serve topped with the creamy mushroom sauce.

Hot and Buttery Chicken Wings

Ready in about: 20 minutes | **Serves:** 16 | **Per serving:** Calories 50; Carbs 1g; Fat 2g; Protein 7g

INGREDIENTS

16 Chicken Wings
1 cup Hot Sauce

1 cup Water
2 tbsp Butter

DIRECTIONS

Add in all ingredients, and seal the lid. Cook on POULTRY for 15 minutes at High. When ready, press CANCEL and release the pressure naturally, for 10 minutes.

Simple Pressure Cooked Whole Chicken

Ready in about: 40 minutes | **Serves:** 4 | **Per serving:** Calories 376; Carbs 0g; Fat 30g; Protein 25g

INGREDIENTS

1 2-pound Whole Chicken
2 tbsp Olive Oil

1 ½ cups Water
Salt and Pepper, to taste

DIRECTIONS

Season chicken all over with salt and pepper. Heat the oil on SAUTÉ, and cook the chicken until browned on all sides. Set aside and wipe clean the cooker.

Insert a rack in your pressure cooker and pour the water in. Lower the chicken onto the rack. Seal the lid. Choose MEAT/STEW setting and adjust the time to 25 minutes at High pressure.

Once the cooking is over, do a quick pressure release, by turning the valve to "open" position.

Chicken Bites Snacks with Chili Sauce

Ready in about: 25 minutes | **Serves:** 6 | **Per serving:** Calories 405; Carbs 18g; Fat 19g; Protein 31g

INGREDIENTS

1 ½ pounds Chicken, cut up, with bones
¼ cup Tomato Sauce
Kosher Salt and Black Pepper to taste

2 tsp dry Basil
¼ cup raw Honey
1 ½ cups Water

FOR CHILI SAUCE:

2 spicy Chili Peppers, halved
½ cup loosely packed Parsley, finely chopped
1 tsp Sugar

1 clove Garlic, chopped
2 tbsp Lime juice
¼ cup Olive Oil

DIRECTIONS

Put a steamer basket in the cooker's pot and pour the water in. Place the meat in the basket, and press PRESSURE COOK button. Seal the lid and cook for 20 minutes at High Pressure.

Meanwhile, prepare the sauce by mixing all the sauce ingredients in a food processor. Blend until the pepper is chopped and all the ingredients are mixed well. Release the pressure quickly. To serve, place the meat in serving bowl and top with the sauce.

Teriyaki Chicken Under Pressure

Ready in about: 25 minutes | **Serves:** 8 | **Per serving:** Calories 352; Carbs 31g; Fat 11g; Protein 31g

INGREDIENTS

1 cup Chicken Broth
¾ cup Brown Sugar
2 tbsp ground Ginger
1 tsp Pepper
3 pounds Boneless and Skinless Chicken Thighs

¼ cup Apple Cider Vinegar
¾ cup low-sodium Soy Sauce
20 ounces canned Pineapple, crushed
2 tbsp Garlic Powder

DIRECTIONS

Stir all of the ingredients, except for the chicken. Add the chicken meat and turn to coat. Seal the lid, choose the POULTRY mode and adjust the time to 20 minutes at High pressure.

Do a quick pressure release, by turning the valve to "open" position.

Turkey and Potatoes with Buffalo Sauce

Ready in about: 30 minutes | **Serves:** 4 | **Per serving:** Calories 377; Carbs 32g; Fat 9g; Protein 14g

INGREDIENTS

3 tbsp Olive Oil
4 tbsp Buffalo Sauce
1 pound Sweet Potatoes, cut into cubes
1 ½ pounds Turkey Breast, cut into pieces

½ tsp Garlic Powder
1 Onion, diced
½ cup Water

DIRECTIONS

Heat 1 tbsp of olive oil on SAUTÉ mode. Stir-fry onion in hot oil for about 3 minutes. Stir in the remaining ingredients. Seal the lid, set to POULTRY mode for 20 minutes at High pressure.

When cooking is over, do a quick pressure release, by turning the valve to "open" position.

Fall-Off-Bone Chicken Drumsticks

Ready in about: 45 minutes | **Serves:** 3 | **Per serving:** Calories 454; Carbs 7g; Fat 27g; Protein 43g

INGREDIENTS

1 tbsp Olive Oil
6 Skinless Chicken Drumsticks
4 Garlic Cloves, smashed
½ Red Bell Pepper, diced

½ Onion, diced
2 tbsp Tomato Paste
2 cups Water

DIRECTIONS

Warm olive oil, and sauté onion and bell pepper, for about 4 minutes, on SAUTÉ.

Add garlic and cook until golden, for a minute. Combine the paste with water and pour into the cooker.

Arrange the drumsticks inside. Seal the lid, set to POULTRY mode for 20 minutes at High pressure.

When it beeps, do a quick pressure release. Serve immediately.

Salsa and Lime Chicken with Rice

Ready in about: 35 minutes | **Serves:** 4 | **Per serving:** Calories 403; Carbs 44g; Fat 16g; Protein 19g

INGREDIENTS

¼ cup Lime Juice
3 tbsp Olive Oil
½ cup Salsa
2 Frozen Chicken Breasts, boneless and skinless
½ tsp Garlic Powder

1 cup Rice
1 cup Water
½ tsp Pepper
½ cup Mexican Cheese Blend
½ cup Tomato Sauce

DIRECTIONS

Lay the chicken into the pressure cooker. Pour lime juice, salt, garlic powder, olive oil, tomato sauce, and pepper, over the chicken. Seal the lid, and cook for 15 minutes on POULTRY.

When ready, do a quick pressure release. Remove the chicken to a plate. Add in rice, cooking juices and water the total liquid in the pressure cooker should be about 2 cups.

Seal the lid and adjust the time to 10 minutes on PRESSURE COOK at High pressure.

Do a quick pressure release and serve with cooked rice.

Sweet Gingery and Garlicky Chicken Thighs

Ready in about: 25 minutes | **Serves:** 4 | **Per serving:** Calories 561; Carbs 61g; Fat 21g; Protein 54g

INGREDIENTS

2 pounds Chicken Thighs
½ cup Honey
3 tsp grated Ginger
2 tbsp Garlic, minced
5 tbsp Brown Sugar

2 cups Chicken Broth
½ cup plus 2 tbsp Soy Sauce
½ cup plus 2 tbsp Hoisin Sauce
4 tbsp Sriracha
2 tbsp Sesame Oil

DIRECTIONS

Lay the chicken at the bottom. Mix the remaining ingredients in a bowl. Pour the mixture over the chicken. Seal the lid, select POULTRY mode and set the time to 20 minutes at High.

When cooking is over, do a quick pressure release, by turning the valve to "open" position.

Sweet and Smoked Slow Cooked Turkey

Ready in about: 4 hours 15 minutes | **Serves:** 4 | **Per serving:** Calories 513; Carbs 15 g; Fat 42g; Protein 65g

INGREDIENTS

1.5 pounds Turkey Breast
2 tsp Smoked Paprika
1 tsp Liquid Smoke
1 tbsp Mustard

3 tbsp Honey
2 Garlic Cloves, minced
4 tbsp Olive Oil
1 cup Chicken Broth

DIRECTIONS

Brush the turkey breast with olive oil and brown it on all sides, for 3-4 minutes, on SAUTÉ. Pour the chicken broth and all remaining ingredients in a bowl. Stir to combine. Pour the mixture over the meat. Seal the lid, set on SLOW COOK mode for 4 hours. Do a quick pressure release.

Chicken Piccata

Ready in about: 20 minutes | **Serves:** 6 | **Per serving:** Calories 318; Carbs 15g; Fat 19g; Protein 19g

INGREDIENTS

6 Chicken Breast Halves
¼ cup Olive Oil
¼ cup Freshly Squeezed Lemon Juice
1 tbsp Sherry Wine
½ cup Flour
4 Shallots, chopped
3 Garlic Cloves, crushed
¾ cup Chicken Broth

1 tsp dried Basil
2 tsp Salt
¼ cup grated Parmesan Cheese
1 tbsp Flour
¼ cup Sour Cream
1 cup Pimento Olives, minced
¼ tsp White Pepper

DIRECTIONS

In a small bowl combine flour with some salt and pepper. Dip the chicken into flour and shake off the excess. Warm olive oil and brown the chicken on all sides for 3-4 minutes, on SAUTÉ. Remove to a plate and set aside.

Add shallots, and garlic and sauté for 2 minutes. Stir in sherry, broth, lemon juice, salt, olives, basil, and pepper. Return the chicken and any juices to the cooker. Seal the lid, set to POULTRY and cook 20 minutes at High. When it beeps, do a quick pressure release. Stir in sour cream and Parmesan cheese.

Cherry Tomato and Basil Chicken Casserole

Ready in about: 30 minutes | **Serves:** 4 | **Per serving:** Calories 337; Carbs 12g; Fat 21g; Protein 27g

INGREDIENTS

8 small Chicken Thighs
½ cup Green Olives
1 pound Cherry Tomatoes
1 cup Water

A handful of Fresh Basil Leaves
1 ½ tsp Garlic, minced
1 tsp dried Oregano
1 tbsp Olive Oil

DIRECTIONS

Season chicken with salt and pepper. Melt the butter on SAUTÉ, and brown the chicken for about 2 minutes per side. Place tomatoes in a plastic bag and smash with a meat pounder. Remove the chicken to a plate.

Combine tomatoes, garlic, water, and oregano in the pressure cooker. Top with the browned chicken and seal the lid. Cook on High for 15 minutes. When ready, do a quick pressure release. Stir in the basil and olives.

Creamy and Garlicky Chicken

Ready in about: 25 minutes | **Serves:** 4 | **Per serving:** Calories 455; Carbs 3g; Fat 26g; Protein 57g

INGREDIENTS

1 cup Spinach, chopped
2 lbs Chicken Breasts, boneless and skinless, cut in half
¾ cup Chicken Broth
2 Garlic Cloves, minced
2 tbsp Olive Oil
¾ cup Heavy Cream
½ cup Sun-Dried Tomatoes
2 tsp Italian Seasoning
½ cup Parmesan Chicken
½ tsp Salt

DIRECTIONS

In a small bowl, combine oil with garlic, salt, and seasonings. Rub the chicken on all sides with this mixture. Heat oil and brown the chicken on all sides, about 4-5 minutes, on SAUTÉ.

Pour the broth in and seal the lid. Press POULTRY and cook for 20 minutes at High pressure. After 9 minutes, hit CANCEL and do a quick pressure release. Open the lid and stir in cream.

Let simmer for 5 minutes with the lid off, on SAUTÉ, and then stir in the cheese. Add in tomatoes and spinach and cook just until the spinach wilts. Serve and enjoy.

Chicken with Mushrooms and Leeks

Ready in about: 25 minutes | **Serves:** 6 | **Per serving:** Calories 321; Carbs 31g; Fat 18g; Protein 39g

INGREDIENTS

2 pounds Chicken Breasts, cubed
4 tbsp Butter
1 ¼ pounds Mushrooms, sliced
½ cup Chicken Broth
2 tbsp Cornstarch
½ cup Milk
¼ tsp Black Pepper
2 Leeks, sliced
¼ tsp Garlic Powder

DIRECTIONS

Melt butter on SAUTÉ mode. Place chicken cubes inside and cook until they are no longer pink, and become slightly golden. Transfer the chicken pieces to a plate.

Add the leeks and sliced mushrooms to the pot and cook for about 3 minutes. Return the chicken to the pressure cooker, season with pepper and garlic powder, and pour in broth.

Give the mixture a good stir to combine everything well, then seal the lid. Set on PRESSURE COOK mode, for 8 minutes at High pressure. When it goes off, release the pressure quickly.

In a bowl, whisk together the milk and cornstarch. Pour the mixture over the chicken and set the pressure cooker to SAUTÉ mode again. Cook until the sauce thickens.

Mexican Chicken

Ready in about: 30 minutes | **Serves:** 6 | **Per serving:** Calories 342; Carbs 11g; Fat 14g; Protein 38g

INGREDIENTS

1 Red Bell Pepper, diced
1 Green Bell Pepper, diced
1 Jalapeno, diced
2 pounds Chicken Breasts
10 ounces canned diced Tomatoes, undrained
1 Red Onion, diced
½ tsp Cumin
¾ tsp Chili Powder
¼ tsp Pepper
Juice of 1 Lime
½ cup Chicken Broth
1 tbsp Olive Oil

DIRECTIONS

Heat oil on SAUTÉ mode. When sizzling, add the onion and bell peppers and cook for about 3-4 minutes, until soft. Add the remaining ingredients and give it a good stir to combine.

Seal the lid, press PRESSURE COOK, and set for 15 minutes at High.

After it beeps, release the pressure quickly. Shred the chicken inside the pot with two forks, then stir to combine it with the juices.

Serve and enjoy!

Chicken in Roasted Red Pepper Sauce

Ready in about: 25 minutes | **Serves:** 6 | **Per serving:** Calories 207; Carbs 5g; Fat 7g; Protein 32g

INGREDIENTS

1 ½ pounds Chicken Breasts, cubed
1 Onion, diced
4 Garlic Cloves
12 ounces Roasted Red Peppers
2 tsp Adobo Sauce
½ cup Beef Broth

1 tbsp Apple Cider Vinegar
1 tsp Cumin
Juice of ½ Lemon
3 tbsp chopped Cilantro
1 tbsp Olive Oil
Salt and Pepper, to taste

DIRECTIONS

Place the garlic, red pepper, adobo sauce, lemon juice, vinegar, cilantro, and some salt and pepper, in a food processor. Process until the mixture becomes smooth.

Set your pressure cooker to SAUTÉ and heat the oil. Add the onion and cook for 2 minutes.

Add the chicken cubes and cook until they are no longer pink. Pour sauce and broth over.

Seal the lid, press PRESSURE COOK button, and set the timer to 8 minutes at High pressure.

After you hear the beeping sound, do a quick pressure release.

Serve and enjoy!

Coconut Chicken with Tomatoes

Ready in about: 25 minutes | **Serves:** 4 | **Per serving:** Calories 278; Carbs 28g; Fat 8g; Protein 19g

INGREDIENTS

1 ½ pounds Chicken Thighs
1 ½ cups chopped Tomatoes
1 Onion, chopped
1 ½ tbsp Butter
2 cups Coconut Milk
½ cup chopped Almonds
2 tsp Paprika

1 tsp Garam Masala
2 tbsp Cilantro, chopped
1 tsp Turmeric
1 tsp Cayenne Powder
1 tsp Ginger Powder
1 ¼ tsp Garlic Powder
Salt and Pepper, to taste

DIRECTIONS

Melt butter on SAUTÉ. Add the onions and sauté until translucent, for about 3 minutes.

Add all spices, and cook for an additional minute, until fragrant. Stir in the tomatoes and coconut milk.

Place the chicken thighs inside and seal the lid. Cook on PRESSURE COOK on High pressure for 13 minutes.

When it goes off, do a quick pressure release.

Serve topped with chopped almonds and cilantro.

Homemade Whole Chicken

Ready in about: 40 minutes | **Serves:** 6 | **Per serving:** Calories 207; Carbs 1g; Fat 8g; Protein 29g

INGREDIENTS

3 - pound Whole Chicken
1 cup Chicken Broth
1 ½ tbsp Olive Oil
1 tsp Paprika
¾ tsp Garlic Powder
¼ tsp Onion Powder

DIRECTIONS

Rinse chicken under cold water, remove the giblets, and pat it dry with some paper towels.

In a small bowl, combine the oil and spices. Rub the chicken well with the mixture. Set your pressure cooker to SAUTÉ. Add the chicken and sear on all sides until golden.

Pour the chicken broth around the chicken not over it), and seal the lid. Cook on PRESSURE COOK, for 25 minutes at High. When the timer goes off, do a quick pressure release. Transfer the chicken to a platter and let sit for about 10 minutes before carving.

Herbed and Garlicky Chicken Wings

Ready in about: 25 minutes | **Serves:** 4 | **Per serving:** Calories 177; Carbs 1g; Fat 10g; Protein 19g

INGREDIENTS

12 Chicken Wings
½ cup Chicken Broth
1 tbsp Basil
1 tbsp Oregano
½ tbsp Tarragon
1 tbsp Garlic, minced
2 tbsp Olive Oil
¼ tsp Pepper
1 cup Water

DIRECTIONS

Pour the water in the pressure cooker and lower the rack. Place all ingredients in a bowl and mix with your hands to combine well. Cover the bowl and let the wings sit for 15 minutes.

Arrange on the rack and seal the lid. Select PRESSURE COOK, and set the timer to 10 minutes at High pressure. When done, do a quick pressure release. Serve drizzled with the cooking liquid and enjoy!

Duck and Green Pea Soup

Ready in about: 30 minutes | **Serves:** 6 | **Per serving:** Calories 191; Carbs 14g; Fat 5g; Protein 21g

INGREDIENTS

1 cup Carrots, diced
4 cups Chicken Stock
1 pound Duck Breasts, chopped
20 ounces diced canned Tomatoes
1 cup Celery, chopped
18 ounces Green Peas
1 cup Onions, diced
2 Garlic Cloves, minced
1 tsp dried Marjoram
½ tsp Pepper
½ tsp Salt

DIRECTIONS

Place all ingredients, except the peas, in your pressure cooker. Stir well to combine and seal the lid. Select SOUP/BROTH mode and set the cooking time to 20 minutes at High.

After the beep, do a quick pressure release. Stir in the peas. Seal the lid again but do NOT turn the pressure cooker on. Let blanch for about 7 minutes. Ladle into serving bowls.

Sweet Potato & Chicken Curry

Ready in about: 30 minutes | **Serves:** 4 | **Per serving:** Calories 343; Carbs 19g; Fat 15g; Protein 26g

INGREDIENTS

1 pound Boneless and Skinless Chicken Breast, cubed
2 cups cubed Sweet Potatoes
2 cups Green Beans
½ Onion, chopped
1 Bell Pepper, sliced
1 ½ tsp Garlic, minced
1 tsp Cumin
1 cup Milk
2 tsp Butter
3 tbsp Curry Powder
1 tsp Turmeric
½ cup Chicken Broth
Salt and Pepper, to taste

DIRECTIONS

Melt butter on SAUTÉ mode. Add the onions and cook for about 3 minutes, until soft. Add the garlic and cook for 30 seconds more. Add the remaining ingredients, except the milk.

Stir well to combine and seal the lid. Hit PRESSURE COOK, and set to 12 minutes at High. Do a quick pressure release. Stir in the milk and set to SAUTÉ again. Cook for 3 minutes, lid off. Serve immediately.

Chicken with Water Chestnuts

Ready in about: 15 minutes | **Serves:** 4 | **Per serving:** Calories 274; Carbs 11g; Fat 8g; Protein 32g

INGREDIENTS

1 pound Ground Chicken
¼ cup Chicken Broth
2 tbsp Balsamic Vinegar
½ cup Water Chestnuts, sliced
¼ cup Soy Sauce
A pinch of Allspice

DIRECTIONS

Place all ingredients in your pressure cooker. Give the mixture a good stir to combine. Seal the lid, and hit PRESSURE COOK. Set the cooking time to 10 minutes at High pressure. Quick-release the pressure.

Chicken with Red Potatoes & Green Beans

Ready in about: 30 minutes | **Serves:** 6 | **Per serving:** Calories 467; Carbs 16g; Fat 33g; Protein 32g

INGREDIENTS

2 pounds Chicken Thighs
1 tbsp Butter
¼ tsp dried Parsley
¼ tsp dried Oregano
½ tsp dried Thyme
Juice of 1 Lemon
½ cup Chicken Broth
2 tbsp Olive Oil
1 Garlic Clove, minced
1 pound Green Beans
1 pound Red Potatoes, halved

DIRECTIONS

Heat oil and butter on SAUTÉ, and cook until they melt. Add the minced garlic and cook for a minute. Place the chicken thighs inside and cook them on both sides, until golden.

Stir in the herbs and the lemon juice and cook for an additional minute, until fragrant. Add all remaining ingredients and stir well to combine. Seal the lid, and cook at High for 15 minutes.

After you hear the beep, release the pressure quickly. Serve immediately.

Creamy Southern Chicken

Ready in about: 25 minutes | **Serves:** 4 | **Per serving:** Calories 291; Carbs 32g; Fat 8g; Protein 31g

INGREDIENTS

1 ½ pounds Boneless Chicken Thighs
2 tsp Paprika
2 Bell Peppers, sliced
1 cup Chicken Broth
½ cup Milk
1 tbsp Chili Powder
¼ cup Lime Juice

1 tsp Cumin
½ tsp Garlic Powder
½ tsp Onion Powder
1 tsp Ground Coriander
½ tsp Cayenne Pepper
1 tbsp Olive Oil
1 tbsp Cornstarch

DIRECTIONS

Warm oil, and cook until hot and sizzling. Meanwhile, combine all spices in a small bowl and rub the mixture all over the chicken. Add the chicken, and cook until golden on both sides.

Pour the broth and lime juice over, and stir in the peppers. Seal the lid, set the timer to 7 minutes at High. Do a quick release. Stir in milk and cornstarch and press SAUTÉ. Cook until the sauce thickens.

Easy Chicken Soup

Ready in about: 30 minutes | **Serves:** 6 | **Per serving:** Calories 272; Carbs 9g; Fat 11g; Protein 33g

INGREDIENTS

1 ½ pounds Boneless and Skinless Chicken Breasts
1 tbsp Chili Powder
2 tsp Garlic, minced
2 cups Chicken Broth
½ cup Water
1 tbsp Cumin

½ tsp Smoked Paprika
1 tsp Oregano
14 ounces canned diced Tomatoes
1 Bell Pepper, sliced
1 Onion, sliced

DIRECTIONS

Place all ingredients in your pressure cooker. Stir well to combine everything and seal the lid. Select PRESSURE COOK, set the timer to 20 minutes, at High pressure.

Do a natural pressure release, for about 10 minutes. Ladle into serving bowls and enjoy!

Pear and Onion Goose

Ready in about: 35 minutes | **Serves:** 6 | **Per serving:** Calories 313; Carbs 14g; Fat 8g; Protein 38g

INGREDIENTS

2 cups Chicken Broth
1 tbsp Butter
½ cup slice Onions
1 ½ pounds Goose, chopped into large pieces
2 tbsp Balsamic Vinegar

1 tsp Cayenne Pepper
3 Pears, peeled and sliced
¼ tsp Garlic Powder
½ tsp Pepper

DIRECTIONS

Melt the butter on SAUTÉ. Add the goose and cook until it becomes golden on all sides. Transfer to a plate. Add the onions and cook for 2 minutes. Return the goose to the cooker.

Add the rest of the ingredients, stir well to combine and seal the lid. Select PRESSURE COOK mode, and set the timer to 18 minutes at High pressure. Do a quick pressure release. Serve and enjoy!

Turkey with Fennel and Celery

Ready in about: 25 minutes | **Serves:** 6 | **Per serving:** Calories 272; Carbs 7g; Fat 4g; Protein 48g

INGREDIENTS

2 pounds Boneless and Skinless Turkey Breast
1 cup Fennel Bulb, chopped
1 cup Celery with leaves, chopped

2 ¼ cups Chicken Stock
¼ tsp Pepper
¼ tsp Garlic Powder

DIRECTIONS

Throw all ingredients in your pressure cooker. Give it a good stir and seal the lid. Press PRESSURE COOK, and cook for 15 minutes at High. Do a quick pressure release. Shred the turkey with two forks.

Stewed Chicken with Kale

Ready in about: 30 minutes | **Serves:** 6 | **Per serving:** Calories 280; Carbs 14g; Fat 15g; Protein 21g

INGREDIENTS

1 pound Ground Chicken
1 cup Tomatoes, chopped
1 cup diced Onions
1 cup Carrots, chopped
1 cup Kale, chopped
½ cup Celery, chopped

6 cups Chicken Broth
2 Thyme Sprigs
1 tbsp Olive Oil
1 tsp Red Pepper Flakes
10 ounces Potato Noodles

DIRECTIONS

Warm oil on SAUTÉ mode. Add the chicken and cook until golden. Stir in the onions, carrots, and celery, and cook for about 5 minutes. Stir in the remaining ingredients, except the noodles.

Seal the lid, select PRESSURE COOK mode, and set the timer to 6 minutes at High pressure. Do a quick pressure release. Stir in the potato noodles and seal the lid again. Cook at High pressure for 4 minutes.

Do a quick pressure release, and serve hot.

Lemon-Garlic Chicken with Herby Stuffed

Ready in about: 50 minutes | **Serves:** 6 | **Per serving:** Calories 376; Carbs 5g; Fat 15g; Protein 48g

INGREDIENTS

4 lb Whole Chicken
1 tbsp Herbes de Provence Seasoning
1 tbsp Olive Oil
Salt and Black Pepper to season
2 cloves Garlic, peeled

1 tsp Garlic Powder
1 Yellow Onion, peeled and quartered
1 Lemon, quartered
1 ¼ cups Chicken Broth

DIRECTIONS

Put the chicken on a clean flat surface and pat it dry using paper towels. Sprinkle the top and cavity with salt, black pepper, and garlic powder. Stuff onion, lemon, Herbes de Provence, and garlic cloves into the cavity.

Arrange the steamer rack inside. Pour in the broth and place the chicken on the rack. Seal the lid, select POULTRY at High for 30 minutes. Do a natural pressure release for 15 minutes, then a quick pressure release to let the remaining steam out. Remove the chicken onto a prepared baking pan, and in an already preheat oven to 350 F.

Broil chicken for 5 minutes untol golden brown color on each side. Dish on a bed of steamed mixed veggies.

Italian-Style Chicken Breasts with Kale Pesto

Ready in about: 30 minutes | **Serves:** 4 | **Per serving:** Calories 372; Carbs 5g; Fat 19g; Protein 35g

INGREDIENTS

4 Chicken Breasts, skinless and boneless
½ cup Heavy Cream
½ cup Chicken Broth
¼ tsp minced Garlic
Salt and Black Pepper to taste

¼ tsp Italian Seasoning
¼ cup Roasted Red Peppers
1 tbsp Tuscan Kale Pesto
1 tbsp Cornstarch

DIRECTIONS

Place the chicken at the bottom of the cooker. Pour the broth over, and add the Italian seasoning, garlic, salt, and pepper. Seal the lid, select POULTRY mode at High pressure for 15 minutes.

Once the timer has ended, do a natural pressure release for 5 minutes, then a quick pressure release to let the remaining steam out, and open the pot. Use a spoon to remove the chicken onto a plate and select SAUTÉ mode.

Scoop out any fat or unwanted chunks from the sauce. In a bowl, add cream, cornstarch, red peppers, and pesto.

Mix them with a spoon. Pour the creamy mixture into the pot and whisk it for 4 minutes until it is well mixed and thickened. Put the chicken back in the pot and let it simmer for 3 minutes. Turn the pot off and dish the sauce onto a serving platter. Serve the chicken with sauce over a bed of cooked quinoa.

Coconut-Lime Chicken Curry

Ready in about: 35 minutes | **Serves:** 4 | **Per serving:** Calories 643; Carbs 30g; Fat 44g; Protein 42g

INGREDIENTS

4 Chicken Breasts
4 tbsp Red Curry Paste
½ cup Chicken Broth
2 cups Coconut Milk
4 tbsp Sugar

Salt and Black Pepper to taste
2 Red Bell Pepper, seeded and cut in 2-inch sliced
2 Yellow Bell Pepper, seeded and cut in 2-inch slices
2 cup Green Beans, cut in half
2 tbsp Lime Juice

DIRECTIONS

Add the chicken, red curry paste, salt, pepper, coconut milk, broth and sugar. Seal the lid, select POULTRY mode at High pressure for 15 minutes. Once the timer has ended, do a quick pressure release, and open the lid.

Remove the chicken onto a cutting board and select SAUTÉ. Add the bell peppers, green beans, and lime juice. Stir the sauce with a spoon and let it simmer for 4 minutes. Slice the chicken with a knife and return it to the pot.

Stir and simmer for a minute. Dish the chicken with sauce and vegetable, and serve with coconut flatbread.

Lemon-Garlic Chicken Thighs

Ready in about: 30 minutes | **Serves:** 4 | **Per serving:** Calories 487; Carbs 8g; Fat 36g; Protein 28g

INGREDIENTS

4 Chicken Thighs
1 ½ tbsp Olive Oil
½ tsp Garlic Powder
Salt and Black Pepper to taste
½ tsp Red Pepper Flakes
½ tsp Smoked Paprika
1 small Onion, chopped

2 cloves Garlic, sliced
½ cup Chicken Broth
1 tsp Italian Seasoning
1 Lemon, zested and juiced
1 ½ tbsp Heavy Cream
Lemon slices to garnish
Chopped parsley to garnish

DIRECTIONS

Warm the olive oil on SAUTÉ, and add the chicken thighs; cook to brown on each side for 3 minutes. Remove the browned chicken onto a plate. Add butter to the pot to melt, then, add garlic, onions, and lemon juice. Stir them with a spoon to deglaze the bottom of the pot and let them cook for 1 minute. Add Italian seasoning, chicken broth, lemon zest, and the chicken. Seal the lid, select POULTRY at High pressure for 15 minutes. Once the timer has ended, let the pot sit closed for 2 minutes, then do a quick pressure release. Open the lid.

Remove the chicken onto a plate and add the heavy cream to the pot. Select SAUTÉ and stir the cream into the sauce until it thickens. Turn off the cooker and return the chicken. Coat the chicken with sauce. Dish the sauce into a serving platter and serve with the steamed kale and spinach mix. Garnish with the lemon and parsley.

Jasmine Rice and Chicken Taco Bowls

Ready in about: 20 minutes | **Serves:** 4 | **Per serving:** Calories 523; Carbs 41g; Fat 22g; Protein 44g

INGREDIENTS

4 Chicken Breasts
2 cups Chicken Broth
2 ¼ packets Taco Seasoning
1 cup Jasmine Rice

To Serve:
Grated Cheese, of your choice
Chopped Cilantro

1 Green Bell Pepper, seeded and diced
1 Red Bell Pepper, seeded and diced
1 cup Salsa
Salt and Black Pepper to taste

Sour Cream
Avocado Slices

DIRECTIONS

Pour in the chicken broth, add the chicken, and pour the taco seasoning over it. Add the salsa and stir it lightly with a spoon. Seal the lid and select POULTRY at High setting for 15 minutes. Do a quick pressure release. Add the rice and peppers, and use a spoon to push them into the sauce. Seal the lid, and select STEAM mode on High pressure for 15 minutes. Once the timer has ended, do a quick pressure release, and open the lid.

Gently stir the mixture, adjust the taste with salt and pepper and spoon the chicken dish into serving bowls. Top it with some sour cream, avocado slices, sprinkle with chopped cilantro and some cheese, to serve.

Hungarian Chicken Thighs in Cherry Tomato Sauce

Ready in about: 30 minutes | **Serves:** 4 | **Per serving:** Calories 437; Carbs 8g; Fat 37g; Protein 24g

INGREDIENTS

4 Chicken Thighs, skinless but with bone
4 tbsp Olive Oil
1 cup Crushed Cherry Tomatoes
2 tbsp Hungarian Paprika
1 large Red Bell Pepper, seeded and diced
1 large Green Bell Pepper, seeded and diced

1 Red Onion, diced
Salt and Black Pepper to taste
1 tbsp chopped Basil
½ cup Chicken Broth
1 bay Leaf
½ tsp dried Oregano

DIRECTIONS

Place the chicken on a clean flat surface and season with hungarian paprika, salt and pepper. Select SAUTÉ mode, on the pressure cooker. Pour the oil in, once heated add the chicken. Brown on both sides for 6 minutes.

Then, add the onions and peppers. Cook until soft for 5 minutes. Add tomatoes, bay leaf, salt, broth, pepper, and oregano. Stir using a spoon. Seal the lid, select POULTRY mode at High pressure for 20 minutes. Do a natural pressure release for 5 minutes, then a quick pressure release to let the remaining steam out. Discard the bay leaf. Dish the chicken with the sauce into a serving bowl and garnish it with the chopped basil. Serve over a bed of steamed squash spaghetti.

Honey-Ginger Shredded Chicken

Ready in about: 35 minutes | **Serves:** 4 | **Per serving:** Calories 462; Carbs 38g; Fat 16g; Protein 37g

INGREDIENTS

4 Chicken Breasts, skinless
¼ cup Sriracha Sauce
2 tbsp Butter
1 tsp grated Ginger
2 cloves Garlic, minced
½ tsp Cayenne Pepper

½ tsp Red Chili Flakes
½ cup Honey
½ cup Chicken Broth
Salt and Black Pepper to taste
Chopped Scallion to garnish

DIRECTIONS

In a bowl, add chicken broth, honey, ginger, sriracha sauce, red pepper flakes, cayenne pepper, and garlic. Use a spoon to mix them well and set aside. Put the chicken on a plate and season them with salt and pepper.

Set aside too. On the cooker, select SAUTÉ mode. Melt the butter, and add the chicken in 2 batches to brown on both sides for about 3 minutes. Add all the chicken back to the pot and pour the pepper sauce over it.

Seal the lid, select POULTRY mode at High pressure for 20 minutes. Once the timer has ended, do a natural pressure release for 5 minutes, then a quick pressure release to let the remaining steam out, and open the lid.

Remove the chicken onto a cutting board and shred them using two forks. Plate the chicken in a serving bowl, pour the sauce over it, and garnish it with the scallions. Serve with a side of sauteéd mushrooms.

Tuscany-Style Sun-Dried Tomato Chicken

Ready in about: 30 minutes | **Serves:** 4 | **Per serving:** Calories 576; Carbs 12g; Fat 44g; Protein 45g

INGREDIENTS

4 Chicken Thighs, cut into 1-inch pieces
1 tbsp Olive Oil
1 ½ cups Chicken Broth
Salt to taste
1 cup chopped Sun-Dried Tomatoes with Herbs

2 tbsp Italian Seasoning
2 cups Baby Spinach
¼ tsp Red Pepper Flakes
6 oz softened Cream Cheese, cut into small cubes
1 cup shredded Pecorino Cheese

DIRECTIONS

Pour the chicken broth in the cooker, and add Italian seasoning, chicken, tomatoes, salt, and red pepper flakes. Stir with a spoon. Seal the lid, select POULTRY mode at High pressure for 15 minutes.

Once the timer has ended, do a quick pressure release, and open the lid. Add and stir in the spinach, parmesan cheese, and cream cheese until the cheese melts and is fully incorporated. Let it stay in the warm for 5 minutes. Dish the Tuscan chicken over a bed of zoodles or a side of steamed asparagus and serve.

Mediterranean Chicken Meatballs

Ready in about: 30 minutes | **Serves:** 4 | **Per serving:** Calories 378; Carbs 13g; Fat 19g; Protein 26g

INGREDIENTS

1 lb Ground Chicken
1 Egg, cracked into a bowl
6 tsp Flour
Salt and Black Pepper to taste
2 tbsp chopped Basil + Extra to garnish
1 tbsp Olive Oil + ½ tbsp Olive Oil

1 ½ tsp Italian Seasoning
1 Red Bell Pepper, seeded and sliced
2 cups chopped Green Beans
½ lb chopped Asparagus
1 cup chopped Tomatoes
1 cup Chicken Broth

DIRECTIONS

In a mixing bowl, add chicken, egg, flour, salt, pepper, 2 tablespoons of basil, 1 tablespoon of olive oil, and Italian seasoning. Mix well with hands, and make 16 large balls out of the mixture. Set the meatballs aside.

Select SAUTÉ mode. Heat half teaspoon of olive oil, add the peppers, green beans, and asparagus. Cook for 3 minutes and set aside. Heat the remaining oil, and then fry the meatballs in batches, for 2 minutes on each side to brown them lightly.Next, put all meatballs back to the pot along with the vegetables and chicken broth. Seal the lid.

Select POULTRY mode at High pressure for 15 minutes. Once it goes off, do a quick pressure release. Dish the meatballs with sauce into a serving bowl and garnish with basil. Serve with over cooked tagliatelle pasta.

Gorgeous Chicken Fajitas with Guacamole

Ready in about: 30 minutes | **Serves:** 4 | **Per serving:** Calories 423; Carbs 9g; Fat 22g; Protein 40g

INGREDIENTS

2 lb Chicken Breasts, skinless and cut in 1-inch slices
½ cup Chicken Broth
1 Yellow Onion, sliced
1 Green Bell Pepper, seeded and sliced
1 Yellow Bell Pepper, seeded and sliced
1 Red Bell Pepper, seeded and sliced

2 tbsp Cumin Powder
2 tbsp Chili Powder
Salt to taste
Half a Lime
Cooking Spray
Fresh cilantro, to garnish

Assembling:
Tacos, Guacamole, Sour Cream, Salsa, Cheese

DIRECTIONS

Grease the pot with cooking spray and line the bottom with the peppers and onion. Lay the chicken on the bed of peppers and sprinkle with salt, chili powder, and cumin powder. Squeeze some lime juice.

Pour the chicken broth over, seal the lid and select POULTRY at High for 20 minutes. Once the timer has ended, do a quick pressure release. Dish the chicken with the vegetables and juice onto a large serving platter. Add the sour cream, cheese, guacamole, salsa, and tacos in one layer on the side of the chicken.

BBQ Sticky Drumettes

Ready in about: 30 minutes | **Serves:** 4 | **Per serving:** Calories 374; Carbs 3g; Fat 11g; Protein 38g

INGREDIENTS

2 lb Chicken Drumettes, bone in and skin in
½ cup Chicken Broth
½ tsp Dry Mustard
½ tsp Sweet Paprika
½ tbsp. Cumin Powder
½ tsp Onion Powder

¼ tsp Cayenne Powder
Salt and Pepper, to taste
1 stick Butter, sliced in 5 to 7 pieces
BBQ Sauce to taste
Cooking Spray

DIRECTIONS

Pour the chicken broth in and insert the trivet. In a zipper bag, pour in dry mustard, cumin powder, onion powder, cayenne powder, salt, and pepper. Add the chicken, then zip, close the bag and shake it to coat the chicken well. After, remove the chicken from the bag and place on the steamer rack. Top with butter slices, seal the lid, select POULTRY mode at High pressure for 20 minutes. Meanwhile, preheat an oven to 350 F.

Once it goes off, do a quick pressure release, and open the lid. Remove the chicken onto a clean flat cutting board and brush with barbecue sauce. Grease a baking tray with cooking spray and arrange the chicken pieces on it. Tuck the tray into the oven and broil the chicken for 4 minutes while paying close attention to prevent burning.

Feta and Spinach Stuffed Chicken Breasts

Ready in about: 30 minutes | **Serves:** 4 | **Per serving:** Calories 417; Carbs 3g; Fat 27g; Protein 33g

INGREDIENTS

4 Chicken Breasts, skinless
Salt and Black Pepper to taste
1 cup Baby Spinach, frozen
½ cup crumbled Feta Cheese
½ tsp dried Oregano

½ tsp Garlic Powder
2 tbsp Olive Oil
2 tsp dried Parsley
1 cup Water

DIRECTIONS

Cover the chicken in plastic wrap and place on a cutting board. Use a rolling pin to pound flat to a quarter inch thickness. Remove the plastic wrap.

In a bowl, mix spinach, salt, feta cheese and scoop the mixture onto the chicken breasts. Wrap the chicken to secure the spinach filling in it. Use some toothpicks to secure the wrap firmly from opening.

Carefully season the chicken pieces with the oregano, parsley, garlic powder, and pepper. Set on SAUTÉ mode. Heat the oil, add the chicken to sear, until golden brown on each side. Work in 2 batches.

Remove the chicken onto a plate and set aside. Pour the water into the pot and use a spoon to scrape the bottom of the pot. Fit the steamer rack into the pot. Transfer the chicken onto the steamer rack.

Seal the lid and select POULTRY mode at High pressure for 15 minutes. Once the timer has ended, do a quick pressure release. Plate the chicken and serve with a side of sautéed asparagus, and slices of tomatoes (optional).

Herby Balsamic Chicken

Ready in about: 50 minutes | **Serves:** 4 | **Per serving:** Calories 412; Carbs 13g; Fat 16g; Protein 38g

INGREDIENTS

2 lb Chicken Thighs, bone in and skin on
2 tbsp Olive Oil
Salt and Pepper, to taste
1 ½ cups diced Tomatoes
¾ cup Yellow Onion

2 tsp minced Garlic
½ cup Balsamic Vinegar
3 tsp chopped fresh Thyme
1 cup Chicken Broth
2 tbsp chopped Oregano

DIRECTIONS

Using paper towels, pat dry the chicken and season with salt and pepper. Select SAUTÉ mode. Warm the olive and add the chicken with skin side down. Cook to golden brown on each side, for about 9 minutes. Set aside.

Then, add the onions and tomatoes, and sauté them for 3 minutes while stirring occasionally. Top the onions with the garlic, and cook for 30 seconds, until fragrant Stir in chicken broth, salt, thyme, and balsamic vinegar.

Add back the chicken, seal the lid, and set on POULTRY at High pressure for 20 minutes.

Meanwhile, preheat oven to 350 F. Do a quick pressure release. Remove the chicken to a baking tray and leave the sauce inside the pot to thicken for about 10 minutes, on SAUTÉ mode.

Tuck the baking tray in the oven and let the chicken broil on each side until golden brown, for about 5 minutes. Remove and set aside to cool slightly.

Adjust the seasoning of the sauce and cook the sauce until desired thickness. Place chicken in a serving bowl and drizzle the sauce all over.

Garnish with parsley and serve with roasted tomatoes, carrots, and sweet potatoes.

Buffalo Chicken Chili

Ready in about: 40 minutes | **Serves:** 4 | **Per serving:** Calories 487; Carbs 8g; Fat 34g; Protein 41g

INGREDIENTS

4 Chicken Breasts, boneless and skinless
½ cup Buffalo Sauce
2 large White Onion, finely chopped
2 cups finely chopped Celery
1 tbsp Olive Oil
1 tsp dried Thyme

3 cups Chicken Broth
1 tsp Garlic Powder
½ cup crumbled Blue Cheese + extra for serving
4 oz Cream Cheese, cubed in small pieces
Salt and Pepper, to taste

DIRECTIONS

Put the chicken on a clean flat surface and season with pepper and salt. Set aside. Select SAUTÉ mode. Heat olive oil, add the onion and celery. Sauté constantly stirring, until they soft and fragrant, for about 5 minutes.

Add the garlic powder and thyme. Stir and cook them for about a minute, and add the chicken, hot sauce, and chicken broth. Season with salt and pepper. Seal the lid, select POULTRY mode at High pressure for 20 minutes.

Meanwhile, add the blue cheese and cream cheese in a bowl, and use a fork to smash them together. Set the mixture aside. Once the timer has ended, do a natural pressure release for 5 minutes.

Remove chicken onto a flat surface with a slotted spoon and use forks to shred it; then return it back the pot. Select SAUTÉ mode. Add the cheese to the pot and stir until is slightly incorporated into the sauce.

Dish the buffalo chicken soup into bowls. Sprinkle the remaining cheese over and serve with sliced baguette.

Side Dish Recipes

Classic Mashed Potatoes

Ready in about: 20 minutes | **Serves:** 4 | **Per serving:** Calories 211; Carbs 34g; Fat 7g; Protein 4g

INGREDIENTS

4 Medium Potatoes
2 tbsp Olive Oil
¼ cup Milk

A pinch of Nutmeg
Sea Salt and Black Pepper
Water, as needed

DIRECTIONS

Wash and peel the potatoes. Place them inside the pressure cooker. Add water, just enough to cover. Seal the lid, press PRESSURE COOK, and set the timer to 8 minutes High pressure.

Once it goes off, release the pressure quickly. Transfer the potatoes to a bowl. Grab a potato masher and mash the cooked potatoes well until there are no more lumps left.

Stir in the remaining ingredients until the mixture is thoroughly combined and smooth.

Garlic & Herb Potatoes

Ready in about: 15 minutes | **Serves:** 2 | **Per serving:** Calories 322; Carbs 43g; Fat 15g; Protein 6g

INGREDIENTS

1 pound Potatoes, peeled and quartered
1 tbsp Cilantro, chopped
1 tbsp Parsley, chopped
1 tbsp Basil, chopped

3 tsp Garlic, minced
3 tbsp Olive Oil
1 cup Water

DIRECTIONS

Pour the water into the pressure cooker and lower the trivet. Place the potatoes in a baking dish that fits into the cooker. Sprinkle herbs and garlic over, and drizzle with olive oil.

Place the baking dish on top of the trivet and seal t the lid. Select PRESSURE COOK mode, and set the timer to 6 minutes High pressure. When ready, do a quick pressure release.

Lime Cabbage with Coconut

Ready in about: 20 minutes | **Serves:** 4 | **Per serving:** Calories 191; Carbs 21g; Fat 11g; Protein 5g

INGREDIENTS

1 tbsp Coconut Oil
½ cup desiccated Coconut
½ cup Lime Juice
1 Cabbage, shredded
1 Onion, sliced

1 Carrot, sliced
1 tsp Garlic, minced
½ tsp Curry Powder
¼ tsp Turmeric Powder

DIRECTIONS

Melt coconut oil on SAUTÉ mode, add the onion slices and cook for about 3-4 minutes. When softened, add the garlic and saute for another minute. Stir in the remaining ingredients. Seal the lid.

Press PRESSURE COOK, and set to 5 minutes at High pressure. Do a quick pressure release, and serve.

Turmeric Carrot Mash

Ready in about: 15 minutes | **Serves:** 4 | **Per serving:** Calories 77; Carbs 16g; Fat 2g; Protein 2g

INGREDIENTS

1 tsp Turmeric Powder
¼ tsp Black Pepper
¼ tsp Sea Salt

1 ½ pounds Carrots, chopped
1 tbsp Heavy Cream
1 ½ cups Water

DIRECTIONS

Pour water into the cooker, and place carrots to the steaming basket, and lower the basket into the pot.

Seal the lid, cook on PRESSURE COOK for 4 minutes at High. Do a quick release. Remove steaming basket and transfer the carrots to a food processor. Add the rest of the ingredients. Process until smooth.

Simple Steamed Potatoes

Ready in about: 15 minutes | **Serves:** 8 | **Per serving:** Calories 132; Carbs 30g; Fat 1g; Protein 3g

INGREDIENTS

3 pounds Potatoes, peeled and quartered
1 tsp Cayenne Pepper
1 tsp Sea Salt

½ tsp Black Pepper
Water, as needed

DIRECTIONS

Place the potatoes inside the pressure cooker. Add enough water to cover them. Seal the lid, choose PRESSURE COOK mode and set the cooking time to 8 minutes at High pressure.

When the timer goes off, do a quick pressure release. Drain the potatoes and place them in a bowl. Cut them if you want, and sprinkle with the seasonings to serve.

Creamy Potato and Scallion Salad

Ready in about: 25 minutes | **Serves:** 6 | **Per serving:** Calories 225; Carbs 39g; Fat 8g; Protein 7g

INGREDIENTS

½ cup chopped Scallions
3 Celery Stalks, chopped
1 Carrot, peeled and chopped
½ Red Onion, sliced
4 Hardboiled Eggs, sliced, optional
1 ½ pounds Potatoes

½ cup Mayonnaise
½ tbsp Vinegar
½ tsp Sea Salt
½ tsp Cayenne Pepper
¼ tsp Black Pepper
2 cups Water

DIRECTIONS

Wash the potatoes thoroughly, scrub them, and place inside the pressure cooker. Pour in water and seal the lid. Select PRESSURE COOK mode, and set the timer to 10 minutes at High.

When it goes off, do a quick pressure release. Transfer the potatoes to a bowl and let them cool slightly. When safe to handle, peel the potatoes and chop them. Season with salt, cayenne, and black pepper.

Place the potatoes in a bowl along with carrot, celery, onion, and scallions. In a small bowl, whisk together mayo and vinegar, and sprinkle over salad. If using eggs, slice them thinly and arrange on top.

Cabbage-Onion Side with Pears

Ready in about: 35 minutes | **Serves:** 4 | **Per serving:** Calories 163; Carbs 24g; Fat 5g; Protein 3g

INGREDIENTS

1 pound Cabbage, shredded
1 cup diced Onions
1 cup Pears, peeled and chopped
1 tbsp Cornstarch
2 tbsp Water

1 ½ cups Veggie Stock
1 tbsp Olive Oil
½ tsp Sea Salt
¼ tsp Pepper
¼ tsp Cumin

DIRECTIONS

Heat the oil on SAUTÉ mode, add the onions and pears, and cook for about 6-7 minutes. When softened, add the rest of the ingredients, except the cornstarch and water.

Seal the lid, select PRESSURE COOK mode, and set the timer to 15 minutes at High.

When it goes off, do a quick pressure release. Whisk together the cornstarch and water, and stir in the mixture in the pot. Cook on SAUTÉ, until the sauce thickens, for about 3 minutes.

Cauliflower and Pea Bowl

Ready in about: 30 minutes | **Serves:** 6 | **Per serving:** Calories 134; Carbs 18g; Fat 4g; Protein 7g

INGREDIENTS

6 cups Cauliflower Florets
2 Sweet Potatoes, peeled and cubed
2 Tomatoes, diced
2 cups Peas
1 tsp Garlic, minced

1 cup Scallions, chopped
1 tbsp Olive Oil
4 cups Vegetable Stock
Salt and Pepper, to taste

DIRECTIONS

Heat oil on SAUTÉ, add the scallions and cook for about 3-4 minutes, until soft. Add the cauliflower, tomatoes, and pour the stock. Seal the lid and cook at High pressure for 6 minutes.

When ready, do a quick pressure release. Stir in the remaining ingredients. Seal the lid, hit PRESSURE COOK once again and set to 10 minutes at High pressure. Do a quick pressure release.

Stewed Yams with Zucchini

Ready in about: 25 minutes | **Serves:** 4 | **Per serving:** Calories 210; Carbs 39g; Fat 4g; Protein 5g

INGREDIENTS

1 pound Yams, peeled and diced
2 Zucchinis, peeled and chopped
2 Large Tomatoes, chopped
1 tsp Garlic, minced
1 Onion, diced

1 cup Chicken Stock
¼ tsp Cayenne Pepper
1 tsp Italian Seasoning
Salt and Pepper, to taste
1 tbsp Olive Oil

DIRECTIONS

Heat the oil, on SAUTÉ mode. Add the onions and cook for about 4 minutes. When soft, add the garlic and cook for another minute. Stir in the remaining ingredients and seal the lid.

Select PRESSURE COOK mode, and set to 10 minutes at High pressure. Do a quick pressure release.

Potatoes and Green Beans

Ready in about: 20 minutes | **Serves:** 6 | **Per serving:** Calories 123; Carbs 14g; Fat 7g; Protein 3g

INGREDIENTS

½ pound Green Beans, chopped
1 ½ pound Potatoes, peeled and chopped
1 tsp Garlic, minced
1 Onion, diced
½ tsp Turmeric Powder

¼ tsp Hot Paprika
1 tbsp Olive Oil
Salt and Pepper, to taste
Water, as needed

DIRECTIONS

Heat olive oil on SAUTÉ. Add the onions and cook them for about 3 minutes. Once softened, add the garlic and saute for a minute. Add the potatoes and cover them with water. Seal the lid.

Select PRESSURE COOK mode and set to 5 minutes at High pressure. Do a quick pressure release. Stir in the green beans, and seal the lid again. Cook for 3 more minutes on PRESSURE COOK at High.

Do a quick release. Season with turmeric, paprika, salt, and pepper.

Lemony Rutabaga and Onion Salad

Ready in about: 20 minutes | **Serves:** 4 | **Per serving:** Calories 185; Carbs 18g; Fat 13g; Protein 3g

INGREDIENTS

1 cup Green Onions, sliced
2 Rutabagas, peeled and cubed
4 tbsp Olive Oil

2 tbsp Lemon Juice
Salt and Pepper, to taste
1 cup Water

DIRECTIONS

Heat 1 tbsp of oil on SAUTÉ. Add the green onions, and cook them for about 2-3 minutes. Add the rutabaga and pour the water. Seal the lid, and cook at High pressure for 5 minutes.

When it goes off, quick release the pressure. Drain rutabaga and green onions, and transfer them to a bowl. Mix the remaining ingredients, in another bowl, and pour over the rutabagas.

Garlicky Sweet Potato Mash

Ready in about: 20 minutes | **Serves:** 6 | **Per serving:** Calories 263; Carbs 43g; Fat 9g; Protein 4g

INGREDIENTS

4 Garlic Cloves, minced
¾ cup Milk
2 tbsp Oil
2 pounds Sweet Potatoes, peeled and chopped
½ tsp Sea Salt

¼ tsp Pepper
A pinch of Nutmeg
A pinch of dried Thyme
Water, as needed

DIRECTIONS

Place the sweet potato chunks inside the pressure cooker. Add enough water to cover the potatoes.

Seal the lid, select PRESSURE COOK mode and cook for 10 minutes at High pressure. When it goes off, release the pressure quickly. Drain the potatoes and place in a bowl.

Add the remaining ingredients and mash with a potato masher until smooth and creamy.

Pea and Sweet Potato Bowl

Ready in about: 20 minutes | **Serves:** 6 | **Per serving:** Calories 155; Carbs 29g; Fat 3g; Protein 4g

INGREDIENTS

1 pound Sweet Potatoes, peeled and cubed
¾ pound Frozen Peas
1 tsp Ginger, minced
1 tsp Garlic, minced
¼ tsp dried Thyme
¼ tsp dried Basil
1 ½ cups Chicken Stock
1 tbsp Olive Oil

DIRECTIONS

Heat oil on SAUTÉ, add the garlic and ginger and cook just for a minute. Add potatoes and pour in the stock. Seal the lid, select PRESSURE COOK, and set to 10 minutes at High.

After the beep, do a quick pressure release. Stir in the peas and seal the lid again. Cook on PRESSURE COOK mode for 4 more minutes at High. Do a quick pressure release again.

Drain the potatoes and peas and transfer to a bowl. Stir in the basil and thyme. Enjoy!

Orange Potatoes with Walnuts

Ready in about: 20 minutes | **Serves:** 6 | **Per serving:** Calories 313; Carbs 45g; Fat 22g; Protein 6g

INGREDIENTS

12 Small Potatoes, peeled and chopped
¾ cup Walnuts, chopped
1 cup Mayonnaise
Juice of 1 Lemon
2 tbsp Olive Oil
¼ tsp Ginger Powder
Salt and Pepper, to taste
2 Oranges, peeled and chopped
Water, as needed

DIRECTIONS

Place the potato chunks inside your pressure cooker and add enough water to cover them. Seal the lid, select PRESSURE COOK modem and cook at High pressure for 10 minutes.

Once done, quick release the pressure. Drain the potatoes, and transfer to a bowl. Add oranges and walnuts. Whisk the remaining ingredients, in a bowl, and pour over the potatoes.

Paprika Hash Browns

Ready in about: 20 minutes | **Serves:** 4 | **Per serving:** Calories 168; Carbs 21g; Fat 8g; Protein 3g

INGREDIENTS

1 pound Potatoes, grated
1 tsp Smoked Paprika
1 ½ tbsp Butter
1 ½ tbsp Corn Oil
½ tsp Pepper
1 tsp Salt
½ small Onion, sliced
1 cup Water

DIRECTIONS

Rinse grated potatoes in cold water to dissolve excess starch, then drain, and pat dry with paper towels. Melt the butter along with the oil on SAUTÉ mode.

Cook onion and potatoes for 6 minutes, until soft, lid off. Season with salt, pepper, and smoked paprika and transfer to a baking dish. Press the potatoes with a metal spatula.

Place a trivet in the pressure cooker and pour water inside. Lower the dish onto the trivet and close the lid. Cook at High on PRESSURE COOK for 15 minutes. Release the pressure immediately, for 5 minutes.

Creamy Goat Cheese Cauliflower

Ready in about: 30 minutes | **Serves:** 4 | **Per serving:** Calories 352; Carbs 7g; Fat 29g; Protein 16g

INGREDIENTS

1 Cauliflower Head, cut into florets
2 tbsp Lemon Juice
2 tbsp Olive Oil

1 cup Vegetable Broth
2 tsp Red Pepper Flakes
Water, as needed

SAUCE:

6 ounces Goat Cheese
1 tsp Nutmeg
½ cup Heavy Cream

1 tbsp Olive Oil
Salt and Black Pepper, to taste

DIRECTIONS

Combine the lemon juice and cauliflower in your pressure cooker and cover with water. Seal the lid, and cook for 4 minutes on STEAM mode, at High pressure.

Release the pressure quickly and transfer to a plate. Discard the liquid and clean the cooker.

Heat the oil on SAUTÉ mode. Add red pepper flakes and cook until fragrant, for about a minute. Add cauliflower and cook for 1 minute uncovered; then return to the bowl.

In a food processor, pulse all sauce ingredients and pour over cauliflower. Serve and enjoy!

Garlicky Zucchini and Carrot Noodles

Ready in about: 15 minutes | **Serves:** 2 | **Per serving:** Calories 198; Carbs 29g; Fat 7g; Protein 4g

INGREDIENTS

4 Carrots, spiralized
2 Zucchinis, spiralized
2 tsp Garlic, minced
1 tbsp Olive Oil

¼ tsp Onion Powder
¼ tsp Black Pepper
¼ tsp Sea Salt
½ cup Tomato Sauce

DIRECTIONS

Heat the olive on SAUTÉ, add the garlic and cook for a minute, until fragrant. Add the noodles and season with salt, pepper, and onion powder. Cook for about 3 minutes.

Stir in the tomato sauce and cook for another 4 to 6 minutes. Serve as a side and enjoy!

Rosemary and Garlic Potatoes

Ready in about: 30 minutes | **Serves:** 4 | **Per serving:** Calories 231; Carbs 41g; Fat 5g; Protein 6g

INGREDIENTS

2 pounds Baby Potatoes
4 tsp Olive Oil
1 cup Vegetable Stock

2 tsp Garlic, minced
1 ½ tsp dried Rosemary
Salt and Black Pepper, to taste

DIRECTIONS

Heat oil on SAUTÉ mode, and add the potatoes, garlic, and rosemary. Sprinkle with salt and pepper, and cook for 5 - 7 minutes, stirring occasionally, until nice and soft. Stir in the stock and seal the lid.

Cook for 8 minutes on RICE mode at High pressure. Release the pressure naturally for 10 minutes.

Simple Mediterranean Asparagus

Ready in about: 5 minutes | **Serves:** 4 | **Per serving:** Calories 101; Carbs 5g; Fat 9g; Protein 3g

INGREDIENTS

1 pound Asparagus Spears, rough ends trimmed
1 Garlic Clove, minced
1 tbsp Shallot, minced
2 ½ tbsp Olive Oil
1 tbsp Lemon Juice
1 cup Water

DIRECTIONS

Place the asparagus and pour water in your pressure cooker. Seal the lid, and cook for 3 minutes on STEAM mode, at High. Once done, release the pressure quickly.

Toss the asparagus with the remaining ingredients to combine thoroughly, and serve.

Orange Broccoli Parmesan

Ready in about: 5 minutes | **Serves:** 4 | **Per serving:** Calories 60; Carbs 3g; Fat 4g; Protein 3g

INGREDIENTS

2 cups Broccoli Florets
¼ cup freshly grated Parmesan Cheese
1 tbsp Orange Juice
¾ cup Water
2 tbsp Butter, melted
A pinch of Salt

DIRECTIONS

Pour the water and add the broccoli. Seal the lid and cook at High pressure mode on STEAM mode, for 3 minutes. When ready, release the pressure quickly and transfer florets to a bowl.

Add the remaining ingredients and toss to combine. Serve and enjoy!

Kale and Carrots Side

Ready in about: 15 minutes | **Serves:** 6 | **Per serving:** Calories 54; Carbs 6g; Fat 3g; Protein 3g

INGREDIENTS

10 ounces chopped Kale
3 Carrots, sliced
½ Onion, chopped
½ cup Broth
1 tbsp Olive Oil
4 Garlic Cloves, minced
1 tbsp Lemon Juice
Salt and Black Pepper, to taste

DIRECTIONS

Heat oil on SAUTÉ, add garlic and cook for a minute, until fragrant. Stir in the remaining ingredients. Seal the lid and cook for 10 minutes on RICE at High. Release the pressure quickly, drain and serve.

Balsamic Capers Beets

Ready in about: 45 minutes | **Serves:** 4 | **Per serving:** Calories 78; Carbs 11g; Fat 4g; Protein 2g

INGREDIENTS

4 Beets
1 tbsp Olive Oil
2 tbsp Capers
1 tsp Garlic, minced
1 tbsp chopped Parsley
2 tbsp Balsamic Vinegar
Salt and Pepper, to taste
Water, as needed

DIRECTIONS

Place the beets in the pressure cooker and cover with water. Seal the lid and cook on MEAT/STEW for 20 minutes, at High. Release the pressure quickly. Let the beets cool.

Whisk together the remaining ingredients, in a bowl. Slice beets and combine with dressing, to serve.

Flavorful Bell Peppers

Ready in about: 15 minutes | **Serves:** 4 | **Per serving:** Calories 214; Carbs 22g; Fat 13g; Protein 6g

INGREDIENTS

1 ½ pounds Red Bell Peppers
½ cup Stock
¾ cup Tomato Soup
½ cup chopped Scallions
½ tbsp Miso Paste

½ Butter Stick
1 tsp Garlic, minced
2 tbsp Champagne Vinegar
Salt and Pepper, to taste

DIRECTIONS

Melt the butter on SAUTÉ mode, and cook the scallions for 3 minutes, until soft. Add garlic and cook for a minute, until fragrant. Stir in the remaining ingredients.

Seal the lid and cook for 3 minutes on STEAM mode at High pressure. Release the pressure quickly.

Sweet and Mustardy Carrots

Ready in about: 20 minutes | **Serves:** 4 | **Per serving:** Calories 122; Carbs 21g; Fat 4g; Protein 2g

INGREDIENTS

1 pound Carrots
2 tbsp Mustard
2 tbsp Butter
2 tbsp Honey

2 tsp Garlic, minced
1 tsp Paprika
Salt and Black Pepper, to taste

DIRECTIONS

Place the carrots and a cup of water in the pressure cooker. Seal the lid, and cook on RICE mode for 10 minutes at High pressure. When ready, release the pressure quickly.

Whisk together the remaining ingredients, in a bowl. Brush over the carrots, and serve.

Zucchini and Cherry Tomato Delight

Ready in about: 20 minutes | **Serves:** 8 | **Per serving:** Calories 60; Carbs 11g; Fat 2g; Protein 1g

INGREDIENTS

1 pound Cherry Tomatoes
2 small Onion, chopped
6 medium Zucchinis, chopped
1 ½ tsp Garlic, minced

1 tbsp Olive Oil
1 cup Water
2 tbsp Basil, chopped
Salt and Pepper, to taste

DIRECTIONS

Heat oil on SAUTÉ mode. Stir onions and cook for 3 minutes, until soft and translucent. Add garlic and cook for 1 minute, until fragrant. Stir in tomatoes and zucchini.

Cook for 2 minutes, until soft, and pour in the water. Seal the lid and cook for 5 minutes on PRESSURE COOK at High. Do a quick pressure release, stir in the basil and season with salt and pepper, to serve.

Basil Eggplant Delight

Ready in about: 40 minutes | **Serves:** 4 | **Per serving:** Calories 183; Carbs 6g; Fat 18g; Protein 1g

INGREDIENTS

2 cups Eggplants, cubed
¼ cup Olive Oil
½ cup freshly Basil, chopped
2 tsp Garlic, minced

1 cup Red Onion, sliced
2 tbsp Red Wine
½ cup Water
1 tbsp Salt

DIRECTIONS

Sprinkle the eggplants with the salt and place them in a colander for 20 minutes. Rinse and squeeze them, reserving the liquid. Heat oil on SAUTÉ mode.

Cook the eggplants, garlic, and onion for a few minutes, until soft and lightly browned. Pour in the wine, water, and reserved liquid. Seal the lid and cook for 7 minutes on STEAM at High.

When ready, release the pressure quickly. Serve topped with freshly chopped basil.

Spicy Cauliflower with Peas

Ready in about: 25 minutes | **Serves:** 8 | **Per serving:** Calories 173; Carbs 24g; Fat 4g; Protein 10g

INGREDIENTS

2 Tomatoes, diced
2 ¼ cups Green Peas
2 pounds Cauliflower, broken into florets
2 tbsp Garlic, minced
7 cups Stock
2 Yams, cubed
2 tbsp Butter

½ tsp Salt
¼ tsp Pepper
½ tsp Paprika
½ tsp Chili Powder
¼ tsp Red Pepper Flakes
¼ tsp Cayenne Pepper
½ tsp Onion Powder

DIRECTIONS

Melt butter on SAUTÉ, and cook the garlic and spices for 1 minute. Stir in the remaining ingredients. Seal the lid and set for 10 minutes on RICE at High. Do a quick release, drain and serve the veggies.

Spinach with Cottage Cheese

Ready in about: 25 minutes | **Serves:** 4 | **Per serving:** Calories 152; Carbs 15g; Fat 6g; Protein 13g

INGREDIENTS

18 ounces Spinach, chopped
10 ounces Cottage Cheese
1 Onion, chopped
8 Garlic Cloves, minced
1 tbsp Butter

2 tbsp Corn Flour
1 tsp Cumin
½ cup Water
½ tsp Coriander
1 tsp grated Ginger

DIRECTIONS

Melt the butter on SAUTÉ mode, and cook the onions, ginger, and garlic for 2 minutes, until soft. Stir in the spices and spinach and cook for 2 minutes, until tender.

Pour in the water and stir in flour. Seal the lid, and cook for 3 minutes on STEAM at High. When ready, do a quick pressure release, and stir in the cottage cheese.

Mushroom and Zucchini Platter

Ready in about: 25 minutes | **Serves:** 8 | **Per serving:** Calories 44; Carbs 5g; Fat 2g; Protein 2g

INGREDIENTS

12 ounces Mushrooms, sliced
4 medium Zucchinis, sliced
15 ounces canned Tomatoes, undrained
1 cup chopped Onion

1 Garlic Clove, minced
1 tbsp chopped Parsley
¼ tsp Red Pepper Flakes
2 tbsp Butter

DIRECTIONS

Melt butter on SAUTÉ mode. Add onion and garlic and cook for 2 minutes, until soft and crispy. Add mushrooms and cook for 5 minutes, until soft. Add zucchini and top with tomatoes. Seal the lid.

Cook for 2 minutes at High. Quick release the pressure. Stir in parsley and flakes and season to taste.

Cabbage and Pepper Side

Ready in about: 20 minutes | **Serves:** 8 | **Per serving:** Calories 60; Carbs 10g; Fat 2g; Protein 2g

INGREDIENTS

2 pounds Cabbage, shredded
1 cup Bell Peppers, diced sliced
¼ cup White Wine
½ cup Veggie Stock
1 cup Scallions, chopped

¼ cup Parsley, chopped
1 tbsp Oil
½ tsp Salt
¼ tsp Pepper

DIRECTIONS

Heat oil on SAUTÉ mode. Add scallions and cook until soft, for about 3 minutes. Stir in the remaining ingredients. Seal the lid and cook for 10 minutes on STEAM mode at High.

Once done, release the pressure quickly. Serve topped with freshly chopped parsley.

Gnocchi with Butternut Squash and Tomatoes

Ready in about: 20 minutes | **Serves:** 4 | **Per serving:** Calories 485; Carbs 67g; Fat 12g; Protein 21g

INGREDIENTS

1 lb Potato Gnocchi
10 oz Butternut squash, peeled, deseeded and diced
1 cup Green Onions, white parts only
1 cup Bell Peppers, stemmed, cored, and chopped
1 ½ cups Water
1 sprig dry Rosemary, crushed

¼ tsp ground Black Pepper
¼ tsp Salt
½ tsp Garlic powder
3 tsp Olive Oil
20 ounces canned diced Tomatoes

DIRECTIONS

Heat oil on SAUTÉ and add in the leeks. Cook for 3-4 minutes, stirring constantly.

Stir in squash and bell peppers, and continue to cook for 2 more minutes. Add in tomatoes, rosemary, water, garlic powder, salt, black pepper, and wine vinegar. Press CANCEL.

Throw in the gnocchi and stir with a wooden spoon until it is well coated. Seal the lid, switch the pressure release valve to close and set to PRESSURE COOK mode, for 8 minutes, for al dente taste.

Once done, do a quick pressure release. Serve topped with fresh chives and grated parmesan.

Frascati and Sage Broccoli

Ready in about: 15 minutes | **Serves:** 6 | **Per serving:** Calories 73; Carbs 9g; Fat 3g; Protein 4g

INGREDIENTS

1 ½ pounds Broccoli, broken into florets
1 large Sweet Onion, sliced
1 cup Frascati, Italian White Wine
½ cup Water

2 tsp Sage
3 tsp Olive Oil
1 tsp Garlic Paste
Salt and Pepper, to taste

DIRECTIONS

Heat the oil on SAUTÉ and cook the onions until soft, for about 3 minutes. Add garlic paste and cook for 1 minute until fragrant. Stir in the remaining ingredients.

Seal the lid and cook for 4 minutes on STEAM mode at High pressure. Do a quick release and serve.

Easy Mushroom Pâté

Ready in about: 30 minutes| **Serves:** 8 | **Per serving:** Calories 55; Carbs 4g; Fat 4g; Protein 1g;

INGREDIENTS

½ cup White Wine
2 Onions, peeled and sliced
1 ½ pounds Button Mushrooms, thinly sliced
1 ½ cups boiling Water

½ tsp Salt
¼ tsp Black Pepper, freshly cracked
1 cup dried Porcini Mushrooms, washed
3 tbsps Butter

DIRECTIONS

Combine the mushrooms and boiling water in a heatproof cup. Cover and set aside. The mushrooms will soak up the water. Melt butter on SAUTÉ. Add in onions and cook for 3 minutes, until soft.

Stir in mushrooms and sauté them until golden brown, for about 4 minutes. Pour in wine and let it fully evaporate. Stir in the soaked mushrooms and adjust the seasoning. Seal the lid.

Select PRESSURE COOK and cook for 10 minutes at High. Do a quick release. To prepare the paté, blend the ingredients with an immersion blender, for about 5 minutes. Refrigerate and serve chilled.

Lemony Buckwheat Salad

Ready in: 15 minutes + chilling time | **Serves:** 6 | **Per serving:** Calories 286; Carbs 51g; Fat 9g; Protein 12g

INGREDIENTS

¼ cup Extra-Virgin Olive Oil
¼ cup fresh Basil, minced
½ tsp Sea Salt
1 tsp Cayenne Pepper
5 cups Water
3 tsp Vegetable Oil

¼ cup fresh Lemon Juice
2 cups Buckwheat, rinsed and drained
½ cup Green Bell Pepper, seeded and chopped
1 cup Red Onions, minced
1 ½ cups Zucchini, diced
Sea Salt and freshly cracked Black Pepper

DIRECTIONS

Add water, buckwheat, salt, oil, and cayenne pepper into your pressure cooker. Seal the lid, set on PRESSURE COOK, and cook for 8 minutes at High Pressure.

Once the cooking is complete, allow for a natural pressure release, for about 10 minutes. Carefully open the lid, and stir in the remaining ingredients. Refrigerate and serve chilled.

Ricotta Cheese Lasagna with Mushrooms

Ready in about: 40 minutes | **Serves:** 6 | **Per serving:** Calories 613; Carbs 86g; Fat 11g; Protein 28g

INGREDIENTS

2 Cloves Garlic, minced
2 pounds dry lasagna Noodles
2 cups Pasta Sauce
2 cups Ricotta Cheese
1 tsp Red Pepper flakes, crushed
½ tsp Sea Salt
½ tsp dried Oregano
½ tsp ground Black Pepper
2 cups Mushrooms, thinly sliced
¼ cup chopped fresh Basil, plus more for garnish
Non-stick Cooking Spray, for greasing
2 cups Water

DIRECTIONS

Grease spring-form pan with cooking spray. Place the lasagna noodles at the bottom and spread the pasta sauce evenly on top. Then place a layer of ricotta cheese and sprinkle roughly with mushrooms.

Season with garlic, herbs, and spices and repeat the process until you run out of products. Cover with aluminum foil. Place the trivet at the bottom of your cooker, and pour 2 cups water.

Place down the spring-form pan on the trivet and seal the lid. Cook for 25 minutes on PRESSURE COOK at High pressure. Do a quick pressure release. Garnish with basil to serve.

Cajun Potatoes with Brussel Sprouts

Ready in about: 20 minutes | **Serves:** 6 | **Per serving:** Calories 131; Carbs 27g; Fat 1g; Protein 5g

INGREDIENTS

1 ½ pounds Potatoes, chopped
½ pound Brussel Sprouts, halved
1 tsp Cajun Seasoning
½ Onion, chopped
1 Garlic Clove, minced
1 ½ cups Chicken Stock
1 tbsp Oil

DIRECTIONS

Heat oil on SAUTÉ mode, and cook the onions and garlic for 2 minutes, until soft and fragrant. Pour the stock and add potatoes. Seal the lid and cook for 6 minutes at High pressure.

When ready, release the pressure, add the Brussel sprouts, and continue cooking for 4 more minutes, lid off, on SAUTÉ. Drain and transfer to a plate. Season with Cajun, and serve.

Turmeric Kale with Shallots

Ready in about: 20 minutes | **Serves:** 3 | **Per serving:** Calories 102; Carbs 14g; Fat 4g; Protein 5g

INGREDIENTS

10 ounces Kale, chopped
5 Shallots, chopped
1 tsp Turmeric Powder
2 tsp Olive Oil
½ tsp Coriander Seeds
½ tsp Cumin
Salt and Black Pepper, to taste
1 cup Water

DIRECTIONS

Pour 1 cup of water and place the kale in the steaming basket. Seal the lid and cook on STEAM for 3 minutes at High pressure. When ready, do a quick pressure release.

Transfer to a plate. Discard the water and heat the oil on SAUTÉ mode. Add the spices and shallots and cook until soft, for about 5-6 minutes. Stir in the kale, serve and enjoy!

Sour Cream Veggies

Ready in about: 20 minutes | **Serves:** 4 | **Per serving:** Calories 399; Carbs 42g; Fat 21g; Protein 12g

INGREDIENTS

4 Bacon slices, chopped
2 Carrots, chopped
½ Onion, chopped
1 Garlic Clove, minced
2 Potatoes, chopped
1 cup Broccoli Florets
1 cup Cauliflower Florets
1 tbsp Lemon Juice
1 tbsp Olive Oil
1 cup Sour Cream
1 ½ cups Chicken Stock
Salt and Pepper, to taste

DIRECTIONS

Cook the bacon until crispy on SAUTÉ mode. Remove to a plate. Add the onion and garlic and cook for 2 minutes, until soft. Add the potatoes and carrots and cook for 2 more minutes.

Pour the stock and seal the lid. Cook for 5 minutes at High pressure. Do a quick release. Stir in sour cream and lemon juice. Adjust the seasoning. Serve topped with crispy bacon slices.

Red Cabbage with Apple

Ready in about: 30 minutes | **Serves:** 4 | **Per serving:** Calories 183; Carbs 18g; Fat 5g; Protein 5g

INGREDIENTS

1 small head Red Cabbage, shredded and stems removed
1 ½ cups Vegetable Stock
½ cup dry Red wine
1 Onion, diced
¼ tsp Allspice
½ tsp ground Black Pepper
1 tsp Salt
2 tbsp Olive Oil
2 apples, peeled, cored and diced
½ tbsp Cornstarch dissolved in 6 tsp dry Red Wine

DIRECTIONS

Warm the oil on SAUTÉ mode. Stir in the apples, and onions and sauté until soft, for about 5 minutes.

Add in the remaining ingredients, except for cornstarch slurry. Select PRESSURE COOK mode and cook for 15 minutes at High. Do a quick pressure release. Stir in the already prepared cornstarch slurry.

Boil for another 5 minutes, lid off, on SAUTÉ. It has to thicken before it is ready to be served. Serve hot.

Spinach and Tomato Side

Ready in about: 25 minutes | **Serves:** 6 | **Per serving:** Calories 45; Carbs 8g; Fat 1g; Protein 3g

INGREDIENTS

10 cups Spinach
1 cup Tomatoes, chopped
1 tbsp Garlic, minced
1 Onion, diced
1 ¼ cups Veggie Broth
1 tbsp Lemon Juice
½ cup Tomato Puree
Salt and Black Pepper, to taste
Cooking Spray, to grease

DIRECTIONS

Coat the pressure cooker with cooking spray and cook the onion for a few minutes, until soft. Add garlic and cook for one more minute. Stir in the remaining ingredients and seal the lid.

Cook for 3 minutes at High pressure. When ready, do a natural release, for about 10 minutes.

Smoky Asian-Style Tomato Chutney

Ready in: 20 minutes + chilling time | **Serves:** 12 | **Per serving:** Calories 155; Carbs 32g; Fat 1g; Protein 2g

INGREDIENTS

½ tbsp Curry Paste
½ tsp ground Ginger
1 clove Garlic, peeled and minced
2 cups Dark Brown Sugar
1 cup Onions, peeled and diced

3 pounds Cherry Tomatoes, blanched, chopped and pureed
1 tbsp Paprika
2 tbsp Golden Sultanas
½ Pomegranate, seeded, to garnish
½ cup Water

DIRECTIONS

Add all ingredients in your pressure cooker. Give it a good stir and select PRESSURE COOK. Seal the lid and cook for 15 minutes at High. When done, do a quick pressure release. Refrigerate before serving.

Vegetable Soup

Ready in about: 20 minutes | **Serves:** 8 | **Per serving:** Calories 115; Carbs 16g; Fat 4g; Protein 4g

INGREDIENTS

2 cups canned diced Tomatoes
1 cup Fennel Bulb, trimmed and chopped
1 lb Green Beans, trimmed, cut into bite-sized pieces
5 cups Vegetable Broth
2 tbsp Butter

1 tbsp Olive Oil
½ tsp ground Black Pepper
½ tsp Salt
1 cup Onions, cut into rings
1 ½ cups fresh corn kernels

DIRECTIONS

Heat oil and butter on SAUTÉ. Stir-fry the onion for about 3-4 minutes. Add in broth, tomatoes, fennel bulb, and dill. Season to taste, and seal the lid. Cook on SOUP/BROTH for 10 minutes at High.

Once the cooking is complete, perform a quick pressure release. Add in the corn and green beans. Cook for another 5 more minutes without the lid on SAUTÉ mode. Serve immediately.

Savoy Cabbage and Beetroot Borscht Soup

Ready in about: 15 minutes | **Serves:** 5 | **Per serving:** Calories 202; Fat 10g; Carbs 18g; Protein 11g

INGREDIENTS

1 ½ cups Savoy Cabbage, shredded
1 cup Red Onions, sliced
1 ½ cups Beetroot, trimmed and chopped
2 Potatoes, chopped
½ cup Sour Cream

1 tsp Cayenne Pepper
3 tsp Olive Oil
Salt and Black Pepper, to taste
1 Garlic clove, minced
5 cups Vegetable Broth

DIRECTIONS

Heat oil on SAUTÉ. Add in the onions and garlic; stir-fry for about 3-4 minutes, or until translucent.

Add cabbage, beetroots, potatoes, broth, and cayenne pepper. Seal the lid, press SOUP/BROTH and cook for 10 minutes at High pressure. Once the cooking is complete, do a quick pressure release.

Season to taste. Top with a scoop of sour cream and serve.

Hearty Artichokes and Garlic Green Beans

Ready in about: 25 minutes | **Serves:** 8 | **Per serving:** Calories 163; Carbs 21g; Fat 6g; Protein 8g

INGREDIENTS

2 pounds Artichoke, cut into small florets
2 ¼ cups fresh Green Beans
2 Tomatoes, diced
2 tbsp Green Garlic, finely minced
½ tsp Salt
½ tsp Red Pepper flakes, crushed
½ tsp ground Black Pepper
1 cup Scallions, white parts only, sliced
2 tsp Butter
½ tbsp Olive Oil
8 cups Vegetable Stock

DIRECTIONS

Melt the butter and oil on SAUTÉ mode. Stir-fry the scallions, for about 3 minutes, until softened. Add in the tomatoes, artichokes, garlic, and stock. Season with salt, black and red pepper, and seal the lid.

Select PRESSURE COOK and cook for 8 minutes at High. Once ready, do a quick pressure release.

Stir in green beans and continue to cook for another 10 minutes, lid off on SAUTÉ. Serve immediately.

Silky Cheese and Cauli Soup

Ready in about: 40 minutes | **Serves:** 4 | **Per serving:** Calories 155; Carbs 12g; Fat 6g; Protein 8g

INGREDIENTS

¾ cups Vegetable Broth
½ cup Onions, chopped
½ cup Parsnip, finely chopped
1 cup Carrots, sliced
¼ cup ground Black Pepper, to taste
1 tsp Salt
1 cup Bell Pepper, seeded and chopped
1 cup Celery stalks, finely chopped
2 cups Cauliflower, broken into small florets
½ cup Colby cheese, grated

DIRECTIONS

Place all ingredients, except for the Colby cheese, in your pressure cooker. Seal the lid. Select SAUTÉ mode and cook for 35 minutes at High Preesure. Do a quick pressure release.

Purée soup with an electric mixer or hand blender. Serve soup topped with freshly grated Colby cheese.

Warm Chili Soup

Ready in about: 45 minutes | **Serves:** 4 | **Per serving:** Calories 135; Carbs 15g; Fat 7g; Protein 6g

INGREDIENTS

4 cups Vegetable Stock
2 pickled Chili Peppers, chopped
2 Onions, finely chopped
½ tsp ground cumin
½ tsp dried Thyme
1 cup Parsnips, chopped
2 tbsp Olive Oil
1 ½ cups Carrots, chopped
½ cup Celery stalk, chopped
1 cup Croutons, for garnish

DIRECTIONS

Heat oil on SAUTÉ mode. Add in celery, parsnips, carrots, onion and chili peppers, and sauté the vegetables for about 5 minutes. Add the remaining ingredients.

Seal the lid, press SOUP/BROTH, and cook for 30 minutes at High. Once the cooking is complete, perform a quick pressure release. Serve with croutons.

Cheesy Soup with Tortillas

Ready in about: 30 minutes | **Serves:** 4 | **Per serving:** Calories 388; Carbs 51g; Fat 19g; Protein 13g

INGREDIENTS

1 cup Water
2 tbsp Butter
3 cups Vegetable Stock
1 cup Shallots, chopped
¼ cup fresh Lime Juice
6 ounces frozen Green peas
1 ½ cups canned Pumpkin Puree
½ habanero Pepper, seeded and diced
2 Green Bell Peppers, seeded and diced
1 cup Summer Squash, cut into bite-size pieces
3 Garlic Cloves, minced

Non-stick Cooking Spray
6 corn Tortillas, cut into wide strips
2 ripe Tomatoes, chopped
¼ tsp ground Black Pepper
½ tsp ground Cumin
½ tsp dry Basil
1 tsp Sea Salt
½ tsp Chili powder
½ tsp dried Oregano
Gruyere cheese, grated, for serving

DIRECTIONS

Preheat oven to 400 degrees F. Line a baking sheet with parchment paper.

Lightly spray both sides of each tortilla with a nonstick cooking spray. Spread the tortilla strips onto the baking sheet.

Bake until they are crisp, turning once halfway through baking. It will take about 9 minutes.

Melt butter on SAUTÉ. Cook the shallots for about 3 minutes. Add squash, peppers, garlic, and lime juice.

Bring to a boil and let the liquid reduce by half. Add tomatoes, pumpkin puree, herbs, spices, water, and vegetable stock. Seal the lid, press SOUP/BROTH and cook for 10 minutes at High.

Stir in the peas. Let it simmer, uncovered, for approximately 3 minutes.

To serve, ladle the soup into bowls; top with crushed tortilla chips and Gruyere cheese.

Power Kale and Chickpea Soup

Ready in about: 20 minutes | **Serves:** 6 | **Per serving:** Calories 315; Carbs 41g; Fat 9g; Protein 11g

INGREDIENTS

1 (15.5 oz) can Chickpeas, rinsed, drained
2 cups Kale, torn into large pieces
3 tbsp dry White Wine
½ cup White Rice
3 tbsp Olive Oil
2 serrano Peppers, seeded and chopped
½ tsp Kosher Salt

½ tsp ground Black Pepper
1 Tomato, finely chopped
1 ½ cups Red Onions, white part only, sliced
1 cup Greek yogurt, room temperature
½ cup Celery with leaves, chopped
7 cups Vegetable Stock

DIRECTIONS

Heat oil on SAUTÉ, and fry onions, peppers, and celery, for about 4 minutes.

Add in rice and cook for 3 minutes. Pour in stock, and stir in salt, black pepper, wine, chickpeas, chopped tomatoes, and kale.

Seal the lid, select SOUP/BROTH mode and cook for 8 minutes at High Pressure.

Once ready, perform a quick pressure release.

Divide soup among bowls. Add a dollop of yogurt and serve hot.

Sicilian Eggplant Delight

Ready in about: 40 minutes | **Serves:** 4 | **Per serving:** Calories 184; Carbs 7g; Fat 15g; Protein 1g

INGREDIENTS

1 cup Red Onion, sliced
3 tbsp Red wine
½ cup Olive Oil
½ cup Water

2 cups Eggplant, unpeeled and cubed, Salted
1 tbsp Salt
2 Garlic Cloves, chopped
½ cup fresh Basil, chopped

DIRECTIONS

Place cubed and salted eggplant in kitchen sieve and let them stand for 35 minutes. Then, rinse, squeeze and set aside. Heat oil on SAUTÉ. Stir-fry garlic, onion, and eggplant, for about 2-3 minutes.

Pour in red wine and water. Seal the lid and cook for 8 minutes on PRESSURE COOKER at High Pressure. Once the cooking is over, do a quick pressure release. Sprinkle with fresh basil to serve.

Miso Sweet Potato Mash

Ready in about: 20 minutes | **Serves:** 6 | **Per serving:** Calories 264; Carbs 43g; Fat 9g; Protein 4g;

INGREDIENTS

3 tbsp cold Butter, cut into pieces
½ tsp Miso Paste
¾ cup Milk
2 pounds Sweet Potatoes, peeled and cut into chunks
1 sprig dried Thyme, crushed

¾ tsp Red Pepper flakes, crushed
¼ tsp ground Black Pepper
2 sprigs dried Rosemary, crushed
½ tsp Salt
2 tbsp Pumpkin Seeds, toasted

DIRECTIONS

Place the potatoes in your pressure cooker and fill with the water to cover them. Sprinkle with the salt and lock the lid. Select PRESSURE COOK mode and cook for 10 minutes at High Pressure.

Do a quick release. Drain the potatoes in a colander. Mash with a potato masher, and season with red and black pepper, rosemary, thyme, and miso paste. Add butter and milk, and stir softly until smooth.

Spoon the mash into a serving bowl, top with the toasted seeds and serve.

Vegetable and Cannellini Beans Pottage

Ready in about: 28 minutes | **Serves:** 4 | **Per serving:** Calories 386; Carbs 49g; Fat 21g; Protein 14g

INGREDIENTS

¼ cup Butter
1 cup Cannellini Beans, soaked overnight
1 cup Scallions, chopped
1 tbsp fresh Ginger, minced
½ pound Potatoes, peeled and cubed
1 ½ cups Tomato Puree

2 cups Vegetable Broth
2 tsp Sesame Oil
2 Red Bell Peppers, chopped
Salt and Black Pepper, to taste
1 tsp Garlic, finely minced
2 cups Water

DIRECTIONS

Melt the butter and sauté the scallions, garlic, and peppers for 3-4 minutes, on SAUTÉ mode. Add the rest of the ingredients. Seal the lid, select SOUP/BROTH mode cook for 15 minutes at High Pressure.

Once the cooking is complete, perform a quick pressure release. Carefully open the lid and serve hot!

Cauliflower Side with Pomegranate and Walnuts

Ready in about: 20 minutes | **Serves:** 8 | **Per serving:** Calories 158; Carbs 20g; Fat 9g; Protein 4g

INGREDIENTS

2 cups Pomegranate Seeds
3 medium Cauliflower Heads, broken into florets
¼ cup Hazelnuts, toasted
1 tbsp Capers

3 tbsp Olive Oil
3 tbsp Orange Juice
1 cup Water

DIRECTIONS

Add 1 cup of water and place cauliflower in the steaming basket. Seal the lid and cook for 3 minutes on STEAM at High. Do a quick release, transfer to a bowl, and stir in the remaining ingredients to serve.

Creamy Coconut Squash Soup

Ready in about: 25 minutes | **Serves:** 6 | **Per serving:** Calories 210; Carbs 21g; Fat 17g; Protein 6g

INGREDIENTS

1 ½ pounds Butternut squash, cut into small pieces
5 cups Vegetable Broth
2 Shallots, diced
1 cup Coconut Milk
4 tsp Olive Oil

2 Garlic Cloves, finely minced
A pinch of Black Pepper
A pinch of Salt
½ tsp Smoked Cayenne Pepper
Fresh Cilantro to garnish

DIRECTIONS

Press the SAUTÉ button and warm the oil. Cook the shallots until tender and translucent, about 3 minutes. Add the squash, garlic, salt, black pepper, and cayenne pepper; sauté for 4 minutes.

Pour in the broth. Seal the lid, select SOUP/BROTH mode and cook for 10 minutes at High Pressure.

Do a quick release. Add ¾ cup coconut milk and purée the soup using an immersion blender. Divide soup between six bowls. Add a drizzle of the remaining coconut milk, and top with fresh cilantro.

Creamy Tomato and Basil Soup

Ready in about: 15 minutes | **Serves:** 6 | **Per serving:** Calories 123; Carbs 14g; Fat 5g; Protein 7g

INGREDIENTS

1 pound fresh Cherry Tomatoes, finely chopped
1 cup Heavy Cream
2 cups Tomato Puree
1 tsp Garlic, minced
6 cups Vegetable Broth

1 Onion, chopped
1 ½ tbsp Olive Oil
1 tsp Oregano
Salt and Black Pepper, to taste
1 tbsp fresh chopped Basil

DIRECTIONS

Warm oil on SAUTÉ. Stir in onions and cook for about 3 minutes, until soft. Add the rest of the ingredients, except for the heavy cream. Seal the lid, select SOUP/BROTH and cook for 15 minutes at High.

Once the cooking process has completed, quick release the pressure. Blend soup inside the cooker with an immersion blender until smooth; add in the cream. Give it a gentle stir and serve right away.

Vegetarian and Vegan

Mashed Broccoli with Mascarpone

Ready in about: 10 minutes | **Serves:** 4 | **Per serving:** Calories 166; Carbs 6g; Fat 13g; Protein 7g

INGREDIENTS

3 heads Broccoli, chopped
6 oz Mascarpone
2 cloves Garlic, crushed
2 tbsp Butter, unsalted
Salt and Black Pepper to taste
1 cup Water

DIRECTIONS

Select SAUTÉ mode at High. Melt the butter, and add the garlic. Cook it for 30 seconds, stirring frequently to prevent the garlic from burning. Then, add the broccoli, mascarpone, water, salt, and pepper.

Seal the lid, and select STEAM at High for 3 minutes. Do a quick pressure release and use a stick blender to mash the ingredients until smooth. Adjust the taste, and serve as a side dish to a sauce of your choice.

Simple Spaghetti Squash with Spinach Dip

Ready in about: 15 minutes | **Serves:** 4 | **Per serving:** Calories 275; Carbs 46g; Fat 9g; Protein 5g

INGREDIENTS

4 lb Spaghetti Squash
For the Dip
½ cup spinach, chopped
2 tbsp Walnuts
2 Garlic Cloves, minced
1 cup Water

Zest and juice from 1/2 lemon
Salt and ground pepper, to taste
¼ cup extra virgin olive oil

DIRECTIONS

In a food processor put all pesto ingredients and blend until well incorporated. Season to taste and set aside.

Put the squash on a flat surface and use a knife to slice in half lengthwise. Use a spoon to scoop out all seeds and discard them. Next, pour the water in the pressure cooker, and fit the trivet at the bottom.

Place the squash halves on the trivet, seal the lid, and select STEAM at High pressure for 6 minutes. Do a quick pressure release. Remove the squash halves onto a cutting board and use a fork to separate the pulp strands into spaghetti-like pieces. Scoop the spaghetti squash into serving plates and drizzle over the spinach pesto.

One-Pot Mushroom and Brown Rice

Ready in about: 30 minutes | **Serves:** 4 | **Per serving:** Calories 417; Carbs 72g; Fat 7g; Protein 12g

INGREDIENTS

2 cups Brown Rice, rinsed
4 cups Vegetable Broth
3 teaspoons Olive oil
1 cup Portobello Mushrooms, thinly sliced
Salt to taste
2 sprigs Parsley, chopped to garnish

DIRECTIONS

Heat oil on SAUTÉ mode and cook the mushrooms for 3 minutes until golden. Season with salt and add rice and broth. Seal the lid and select MANUAL mode at High pressure for 20 minutes.

Once the timer has ended, do a quick pressure release. Plate the pilaf, fluff with a fork and top with parsley.

Eggplant and Goat Cheese Homemade Lasagna

Ready in about: 20 minutes | **Serves:** 4 | **Per serving:** Calories 288; Carbs 38g; Fat 5g; Protein 19g

INGREDIENTS

3 large Eggplants, sliced in uniform ¼ inches
4 ¼ cups Marinara Sauce
1 ½ cups crumbled Goat Cheese
Cooking Spray
Chopped Fresh Basil to garnish

DIRECTIONS

Grease the pot with cooking spray. Arrange the eggplant slices in a single layer at the bottom of the pot and sprinkle some cheese all over. Arrange another layer of eggplant slices on top, layer with cheese again.

Repeat the layering until you run out of ingredients. Lightly spray the eggplant with cooking spray and pour the marinara sauce all over it. Seal the lid and select MANUAL mode at High pressure for 8 minutes.

Do a quick pressure release. With two napkins, gently remove the inner pot. Then, place a plate to cover this pot and turn the eggplant over on the plate. Garnish the eggplant and cheese with basil and serve as a side dish.

Sautéed Leafy Greens

Ready in about: 10 minutes | **Serves:** 4 | **Per serving:** Calories 130; Carbs 15g; Fat 4g; Protein 13g

INGREDIENTS

2 lb Baby Spinach
1 lb Kale Leaves
½ lb Swiss Chard
1 tbsp dried Basil
Salt and Black Pepper to season
½ tbsp Butter
½ cup Water

DIRECTIONS

Pour water in the pressure cooker and fit the trivet at the bottom. Put the spinach, swiss chard, and kale on the trivet. Seal the lid, and select STEAM mode at Low pressure for 3 minutes. Do a quick pressure release.

Remove the trivet with the wilted greens onto a plate and discard the water in the pot. Select SAUTÉ mode and add the butter. Once it melts, add the spinachkale back to the pot, and add dried basil. Season with salt and pepper and stir it. Dish the sautéed greens into serving plates and serve as a side dish.

Celery-Pumpkin Autumn Soup

Ready in about: 30 minutes | **Serves:** 4 | **Per serving:** Calories 98; Carbs 15g; Fat 2g; Protein 6g

INGREDIENTS

1 Celeriac, peeled and cubed
16 oz Pumpkin Puree
5 stalks Celery, chopped
1 White Onion, chopped
1 lb Green Beans, cut in 5 to 6 strips each
2 cups Vegetable Broth
3 cups Spinach Leaves
1 tbsp chopped Basil Leaves
¼ tsp dried Thyme
¼ tsp rubbed Sage
Salt to taste

DIRECTIONS

Pour in the celeriac, pumpkin puree, celery, onion, green beans, vegetable broth, basil leaves, thyme, sage, and a little bit of salt. Seal the lid, and select STEAM mode on High pressure for 3 minutes. Do a quick pressure release.

Add the spinach and stir it in using a spoon. Cover the pot and let the spinach sit in for 3 minutes or until it wilts. Use a soup spoon to fetch the soup into serving bowls.

Stuffed Red Peppers with Quinoa and Zucchini

Ready in about: 40 minutes | **Serves:** 4 | **Per serving:** Calories 409; Carbs 42g; Fat 17g; Protein 20g

INGREDIENTS

4 Red Bell Peppers
2 large Tomatoes, chopped
1 small Onion, chopped
2 cloves Garlic, minced
1 tbsp Olive Oil
1 cup Quinoa, rinsed
2 cups Chicken Broth

1 small Zucchini, chopped
1 ½ cup Water
½ tsp Smoked Paprika
½ cup chopped Mushrooms
Salt and Black Pepper to taste
1 cup grated Gouda Cheese

DIRECTIONS

Select SAUTÉ mode at High. Warm the olive oil and sauté the onion and garlic, for 3 minutes until soft, stirring occasionally. Add the tomatoes, cook them for 3 minutes, and then add quinoa, zucchinis, and mushrooms.

Season with paprika, salt, and black pepper and stir well. Cook them for 5 to 7 minutes, then, turn the cooker off. Use a knife to cut the bell peppers in halves (lengthwise) and remove their seeds and stems.

Spoon the quinoa mixture into the bell peppers leaving about a quarter space at the top of the peppers for the cheese. Sprinkle them with the gouda cheese. Put the peppers in a greased baking dish and pour the broth over.

Wipe the pot clean with some paper towels, and pour in the water. Fit the steamer rack at the bottom of the pot. Place the baking dish on top of the steamer rack, seal the li and select STEAM mode at High for 15 minutes.

Do a quick pressure release. Serve right away or as a side to a meat dish.

Asian-Style Tofu Noddle Soup

Ready in about: 25 minutes | **Serves:** 4 | **Per serving:** Calories 343; Carbs 42g; Fat 21g; Protein 14g

INGREDIENTS

16 oz firm Tofu, cubed
7 cloves Garlic, minced
2 tbsp Korean red pepper flakes (gochugaru)
1 tbsp Sugar
1 tbsp Olive Oil
2 tbsp Ginger Paste

¼ cup Soy Sauce
3 cup sliced Bok Choy
6 ounces dry Egg Noodles
4 cups Vegetable Broth
1 cup sliced Shitake Mushrooms
½ cup chopped Cilantro

DIRECTIONS

Select SAUTÉ at High. Heat the oil, add the garlic and ginger, and sauté them for 1 minute. Add sugar, broth, and soy sauce. Stir the mixture and cook for 30 seconds. Add tofu, mushrooms, bok choy, and gochugaru; seal the lid and select STEAM at High for 10 minutes.

Do a quick pressure release. Add the noodles, give it a good stir using a spoon, and close the lid. Let the soup sit for 4 minutes. Add the cilantro and stir with the spoon. Fetch the soup into soup bowls to serve.

Hearty Colorful Vegetable Soup

Ready in about: 20 minutes | **Serves:** 4 | **Per serving:** Calories 198; Carbs 28g; Fat 4g; Protein 4g

INGREDIENTS

1 (15.5 oz) can Cannellini Beans
1 Potato, peeled and diced
1 Carrot, peeled and chopped

1 cup chopped Butternut Squash
2 small Red Onions, cut in wedges
1 cup chopped Celery

1 tbsp chopped Fresh Rosemary
8 Sage Leaves, chopped finely
1 Bay Leaf
4 cups Vegetable Broth
Salt and Pepper, to taste
2 tsp Olive Oil
2 tbsp chopped Parsley

DIRECTIONS

Add in the beans, potato, carrot, squash, onion, celery, rosemary, sage leaves, bay leaf, vegetable broth, salt, pepper, and olive oil. Seal the lid and select STEAM mode at High pressure for 5 minutes.

Do a quick pressure release. Stir in parsley and fetch the soup into bowls. Serve with a side of crusted bread.

Kale and Spinach Cream Soup

Ready in about: 15 minutes | **Serves:** 4 | **Per serving:** Calories 269; Carbs 14g; Fat 14g; Protein 12g

INGREDIENTS

½ lb Kale Leaves, chopped
½ lb Spinach Leaves, chopped
½ lb Swiss Chard Leaves, chopped
1 tbsp Olive Oil
1 Onion, chopped
4 cloves Garlic, minced
4 cups Vegetable Broth
1 ¼ cup Heavy Cream
Salt and Pepper, to taste
1 ½ tbsp. White Wine Vinegar
Chopped Peanuts to garnish

DIRECTIONS

Select SAUTÉ mode at High. Warm the olive oil, and sauté the onion and garlic, for 1 minute. Add greens and vegetable broth. Seal the lid, and select STEAM mode at High for 5 minutes. Do a quick pressure release.

Add the white wine vinegar, salt, and pepper. Use a stick blender to puree the ingredients in the pot. Stir in the heavy cream. Spoon the soup into bowls, sprinkle with peanuts, and serve.

Spiced Bok Choy Soup with Spiralized Zucchini

Ready in about: 35 minutes | **Serves:** 6 | **Per serving:** Calories 115; Carbs 15g; Fat 6g; Protein 2g

INGREDIENTS

1 lb Baby Bok Choy, stems removed
6 oz Shitake Mushrooms, stems removed and sliced to a 2-inch thickness
3 Carrots, peeled and sliced diagonally
2 Zucchinis, spiralized
2 Sweet Onion, chopped
2-inch Ginger, chopped
2 cloves Garlic, peeled
2 tbsp Sesame Oil
2 tbsp Soy Sauce
2 tbsp Chili Paste
6 cups Water
Salt to taste
Chopped Green Onion to garnish
Sesame Seeds to garnish

DIRECTIONS

In a food processor, add the chili paste, ginger, onion, and garlic; and process until pureed. Set the pressure cooker on SAUTÉ at High. Warm the oil, and cook the puree for 4 minutes, stirring constantly to prevent burning.

Pour in the water, mushrooms, soy sauce, and carrots. Stir, seal the lid and select STEAM mode at High pressure for 3 minutes. Do a quick pressure release. Stir in the zoodles and bok choy.

Make sure that they are well submerged in the liquid. Season with salt, cover, and let the veggies sit for 10 minutes. Dish the soup with veggies into soup bowls. Sprinkle with green onions and sesame seeds.

Fake Mushroom Risotto the Paleo Way

Ready in about: 15 minutes | **Serves:** 4 | **Per serving:** Calories 123; Carbs 13g; Fat 11g; Protein 3g

INGREDIENTS

1 ½ head Cauliflower
2 cups Mushrooms, sliced
1 Garlic Clove, minced
1 tsp dried Basil

1 Carrot, grated
1 cup Veggie Broth
1 tbsp Olive Oil
½ Onion, diced

DIRECTIONS

Cut the cauliflower into pieces and place them in your food processor. Process until ground, rice-like. You should have about 6 cups of cauliflower rice. Heat the oil and sauté the carrots, and onions for 3 minutes, on SAUTÉ mode. Add the garlic and cook for one more minute.

Stir in all of the remaining ingredients. Seal the lid, set to PRESSURE COOK for 10 minutes at High. It may take a few minutes before pressure is built inside the cooker. Do a quick pressure release.

Potato Chili

Ready in about: 30 minutes | **Serves:** 4 | **Per serving:** Calories 297; Carbs 53g; Fat 4g; Protein 16g

INGREDIENTS

15 ounces canned Black Beans, rinsed and drained
2 cups Vegetable Broth
28 ounces canned diced Tomatoes
15 ounces canned Kidney Beans, rinsed and drained
1 Sweet Potato, chopped
1 Red Onion, chopped
1 Red Bell Pepper, chopped

1 Green Bell Pepper, chopped
1 tbsp Olive Oil
1 tbsp Chili Powder
¼ tsp Cinnamon
1 tsp Cumin
1 tsp Cayenne
Pepper Salt, to taste

DIRECTIONS

Heat olive oil in and sauté onions, peppers, and potatoes until the onions become translucent, about 3-4 minutes, on SAUTÉ mode. Stir in the rest of the ingredients.

Seal the lid, cook for 16 minutes at High pressure. Once ready, do a quick pressure release.

White Wine Red Peppers

Ready in about: 15 minutes | **Serves:** 6 | **Per serving:** Calories 97; Carbs 7g; Fat 8g; Protein 2g

INGREDIENTS

1 ½ pounds Red Bell Peppers, deveined and sliced
1 cup Tomato Puree
½ cup Vegetable Broth
½ tbsp miso paste
1 tbsp Garlic, crushed

½ cup Green Onions, chopped
3 tbsp Butter, melted
Sea Salt and freshly ground Black Pepper
2 tbsp White Wine

DIRECTIONS

Melt butter on SAUTÉ and sauté onions, until soft, for about 3 minutes. Add garlic and stir for about a minute, until fragrant. Pour broth, tomato and pesto sauce, salt, and pepper.

Seal the lid, press PRESSURE COOK button and cook for 10 minutes at High pressure. When ready, do a quick release. Season with salt, and black pepper. Serve drizzled with white wine.

Meatless Shepherd's Pie

Ready in about: 17 minutes | **Serves:** 4 | **Per serving:** Calories 224; Carbs 6g; Fat 15g; Protein 16g

INGREDIENTS

½ cup diced Celery
1 cup diced Onion
2 cups Cauliflower, steamed and mashed
1 tbsp Olive Oil
½ cup diced Turnips
1 ¾ cup Veggie Broth
1 cup diced Tomatoes
1 cup grated Potatoes
½ cup diced Carrot
½ cup Water

DIRECTIONS

Heat olive oil and cook onions, carrots, celery, for 3 minutes, on SAUTÉ mode. Stir in turnips, potatoes, and veggie broth. Seal the lid, set to BEANS/CHILI for 25 minutes at LOW.

After 10 minutes, press CANCEL and do a quick release. Stir in tomatoes. Transfer the mixture to 4 ramekins. Top each ramekin with ½ cup of mashed cauliflower. Pour the water into your pressure cooker and place a trivet at the bottom. Seal the lid, and continue cooking. Do a quick pressure release.

Mediterranean Steamed Asparagus with Pine Nuts

Ready in about: 10 minutes | **Serves:** 4 | **Per serving:** Calories 182; Carbs 13g; Fat 15g; Protein 7g

INGREDIENTS

1 ½ lb Asparagus, ends trimmed
Salt and Pepper, to taste
1 cup Water
¼ cup Pomegranate seeds
½ cup chopped Pine Nuts
1 tbsp Olive Oil to garnish

DIRECTIONS

Pour the water in the pressure cooker, and fit the steamer rack at the bottom. Place the asparagus on the steamer rack, seal the lid and select STEAM mode on Low pressure for 3 minutes.

Once the timer is done, do a quick pressure release. Remove asparagus with tongs onto a plate and sprinkle with salt and pepper. Scatter over the pomegranate seeds and pine nuts, and drizzle olive oil.

Vegetarian Spaghetti Bolognese

Ready in about: 25 minutes | **Serves:** 8 | **Per serving:** Calories 360; Carbs 63g; Fat 3g; Protein 15g

INGREDIENTS

8 cups cooked Spaghetti
1 cup Cauliflower Florets
2 cups Shredded Carrots
6 Garlic Cloves, minced
2 tbsp Tomato Paste
2 tbsp Agave Nectar
1 ½ tbsp dried Oregano
56 ounces canned crushed Tomatoes, undrained
2 tbsp Balsamic Vinegar
1 tbsp dried Basil
10 ounces Mushrooms
2 cups chopped Eggplant
2 cups Water
1 ½ tsp dried Rosemary
Salt and Black Pepper, to taste

DIRECTIONS

Add cauliflower, mushrooms, eggplant, and carrots to a food processor and process until finely ground. Transfer to the pressure cooker. Stir in the rest of the ingredients. Seal the lid and cook for 10 minutes on PRESSURE COOK mode at High pressure. When ready, release the pressure naturally for 10 minutes. Serve the sauce over spaghetti.

Veggie Burger Patties

Ready in about: 30 minutes | **Serves:** 4 | **Per serving:** Calories 221; Carbs 34g; Fat 7g; Protein 4g

INGREDIENTS

1 Zucchini, peeled and grated
3 cups Cauliflower Florets
1 Carrot, grated
1 cup Veggie Broth
2 cups Broccoli Florets
½ Onion, diced
½ tsp Turmeric Powder
2 tbsp Olive Oil
2 cups Sweet Potato cubes
¼ tsp Black Pepper

DIRECTIONS

Heat 1 tbsp oil and sauté the onions for about 3 minutes, on SAUTÉ mode. Add the carrots and cook for an additional minute. Pour the broth and add the potatoes. Seal the lid, set on PRESSURE COOK for 13 minutes at High pressure. Do a quick release. Stir in the remaining veggies. Seal the lid, and cook for 3 minutes at High. Do a quick pressure release.

Mash veggies with a potato masher and stir in the seasonings. Let cool for a few minutes and make burger patties out of the mixture. On SAUTÉ, heat remaining oil. Cook patties for a minute on each side.

Spicy Moong Beans

Ready in about: 30 minutes | **Serves:** 8 | **Per serving:** Calories 328; Carbs 62g; Fat 5g; Protein 10g

INGREDIENTS

1 tsp Paprika
2 tsp Curry Powder
4 cups Moong Beans, soaked and drained
1 Onion, diced
1 tsp Turmeric
Juice of 1 Lime
1 Jalapeno Pepper, chopped
1 Sprig Curry Leaves
4 Garlic Cloves, minced
2 tbsp Olive Oil
1 ½ tsp Cumin Seeds
2 Tomatoes, chopped
Salt, to taste
1-inch piece of Ginger, grated

DIRECTIONS

Heat the oil and cook cumin seeds for minute, on SAUTÉ mode. Add onion and garlic along with curry, turmeric, ginger, and some salt. Cook for 3-4 minutes.

Stir in jalapeno, and tomatoes and cook for 5 minutes, or until soft. Add the beans and pour water to cover the ingredients, by at least 2 inches. Sprinkle with lime juice and curry leaves. Seal the lid, set on BEANS/CHILI for 25 minutes at High. Do a quick pressure release. Serve hot.

Sweet Potato and Baby Carrot Medley

Ready in about: 30 minutes | **Serves:** 4 | **Per serving:** Calories 415; Carbs 78g; Fat 8g; Protein 7g

INGREDIENTS

1 tsp dried Oregano
2 tbsp Olive Oil
½ cup Veggie Broth
1 Onion, finely chopped
2 pounds Sweet Potatoes, cubed
2 pounds Baby Carrots, halved

DIRECTIONS

Heat olive oil and cook onions for 3 minutes, on SAUTÉ. Stir in the carrots and cook for 3 more minutes. Add potatoes, carrots, broth, and oregano. Seal the lid, set on PRESSURE COOK for 15 minutes at High. Once the cooking is over, do a quick pressure release.

Tamari Tofu with Sweet Potatoes and Broccoli

Ready in about: 10 minutes | **Serves:** 4 | **Per serving:** Calories 250; Carbs 22g; Fat 12g; Protein 17g

INGREDIENTS

1 pound Tofu, cubed
3 Garlic Cloves, minced
2 tbsp Tamari
2 tbsp Sesame Seeds
2 tsp Sesame Oil
2 tbsp Tahini

1 tbsp Rice Vinegar
1 cup Vegetable Stock
2 cups Onion slices
2 cups Broccoli Florets
1 cup diced Sweet Potato
2 tbsp Sriracha

DIRECTIONS

Heat oil and cook onion and sweet potatoes for 2 minutes, on SAUTÉ mode. Add garlic and half of the sesame seeds, and cook for a minute. Stir in tamari, broth, tofu, and vinegar.

Seal the lid, select PRESSURE COOK for 8 minutes at High pressure. Do a quick pressure release. Open the lid and add in broccoli, and cook for 2 minutes, lid off. Stir in sriracha and tahini before serving.

Tomato Zoodles

Ready in about: 20 minutes | **Serves:** 4 | **Per serving:** Calories 102; Carbs 10g; Fat 4g; Protein 2g

INGREDIENTS

4 cups Zoodles
2 Garlic Cloves, minced
8 cups Boiling Water
1 tbsp Olive Oil

½ cup Tomato Paste
2 cups canned Tomatoes, diced
2 tbsp chopped Basil

DIRECTIONS

Place the zoodles in a bowl filled with boiling water. After one minute, drain them and set aside. Heat oil and cook garlic for about a minute, until fragrant, on SAUTÉ.

Add tomato paste, and 1 cup water and basil. Stir in the zoodles, coating them well with the sauce. Seal the lid, cook for 8 minutes at High. Do a quick pressure release.

Leafy Green Risotto

Ready in about: 15 minutes | **Serves:** 6 | **Per serving:** Calories 272; Carbs 40g; Fat 11g; Protein 6g

INGREDIENTS

3 ½ cups Veggie Broth
1 cup Spinach Leaves, packed
1 cup Kale Leaves, packed
¼ cup Parmesan Cheese, grated
¼ cup diced Onion
3 tbsp Butter

2 tsp Olive Oil
1 ½ cups Arborio Rice
4 Sun-dried Tomatoes, chopped
A pinch of Nutmeg
Salt and Pepper, to taste

DIRECTIONS

Heat olive oil and cook onions until soft, about 3 minutes. Add rice and cook for 3-4 minutes, on SAUTÉ mode. Pour in broth. Seal the lid, cook for 12 minutes at High. Do a quick pressure release.

Stir in the remaining ingredients. Leave for a 1-2 minutes, or until greens wilt. Serve and enjoy.

Tropical Salsa Mash

Ready in about: 10 minutes | **Serves:** 4 | **Per serving:** Calories 122; Carbs 24g; Fat 4g; Protein 2g

INGREDIENTS

¼ cup Red Onions, chopped
1 cup Mango, chopped
1 cup Apples, chopped
1 cup Tomatoes, chopped
1 cup Pineapples, diced
2 tbsp chopped Mint
2 Jalapenos, minced

1 Garlic Clove, minced
2 tbsp Cilantro, chopped
¼ cup Lime Juice
1 tbsp Olive Oil
¼ tsp Sea Salt
¼ tsp Pepper

DIRECTIONS

Heat oil on SAUTÉ, add the onions and cook for 2 minutes, until translucent. Add apples, pineapples, tomatoes, and mangos, and cook for 3 more minutes.

Stir in the garlic, salt, and pepper, and cook for another minute. Transfer the mixture to a bowl. Stir in the remaining ingredients. Remove the mixture to a food processor.

Pulse for two seconds. The mixture should not be smooth, but chunky. Serve and enjoy!

Roasted Potatoes with Gorgonzola

Ready in about: 20 minutes | **Serves:** 4 | **Per serving:** Calories 377; Carbs 28g; Fat 12g; Protein 11g

INGREDIENTS

1 ½ pounds Fingerling Potatoes,
1 cup Gorgonzola Cheese, grated
½ cup Vegetable Broth
4 tbsp Butter, melted

½ tsp Kosher Salt
½ tsp Thyme
½ tsp Cayenne Pepper

DIRECTIONS

In your pressure cooker, add the butter, potatoes and broth. Seal the lid and switch the pressure release valve to close. Set on PRESSURE COOK mode and cook for 15 minutes at High pressure10 minutes.

Do a quick release. Sprinkle with cayenne pepper, thyme and grated Gorgonzola cheese. Serve hot.

Cheddar and Swiss Chard Relish

Ready in about: 11 minutes | **Serves:** 4 | **Per serving:** Calories 324; Carbs 4g; Fat 24g; Protein 22g

INGREDIENTS

½ pound Cheddar cheese, sliced
3 cups Swiss chard, chopped
2 ½ cups stock
½ cup Onions, chopped

2 Cloves Garlic, crushed
1 tbsp dry Thyme
Sea Salt and ground Black Pepper, to taste

DIRECTIONS

Fry garlic and onions for about 2 minutes, on SAUTÉ. Add the rest of the ingredients and seal the lid. Select PRESSURE COOK and cook for 5 minutes at High.

Once the cooking process has completed, quick release the pressure. Serve immediately.

Cheesy Acorn Squash Relish

Ready in about: 15 minutes | **Serves:** 6 | **Per serving:** Calories 167; Carbs 8g; Fat 15g; Protein 1g

INGREDIENTS

1 cup Water
1 tsp baking soda
1 cup Parmesan cheese, grated
¼ cup Milk
1 tsp Sesame Seeds, toasted

½ tsp Sea Salt
¼ tsp Black Pepper
½ cup Butter, melted
1 pound Acorn Squash, halved
2 tbsp Apple Cider Vinegar

DIRECTIONS

Select STEAM mode, and add water and acorn squash. Drizzle with apple cider and stir in the remaining ingredients. Seal the lid, switch the pressure release valve to close and cook for 10 minutes.

When it goes off, quick release the pressure. Put the squash in a food processor along with parmesan cheese, and blend until smooth, then add in the milk while the machine is running.

Spoon the dip into a serving bowl and sprinkle with sesame seeds to serve.

Pickled Pepperoncini and Parmesan Dip

Ready in about: 15 minutes | **Serves:** 10 | **Per serving:** Calories 146; Carbs 5g; Fat 11g; Protein 8g

INGREDIENTS

1 tbsp minced pickled Pepperoncini Peppers
12 ounces Parmesan cheese, shredded
1 ½ tbsp Flour
1 cup Tomato paste
2 tsp Olive Oil

1 cup Milk
½ tsp Cayenne Pepper
½ tsp basil
Salt and Black Pepper, to taste

DIRECTIONS

Heat oil on SAUTÉ. Slowly stir in flour and keep stirring until you obtain a paste. Pour the milk and stir until the mixture thickens, then bring to a boil. Add the cheese and stir until melted.

Add the remaining ingredients. Seal the lid, press PRESSURE COOK and cook for 5 minutes at High Pressure. Do a quick release the pressure.

Easy Buttery Corn on the Cob

Ready in about: 15 minutes | **Serves:** 4 | **Per serving:** Calories 168; Carbs 11g; Fat 14g; Protein 2g

INGREDIENTS

4 corn on the cob, husked
½ cup Butter, melted
1 ½ cups Water

Salt and white Pepper, to taste
2 tbsp finely chopped fresh Parsley

DIRECTIONS

Place a trivet into your pressure cooker. Pour the water and lower the corn on the trivet. Seal the lid Set on PRESSURE COOK mode and cook for 2 minutes at High Pressure.

Once the cooking process has completed, quick release the pressure. Remove the corn to a platter, sprinkle with butter, allspice, parsley, and salt, then serve.

Delicious Eggs de Provence

Ready in about: 20 minutes | **Serves:** 4 | **Per serving:** Calories 455; Carbs 18g; Fat 29g; Protein 29g

INGREDIENTS

8 Eggs
½ cup Goat Cheese, crumbled
1 cup Cream
1 ½ cups Kale, torn into pieces
2 Shallots, chopped

½ tsp dried Oregano
½ tsp dried Thyme
1 tsp Salt
½ tsp ground Black Pepper
4 tbsp Water + 2 cups

DIRECTIONS

In a deep bowl, whisk the eggs, water, and cream. Stir in the remaining ingredients until well mixed. Transfer the mixture into a heat-proof dish and cover with aluminium foil. Add about 2 cups of water to the bottom of your pressure cooker, and pace the trivet inside.

Lower the dish onto the trivet. Select RICE mode, seal the lid and cook for 15 minutes at High pressure. Once the cooking is complete, do a quick pressure release and serve immediately.

Spicy Tomato Dip

Ready in about: 20 minutes | **Serves:** 10 | **Per serving:** Calories 84; Carbs 9g; Fat 5g; Protein 1g

INGREDIENTS

1 cup Carrot, chopped
½ tsp Sea Salt
1 pound plum Tomatoes, peeled, cored, sliced
2 tbsp Sugar
1 tsp Jalapeno Peppers, seeded and chopped
½ cup shallot, diced

1 cup Bell Pepper, seeded and chopped
black Pepper, to taste
3 tbsp Olive Oil
1 sprig dried Rosemary
½ tsp dried basil
1 cup Water

DIRECTIONS

Heat oil on SAUTÉ, and add the bell pepper, Jalapeño peppers, carrot, shallots. Cook for about 4 minutes, until soft. Stir in the tomatoes, brown sugar, water salt, black pepper, rosemary, and basil.

Seal the lid, press PRESSURE COOK mode and cook for 10 minutes at High Pressure. Do a quick release the pressure. Pour in the olive oil and blend with a blender, until the mixture is smooth.

Herby Steamed Potatoes

Ready in about: 15 minutes | **Serves:** 8 | **Per serving:** Calories 117; Carbs 27g; Fat 0g; Protein 3g

INGREDIENTS

1 cup Water
2 pounds Potatoes, peeled and quartered
1 tsp Salt
1 tbsp Olive Oil
½ tsp ground Black Pepper

1 tsp Cayenne Pepper
¼ tsp Rosemary
¼ tsp dried basil
¼ tsp dried Oregano
¼ tsp dried Sage

DIRECTIONS

Place a trivet into the pressure cooker and pour the water. Lay the potatoes on the trivet, seal the lid and select STEAM mode. Cook for 10 minutes at High Pressure. Do a quick release. Remove the potatoes to a bowl. Add the remaining ingredients and lightly toss to coat.

Creamy Potato Slices with Chives

Ready in about: 10 minutes | **Serves:** 6 | **Per serving:** Calories 168; Carbs 31g; Fat 3g; Protein 4g

INGREDIENTS

6 Potatoes
½ cup Sour Cream
2 tbsp Potato Starch
1 tbsp chopped Chives

½ cup Milk
1 cup Chicken Broth
1 tsp Salt
A pinch of Pepper

DIRECTIONS

Peel and slice the potatoes. Coat them with salt, chives, and pepper. Add broth and potatoes in your Pressure cooker. Seal the lid, and cook for 3 minutes on STEAM mode at High pressure.

Do a quick pressure release. Remove potatoes to a bowl, and reserve the liquid. Whisk in the remaining ingredients into the cooking juices in the pressure cooker.

Select SAUTÉ, and cook for one minute, stirring constantly, until you obtain sauce texture. Pour the sauce over the potatoes and serve immediately.

Sicilian-Style Deviled Eggs

Ready in about: 15 minutes | **Serves:** 6 | **Per serving:** Calories 175; Carbs 5g; Fat 8g; Protein 12g

INGREDIENTS

9 large Eggs
¼ cup Ricotta Cheese
¼ cup Mayonnaise

¼ tsp Garlic powder
1 tsp Shallot powder
Salt and freshly ground Black Pepper, to taste

DIRECTIONS

Pour 1 ½ cups of water and add a trivet to the pressure cooker. Align the eggs in steamer basket, and lower the basket onto the trivet. Seal the lid, set to PRESSURE COOK mode for 5 minutes at High.

Once the cooking is over, do a quick pressure release. Transfer the eggs to cold water to cool. Slice the egg in half and remove the yolk. Mash with a fork, and add the remaining ingredients.

Split the mixture of the yolks on the egg whites and lay on a serving plate.

Spanish Baked Eggs

Ready in about: 10 minutes | **Serves:** 4 | **Per serving:** Calories 425; Carbs 4g; Fat 27g; Protein 37g

INGREDIENTS

8 medium-sized Eggs
8 slices Spanish Manchego cheese
4 thick slices Swiss Cheese

2 tbsp Butter, softened at room temperature
4 tbsp Spring Onions, chopped
2 tbsp fresh coriander, coarsely chopped

DIRECTIONS

Pour 1 ½ cups of water inside your pressure cooker. Place the trivet on the bottom. Coat the bottom and sides of 4 ramekins with butter. Place the manchego cheese at the bottom and crack two eggs into each ramekin.

Add the onions and top with cheese. Lower the ramekins onto the steamer basket and cover with aluminium foil. Seal the lid, select PRESSURE COOK and cook for 5 minutes at High.

Once done, do a quick pressure release and open the lid. Serve with fresh coriander.

Hummus Under Pressure

Ready in about: minutes | **Serves:** 8 | **Per serving:** Calories 161; Carbs 20g; Fat 6g; Protein 8g

INGREDIENTS

1 Onion, quartered
1 Bay Leaf
2 tbsp Soy Sauce
¼ cup Tahini
¾ cup Garbanzo Beans

¼ cup dried Soybeans
¼ cup chopped Parsley
1 cup Vegetable Broth
Juice of 1 Lemon
2 Garlic Cloves, minced

DIRECTIONS

Add garbanzo beans, soybeans, and broth in your pressure cooker. Pour some water over to cover them by one inch. Seal the lid, press SOUP/BROTH, for 20 minutes at High pressure.

When ready, release the pressure naturally for 10 minutes. Drain the beans and save the cooking liquid. Place the beans along with the remaining ingredients into a food processor.

Process until smooth. Add some of the cooking liquid to make hummus thinner, if desired.

Potatoes and Peas Bowl

Ready in about: 20 minutes | **Serves:** 2 | **Per serving:** Calories 185; Carbs 24g; Fat 8g; Protein 8g

INGREDIENTS

3 Sweet Potatoes, diced
1 Onion, chopped
1 cup Green Peas, fresh
2 cups Spinach, chopped
2 tsp Garlic

1 tbsp Tomato Paste
1 tbsp Oil
½ tsp Coriander
1 tsp Cumin
1 ½ cups Water

DIRECTIONS

Heat oil on SAUTÉ mode. Cook the onions and garlic for 2 minutes, until soft and fragrant. Stir in the tomato paste and spices. Pour in the water and tomato paste. Stir to combine.

Add sweet potatoes and seal the lid. Cook for 14 minutes on PRESSURE COOK at High. When done, do a quick pressure release. Stir in spinach and cook until wilted, for a few minutes, on SAUTÉ, lid off.

Collard Greens Hummus

Ready in about: 25 minutes | **Serves:** 12 | **Per serving:** Calories 169; Carbs 22g; Fat 6g; Protein 7g

INGREDIENTS

3 tbsp Tahini
¼ tsp ground Black Pepper
½ tsp Sea Salt
2 cups Chickpeas

1 cup Green Garlic, minced
4 ½ cups Water
2 tbsp Olive Oil
2 cups packed Collard Greens, chopped

DIRECTIONS

Select PRESSURE COOK mode. Pour water in the pressure cooker and add the chickpeas. Seal the lid and adjust the cooking time to 20 minutes. Do a quick release, and drain the chickpeas.

Transfer to a food processor with the greens, garlic, salt, pepper, and tahini. Pulse until you obtain a creamy mixture. Pour gradually the oil while machine is running, until everything is well incorporated.

Saucy BBQ Veggie Meal

Ready in about: 20 minutes | **Serves:** 4 | **Per serving:** Calories 244; Carbs 29g; Fat 9g; Protein 15g

INGREDIENTS

2 Tomatoes, chopped
2 Carrots, chopped
1 cup Peas
2 Onions, chopped
1 cup Parsnips, chopped
2 Bell Peppers, diced
2 Sweet Potatoes, diced
½ cup BBQ Sauce
1 tbsp Oil
1 tbsp Ketchup
¼ tsp Cayenne Pepper
½ tsp Salt
¼ tsp Pepper
1 cup Veggie Stock

DIRECTIONS

Heat oil on SAUTÉ mode. Add onions and cook for 2 minutes, until translucent. Add parsnips and carrots and cook for 3 more minutes, until soft. Stir in the remaining ingredients.

Seal the lid and cook for 10 minutes on PRESSURE COOK mode at High pressure. When ready, and do a quick pressure release. Discard the excess cooking liquid, before serving.

Vegan Swiss Chard Dip

Ready in about: 15 minutes | **Serves:** 12 | **Per serving:** Calories 88; Carbs 3g; Fat 7g; Protein 3g

INGREDIENTS

1 ½ cups Tofu
2 cups Swiss Chard, chopped
1 tsp dried Dill weed
2 tsp fresh Lemon Juice
½ tsp ground Black Pepper
1 tsp Salt
1 ¼ cups Vegan Mayonnaise
1 tsp Lemon Zest, grated for garnish
1 cup Water

DIRECTIONS

Pour 1 cup water. In a baking dish, mix all ingredients, except lemon zest, and stir to combine. Cover the dish with aluminium foil. Then, make a foil sling and lower the dish on the rack.

Seal the lid, switch the pressure release valve to close and cook for 10 minutes at High Pressure. When it goes off, quick release the pressure. Sprinkle with lemon zest and serve.

Cheesy Asparagus and Spinach Dip

Ready in about: 15 minutes | **Serves:** 16 | **Per serving:** Calories 118; Carbs 8g; Fat 8g; Protein 4g

INGREDIENTS

18 oz Asparagus Spears, ends trimmed, chopped
12 ounces Spinach, thawed, drained and chopped
1 ½ cups Mozzarella Cheese, shredded
½ tsp ground Black Pepper
1 tsp Sea Salt
½ cup Mayonnaise
1 cup Heavy Cream

DIRECTIONS

Select PRESSURE COOK mode and insert a trivet in the Pressure Cooker. Pour half cup of water.

In a baking dish, add all ingredients and stir to combine. Cover with aluminium foil and lower on top of the trivet. Seal the lid and cook for 12 minutes at High. Do a quick release, and serve with crackers.

Classic Italian Peperonata

Ready in about: 10 minutes | **Serves:** 4 | **Per serving:** Calories 152; Carbs 17g; Fat 8g; Protein 6g

INGREDIENTS

1 Green Bell Pepper, sliced
2 Yellow Bell Peppers, sliced
2 Red Bell Peppers, sliced
3 Tomatoes, chopped
1 Red Onions, chopped
2 Garlic Cloves, minced
2 cups Veggie Stock
2 tbsp Olive Oil
Salt and Pepper, to taste
4 cup Egg Noodles, cooked optional, to serve

DIRECTIONS

Heat oil on SAUTÉ mode, and cook the onion for 2 minutes, until translucent. Stir in peppers and stir-fry for 2 more minutes. Add garlic and cook for 1 minute, until soft.

Stir in the tomatoes and cook for 2 minutes before pouring in the stock. Seal the lid and cook for 6 minutes on STEAM mode at High. When done, do a quick pressure release.

Check the veggies whether they are soft and cooked through. If not, cook for a few more minutes, lid off, on SAUTÉ mode. Drain and serve over noodles.

Spicy Tomato Sauce

Ready in about: 20 minutes | **Serves:** 16 | **Per serving:** Calories 50; Carbs 5g; Fat 3g; Protein 1g

INGREDIENTS

3 pounds Tomatoes, peeled and diced
1 cup Red Onions, chopped
¼ cup Olive Oil
2 tsp Brown Sugar
½ tsp dried basil
1 Red Chilli, chopped
½ tsp dried Oregano
2 Cloves Garlic, minced
½ tsp dried Sage
Salt and ground Black Pepper, to taste
½ cup Water

DIRECTIONS

Select SAUTÉ mode and heat the oil; cook the green onions and garlic until tender, for about 3 minutes. Add the remaining ingredients and seal the lid. Select PRESSURE COOK mode.

Cook for 10 minutes at High Pressure. Do a quick pressure release. Cool before serving.

Zesty Carrots with Pecans

Ready in about: 10 minutes | **Serves:** 4 | **Per serving:** Calories 276; Carbs 45g; Fat 10g; Protein 5g

INGREDIENTS

2 pounds Carrots, peeled and cut into rounds
½ cup Pecans, toasted and chopped
1 tbsp Butter
¼ cup Raisins
1 cup Water
½ Sea Salt
1 tbsp Vinegar
Freshly ground Black Pepper, to taste

DIRECTIONS

Select SAUTÉ mode and melt the butter. Add in the carrots and cook for 5 minutes until tender. Add the raisins, water, and salt. Seal the lid, press PRESSURE COOK and cook for 3 minutes at High pressure.

When it goes off, do a quick pressure release. Pour in the vinegar, and black pepper, and give it a good stir. Scatter the pecans over the top, to serve.

Pressure Cooked Devilled Eggs

Ready in about: 20 minutes | **Serves:** 4 | **Per serving:** Calories 100; Carbs 1g; Fat 8g; Protein 6g

INGREDIENTS

4 Eggs
1 tsp Paprika
1 tbsp Light Mayonnaise
1 tsp Dijon Mustard
1 cup Water

DIRECTIONS

Place the eggs and water in your pressure cooker. Seal the lid and cook on PRESSURE COOK for 5 minutes at High. Once cooking is over, do a quick pressure release.

Transfer the veggies to a food processor. Place the eggs in an ice bath and let cool for 5 minutes. Peel and cut them in half. Remove yolks to a mixing dish and mash with a fork; add the remaining ingredients excluding the paprika and stir.

Fill the egg halves with the yolk mixture. Sprinkle with paprika to serve.

Lemony and Garlicky Potato and Turnip Dip

Ready in: 15 minutes + chilling time | **Serves:** 4 | **Per serving:** Calories 143; Carbs 12g; Fat 10g; Protein 1g

INGREDIENTS

3 tbsp Olive Oil
6 Whole Garlic Cloves, peeled
2 tbsp Lemon Juice
1 Turnip, cut lengthwise
1 Sweet Potato, cut lengthwise
1 cup Water
2 tbsp Coconut Milk

DIRECTIONS

Pour in water. Place the potato, turnip, and garlic on the rack. Seal the lid, and cook on PRESSURE COOK at High pressure for 10 minutes. When done, do a quick pressure release.

Transfer the veggies to a food processor. Add the remaining ingredients and process until smooth. Transfer to a container with a lid. Refrigerate for about 2 hours before serving.

Easy Street Sweet Corn

Ready in about: 10 minutes | **Serves:** 6 | **Per serving:** Calories 130; Carbs 16g; Fat 5g; Protein 9g

INGREDIENTS

Juice of 2 Limes
1 cup Parmesan Cheese, grated
6 Ears Sweet Corn
2 cups Water
6 tbsp Yogurt
½ tsp Garlic Powder
1 tsp Chili Powder, optional

DIRECTIONS

Pour in water. Put the corn in a steamer basket. Place into the pressure cooker. Seal the lid, and cook on STEAM mode for 3 minutes at High. Combine the remaining ingredients, except the cheese, in a bowl.

Once cooking is over, do a quick pressure release. Let cool for a couple of minutes. Remove husks from the corn and brush them with the mixture. Sprinkle parmesan on top and serve.

Cheesy Sour Veggie Casserole

Ready in about: 35 minutes | **Serves:** 8 | **Per serving:** Calories 379; Carbs 54g; Fat 14g; Protein 11g

INGREDIENTS

6 Potatoes, chopped
½ cup Onion, chopped
1 cup Carrots, chopped
1 cup Bell Peppers, chopped
1 cup Panko Breadcrumbs

½ cup Sour Cream
1 cup Cheddar Cheese, shredded
3 tbsp Butter, melted
2 tbsp Olive Oil
Water, as needed

DIRECTIONS

Heat oil on SAUTÉ mode, and cook the onions for 2 minutes, until translucent. Add the veggies and stir-fry for 2 more minutes. Pour enough water to cover.

Seal the lid and cook for 7 minutes on PRESSURE COOK at High. Do a quick pressure release. Transfer the veggies to a baking pan, that fits in the pressure cooker. Leave the liquid in the cooker.

Place a trivet at the bottom. In the baking pan, stir in the remaining ingredients. Place the pan atop of the trivet, inside the cooker and seal the lid. Cook for 5 more minutes at High. Do a quick release.

Bean and Rice Casserole

Ready in about: 40 minutes | **Serves:** 4 | **Per serving:** Calories 322; Carbs 63g; Fat 2g; Protein 6g

INGREDIENTS

1 cup Black Beans, soaked
5 cups Water
2 tsp Onion Powder
2 tsp Chili Powder, optional

2 cups Brown Rice
6 ounces Tomato Paste
1 tsp Garlic, minced
1 tsp Salt

DIRECTIONS

Add all ingredients in your pressure cooker. Seal the lid, select BEANS/CHILI and adjust the time to 35 minutes at High pressure. When over, do a quick pressure release.

Vegan Sausage and Pepper Casserole

Ready in about: 15 minutes | **Serves:** 4 | **Per serving:** Calories 293; Carbs 42g; Fat 8g; Protein 14g

INGREDIENTS

2 Vegan Sausage Links, sliced
2 Large Potatoes, diced
3 Bell Peppers, chopped
1 Onion, chopped
1 Zucchini, grated
1 Carrot, grated
½ cup Milk

1 cup Veggie Stock
½ tsp Cumin
¼ tsp Pepper
¼ tsp Salt
¼ tsp Turmeric Powder
1 tbsp Olive Oil

DIRECTIONS

Heat oil on SAUTÉ mode, and cook the onions for 1 minute, until translucent. Stir in peppers and cook for 4 more minutes, until soft. Add sausage and cook until browned.

Stir in the spices, stock, and potatoes. Seal the lid and cook for 5 minutes on PRESSURE COOK, at High pressure. When ready, do a quick pressure release. Stir in the remaining ingredients. Cook for 3 more minutes on SAUTÉ, lid off. Drain and serve.

Garlicky and Chili Pomodoro Zoodles

Ready in about: 15 minutes | **Serves:** 4 | **Per serving:** Calories 121; Carbs 16g; Fat 4g; Protein 3g

INGREDIENTS

2 Large Zucchini, spiralized
½ Onion, diced
3 tsp Garlic, minced
1 tbsp Olive Oil
1 cup Tomatoes, diced

¾ cup Tomato Sauce
½ cup Water
1 tbsp freshly Basi, chopped l
2 tsp Chili Powder
Salt and Pepper, to taste

DIRECTIONS

Heat oil on SAUTÉ. Cook the onions for 3 minutes, until translucent. Add garlic and cook for 1 more minute, until fragrant and crispy. Stir in the tomatoes, water and tomato sauce.

Seal the lid and cook for 3 minutes at High. Release the pressure quickly. Stir in the zoodles, and season with salt and pepper. Cook for 3 minutes, lid off, and stir in chili powder. To serve, top with basil.

Buttery Parsley Corn

Ready in about: 10 minutes | **Serves:** 4 | **Per serving:** Calories 310; Carbs 32g; Fat 21g; Protein 5g

INGREDIENTS

4 ears shucked Corn
6 tbsp Butter, melted
½ tsp Salt
1 ¼ cups Water

½ tsp Chili Powder, optional
¼ tsp Sugar
2 tbsp Parsley, minced

DIRECTIONS

Pour the water in your pressure cooker and insert a trivet. Place corn on top of the trivet. Seal the lid and select STEAM mode for 3 minutes at High. Do a quick pressure release.

In a bowl, combine butter, salt, parsley, and chili powder, and pour over the corn, to serve.

Eggplant Escalivada Toast

Ready in about: 30 minutes | **Serves:** 6 | **Per serving:** Calories 164; Carbs 23g; Fat 7g; Protein 5g

INGREDIENTS

6 Bread Sliced, toasted
2 Eggplants, peeled and sliced
1 Red Bell Pepper, peeled and sliced
2 Garlic Cloves
A handful of Black Olives
2 tbsp Olive Oil

1 tbsp Tahini
Juice from 1 Lemon
A pinch of Red Pepper flakes
½ tsp Salt
¼ tsp Black Pepper
1 ½ cups Water

DIRECTIONS

Combine the water, bell pepper and eggplant in the pressure cooker. Seal the lid and cook at High for 6 minutes. When ready, do a quick pressure release.

Drain and place the eggplants in a food processor. Add lemon juice, olive oil, olives, garlic, salt, pepper, and pepper flakes. Pulse until smooth. Spread the mixture over the toasted bread and serve warm.

Mushroom and Veggie Baguette

Ready in about: 20 minutes | **Serves:** 4 | **Per serving:** Calories 227; Carbs 20g; Fat 9g; Protein 17g

INGREDIENTS

1 Baguette, cut into 4 equal pieces
1 ½ cups Mushrooms, chopped
1 Shallot, chopped
1 Carrot, chopped
2 Bell Peppers, chopped
1 Parsnip, chopped

2 Tomatoes, chopped
1 Garlic Clove
1 tbsp Olive Oil
1 ½ cups Vegetable Stock
Salt and Pepper, to taste

DIRECTIONS

Melt oil on SAUTÉ mode, add shallots and garlic and cook for 2 minutes, until soft and fragrant. Stir in the rest of the veggies and cook for 5 minutes, stirring occasionally.

Stir in the remaining ingredients. Seal the lid and cook for 6 minutes on RICE at High. Release the pressure quickly. Remove to a food processor and pulse until smooth. Spread mixture over baguette.

Root Veggie Casserole

Ready in about: 25 minutes | **Serves:** 4 | **Per serving:** Calories 378; Carbs 73g; Fat 7g; Protein 13g

INGREDIENTS

1 Onion, diced
4 pounds Baby Potatoes, halved
2 pounds Baby Carrots
1 tsp Garlic, minced

1 tsp Thyme
1 tsp dried Parsley
2 tbsp Olive Oil
½ cup Veggie Broth

DIRECTIONS

Heat the oil on SAUTÉ. When hot and sizzling, add the onions and cook for 2-3 minutes.

When the onions become translucent, add the garlic and cook for another minute. Add the carrots and cook for another 3 minutes. Stir in the rest of the ingredients and seal the lid.

Press PRESSURE COOK, and set the cooking time to 10 minutes at High. Release the pressure quickly.

Coconut Zucchini Soup

Ready in about: 20 minutes | **Serves:** 2 | **Per serving:** Calories 296; Carbs 12g; Fat 25g; Protein 8g

INGREDIENTS

16 ounces Veggie Broth
10 cups Zucchini, chopped
13 ounces Coconut Milk
1 tbsp Curry Paste
½ tsp Garlic Powder

½ tsp Onion Powder
Freshly ground Black Pepper
1/4 cup Butter, at room temperature
Crème fraîche for garnish

DIRECTIONS

Place all ingredients, except for the coconut milk in the pressure cooker. Give the mixture a good stir to combine, and then seal the lid, select PRESSURE COOK for 10 minutes at High.

When the timer goes off, do a quick pressure release. Remove the ingredients to a deep bowl, add coconut milk and blend with an immersion blender until smooth. Serve right away garnished with crème fraîche and ground black pepper, to enjoy.

Harissa Turnip Stew

Ready in about: 15 minutes | **Serves:** 4 | **Per serving:** Calories 145; Carbs 16g; Fat 8g; Protein 4g

INGREDIENTS

6 Turnip, cut into halves lengthwise
¼ tsp Smoked Paprika
2 tbsp Harissa Paste
1 cup Vegetable Broth

2 tbsp Olive Oil
2 tin Tomatoes, chopped
1 tsp Garlic powder
Kosher Salt and ground Black Pepper, to taste

DIRECTIONS

Stir in all ingredients in the pressure cooker. Seal the lid. Set to PRESSURE COOK and cook for 12 minutes at High. Once ready, do a quick pressure release. Serve warm.

Pressure Cooked Ratatouille

Ready in about: 20 minutes | **Serves:** 4 | **Per serving:** Calories 104; Carbs 11g; Fat 7g; Protein 2g

INGREDIENTS

1 Zucchini, sliced
2 Tomatoes, sliced
1 tbsp Balsamic Vinegar
1 Eggplant, sliced
1 Onion, sliced

1 tbsp dried Thyme
2 tbsp Olive Oil
2 Garlic Cloves, minced
1 cup Water

DIRECTIONS

Add the garlic to a springform pan. Arrange the veggies in a circle. Sprinkle them with thyme and drizzle with olive oil. Pour water in your pressure cooker. Place the pan inside on a trivet. Seal the lid.

Cook for 6 minutes on PRESSURE COOK at High. Release the pressure naturally, for 10 minutes.

Chipotle Pumpkin Soup

Ready in about: 25 minutes | **Serves:** 6 | **Per serving:** Calories 137; Carbs 11g; Fat 3g; Protein 6g

INGREDIENTS

2 Chipotle Peppers, seeded and finely minced
4 cups Vegetable Broth
1 tbsp Olive Oil
1 cup Onions, peeled and chopped
2 cups Water
3 tbsp fresh Cilantro, chopped
½ tsp Cayenne Pepper

¼ tsp Black Pepper
½ tsp Salt
28 ounces canned Pumpkin Puree
1 tsp Garlic, smashed
½ tsp ground Allspice
2 tbsp Pumpkin Seeds, toasted for garnish
1 cup Heavy Cream

DIRECTIONS

Warm oil in the cooker on SAUTÉ, and cook the garlic and onion until brown, for about 3-4 minutes. Add the chipotle peppers, allspice, salt, cayenne pepper, and black pepper, and cook for another 2 minutes.

Then, stir in the pumpkin, broth, and water. Seal the lid, press SOUP/BROTH and cook for 10 minutes at High Pressure. Once ready, do a quick pressure release. Transfer the soup to a food processor.

Blend until smooth and creamy, working in batches if necessary, then pour in the heavy cream. Sprinkle with toasted pumpkin seeds and fresh cilantro to serve.

Beet Borscht

Ready in about: 60 minutes | **Serves:** 8 | **Per serving:** Calories 186; Carbs 42g; Fat 1g; Protein 5g

INGREDIENTS

3 cups Cabbage, shredded
8 cups Beets, diced
3 Celery Stalks, diced
1 Onion, diced
1 Garlic Clove, diced

3 cups Veggie Stock
2 Carrots, diced
1 tsp Thyme
¼ tsp Pepper
1 ½ cups Water

DIRECTIONS

Pour the water in the pressure cooker and lower the steamer basket. Place the beets inside the basket and seal the lid. Select PRESSURE COOK, set to 7 minutes at High pressure.

After the beeping sound, release the pressure quickly. Remove the steamer basket and discard the water. Return the cooked beets to the pot and add the rest of the ingredients.

Stir well to combine and then seal the lid again. Select SOUP/BROTH, and cook for 45 minutes, at High. When the timer goes off, do a natural pressure release, for about 10 minutes.

Potato Chili

Ready in about: 22 minutes | **Serves:** 4 | **Per serving:** Calories 285; Carbs 50g; Fat 5g; Protein 6g

INGREDIENTS

4 cups Vegetable Broth
3 large Russet Potatoes, peeled and diced
2 Jalapeno Peppers, seeded and diced
1 Garlic Clove, minced
½ tsp Cumin

1 tsp Chili Powder
¼ tsp Cayenne Pepper
½ Red Onion, diced
1 tbsp Olive Oil

DIRECTIONS

Warm oil on SAUTÉ. Once hot and sizzling, add onions and cook for 2-3 minutes. When translucent, add the garlic and cook for another minute. Add the remaining ingredients.

Stir well to combine, seal the lid, and cook at High pressure for 8 minutes. After the beep, let the pressure release naturally, by allowing the valve to drop on its own, for about 10 minutes.

Tofu and Veggie 'Stir Fry'

Ready in about: 20 minutes | **Serves:** 4 | **Per serving:** Calories 410; Carbs 18g; Fat 28g; Protein 25g

INGREDIENTS

12 ounces Tofu, mashed
2 Shallots, diced
1 Tomato, diced
1 cup Parsnips, chopped
2 tbsp Olive Oil

2 tsp Sherry
¼ cup Parsley, chopped
1 tsp Garlic, minced
3 cups Water
Salt and Pepper, to taste

DIRECTIONS

Heat oil on SAUTÉ mode. Add shallots, parsnips, garlic, and tomatoes; cook for 3 minutes, stirring occasionally. Stir in tofu, sherry, and season with salt and pepper.

Seal the lid, set on STEAM, and cook for 4 minutes at High. Once done, do a quick release.

Flavorful Tofu Bowl

Ready in about: 10 minutes | **Serves:** 6 | **Per serving:** Calories 275; Carbs 10g; Fat 16g; Protein 26g

INGREDIENTS

20 ounces Firm Tofu, cubed
2 tsp Garlic, minced
1 Onion, chopped
2 tbsp Chives, chopped
1 tsp Ginger, minced

2 cups Veggie Broth
2 tbsp Tamari
2 tbsp White Wine
3 tsp Vegetable Oil
2 cups cooked Rice to serve

DIRECTIONS

Heat oil on SAUTÉ mode. Add tofu and cook until browned, for a few minutes. Meanwhile, place the remaining ingredients, except the rice, in a food processor and pulse until smooth.

Pour this mixture over the tofu. Seal the lid and cook on STEAM for 3 minutes at High. When ready, release the pressure quickly. Stir in the rice and serve.

Veggie Flax Burgers

Ready in about: 30 minutes | **Serves:** 4 | **Per serving:** Calories 123; Carbs 8g; Fat 8g; Protein 2g

INGREDIENTS

2 tbsp Olive Oil
1 bag of Frozen Mixed Veggies Broccoli, Carrots, peas
1 cup Cauliflower Florets

1 cup Flax Meal
1 ½ cups Water

DIRECTIONS

Pour the water into your pressure cooker. Combine the mixed veggies and cauliflower florets in the steaming basket and then lower the basket into the pot. Seal the lid.

Select PRESSURE COOK for 5 minutes at High pressure. After the timer goes off, do a quick pressure release. Transfer the veggies to a bowl and discard the water.

Mash the veggies with a potato masher and allow them to cool a bit, about 10 minutes. When safe to handle, stir in the flax meal and shape the mixture into 4 equal patties.

Wipe the pressure cooker clean, and add olive oil. Set to SAUTÉ and wait until oil heats. When sizzling, add veggie burgers. Cook for 3 minutes then flip over and cook for 3 more minutes. Serve and enjoy!

Tempeh Sandwiches

Ready in about: 30 minutes | **Serves:** 6 | **Per serving:** Calories 428; Carbs 41g; Fat 23g; Protein 15g

INGREDIENTS

12 ounces Tempeh, sliced
6 Brioche Buns
1 tsp Ginger, minced
2 tbsp Brown Mustard
2 tsp Agave Nectar
1 tsp Garlic, minced

½ tsp Smoked Paprika
½ cup Apple Cider Vinegar
½ cup Veggie Stock
2 tbsp Tamari
Salt and Black Pepper, to taste
Cooking spray, to grease

DIRECTIONS

Coat with cooking spray and sauté the tempeh on SAUTÉ mode for a few minutes. Stir in the remaining ingredients, except the buns, and seal the lid. Cook for 2 minutes at High pressure. When ready, release the pressure quickly. Divide the mixture between the buns and serve.

Red Lentil Dhal with Butternut Squash

Ready in about: 25 minutes | **Serves:** 6 | **Per serving:** Calories 325; Carbs 45g; Fat 10g; Protein 12g

INGREDIENTS

4 ½ cups Vegetable Broth
1 ½ cups Tomatoes, diced
1 ½ cups Red Lentils, rinsed
1 heaping tsp Garlic, minced
1 cup Onions, diced
3 tbsp Olive Oil
¼ tsp Black Pepper
½ tsp Cayenne Pepper

1 tsp ground Turmeric
Juice from 1 lemon
1 tsp Salt
2 pounds Butternut squash, roughly chopped
2 tsp Garam Masala
½ cup fresh Cilantro, chopped for garnish
½ cup Natural Yogurt, for garnish

DIRECTIONS

Warm the oil on SAUTÉ mode. Cook the garlic and onions for 2-3 minutes, until soft. Add the squash, Garam masala, cayenne pepper, turmeric, salt, and black pepper. Cook for 3 more minutes.

Then, stir in the broth, lentils, and tomatoes. Lock the lid and switch the pressure release valve to close. Select PRESSURE COOK and cook for 10 minutes at High pressure. Do a quick pressure release.

Stir in lemon juice. Ladle dhal into bowls and garnish with fresh cilantro and yogurt and serve.

Asparagus Dressed in Cheese

Ready in about: 17 minutes | **Serves:** 4 | **Per serving:** Calories 224; Carbs 6g; Fat 15g; Protein 16g

INGREDIENTS

1 pound Asparagus
8 ounces Cheddar cheese

1 cup Water

DIRECTIONS

Pour water into your cooker. Cut off the asparagus' ends. Slice the cheddar cheese in enough strips to wrap around each asparagus spear. Arrange the wrapped asparagus on a steamer basket.

Place the basket inside the pressure cooker. Seal the lid, cook at High for 4 minutes. When cooking is complete, press CANCEL and release the pressure quickly. Serve hot.

Spicy Pinto Bean Chili

Ready in about: 30 minutes | **Serves:** 8 | **Per serving:** Calories 132; Carbs 23g; Fat 3g; Protein 11g

INGREDIENTS

5 cups Vegetable Stock
1 tsp Red Pepper flakes, crushed
20 ounces canned Tomatoes, diced
1 cup Carrots, chopped into sticks
1 Green Bell Pepper, thinly sliced
3 Cloves Garlic, minced

1 cup Red Onion, chopped
½ tsp Cilantro, to garnish
Sea Salt and Black Pepper, to taste
2 ½ cups dried Pinto Beans, rinsed
1 cup Parsnip, chopped

DIRECTIONS

Sauté garlic and onion for 3 minutes on SAUTÉ, with a splash of vegetable stock. Stir in the remaining ingredients, except for the cilantro. Seal the lid, press BEANS/CHILI for 20 minutes at High pressure.

Once the cooking is complete, do a quick pressure release. Garnish with fresh cilantro to serve.

Effortless Cannellini and Black Bean Chili

Ready in about: 30 minutes | **Serves:** 8 | **Per serving:** Calories 136; Carbs 19g; Fat 7g; Protein 4g

INGREDIENTS

2 cups Vegetable Stock
1 tsp Chili Pepper, minced
½ cup Red Bell Pepper, seeded and thinly sliced
1 cup Leeks, thinly sliced
1 tsp Garlic, minced
2 tbsp Vegetable Oil
1 cup Carrots, chopped into sticks
1 ½ cup dried Black Beans, soaked, drained and rinsed
1 ½ cup dried cannellini Beans, soaked, drained and rinsed
¼ tsp Sea Salt, to taste
½ tsp Celery seeds
5-6 Black Peppercorns
½ tsp Red Pepper flakes, crushed
24 ounces canned diced Tomatoes
½ cup Green Onion, chopped

DIRECTIONS

Heat oil on SAUTÉ, and cook the garlic and leeks for 3-4 minutes. Stir in the remaining ingredients, except for the tomatoes. Seal the lid, select PRESSURE COOK and cook for 20 minutes at High Pressure.

Once the cooking is complete, perform a quick pressure release. Add in the tomatoes, and stir occasionally for about 5 minutes. Serve garnished with green onion.

Candied Holiday Yams

Ready in about: 10 minutes | **Serves:** 4 | **Per serving:** Calories 466; Carbs 78g; Fat 16g; Protein 4g

INGREDIENTS

3 Yams, peeled and cubed
4 tbsp Butter
¼ cup Maple Syrup
1 cup Water
½ cup Brown Sugar
1 tsp Cinnamon
2 ½ tbsp Cornstarch
½ cup Pecans, chopped
A pinch of Salt

DIRECTIONS

Combine all ingredients in the pressure cooker. Seal the lid and cook at High pressure, for 5 minutes. When ready, release the pressure quickly, and serve.

Walnut & Cinnamon Coconut Potatoes

Ready in about: 20 minutes | **Serves:** 4 | **Per serving:** Calories 387; Carbs 67g; Fat 15g; Protein 5g

INGREDIENTS

4 Potatoes, boiled and mashed
2 tbsp Coconut Flour
¼ tsp Cinnamon
2 tbsp Coconut Milk
½ cup chopped Walnuts
1 tbsp Coconut Oil
2 tbsp Fresh Orange Juice
1 cup Water

DIRECTIONS

Add the mashed potatoes, coconut milk, cinnamon, orange juice, and coconut oil, to a large bowl. Mix well until the mixture is fully incorporated. Grease a baking dish with cooking spray.

Press well the potato mixture at the bottom. Top with walnuts and sprinkle with coconut flour. Pour the water into the pressure cooker and lower the trivet. Place baking dish on top of the trivet.

Seal the lid, and cook at High pressure for 7 minutes. Do a natural pressure release, for 10 minutes.

Minty Cauliflower Tabbouleh

Ready in about: 10 minutes | **Serves:** 3 | **Per serving:** Calories 232; Carbs 15g; Fat 18g; Protein 3g

INGREDIENTS

2 cups Cauliflower Rice (made in a food processor)
4 tbsp Olive Oil
½ cup Spring Onions, chopped
½ Cucumber, diced
3 tbsp Lime Juice
½ cup Parsley
½ cup Mint
1 tsp Garlic, minced
1 cup diced Tomatoes

DIRECTIONS

Heat a tablespoon of olive oil to the pressure cooker on SAUTÉ. Add the garlic and cook for a minute. Add the tomatoes and cauliflower, and saute them for about 2-3 minutes.

Transfer to a bowl. Add the remaining ingredients to the bowl and give the mixture a good stir to combine well. Divide among 3 serving bowls.

Navy Beans with Parsley and Garlic

Ready in about: 30 minutes | **Serves:** 6 | **Per serving:** Calories 112; Carbs 19g; Fat 1g; Protein 9g

INGREDIENTS

1 Tomato, chopped
2 tbsp Olive Oil
1 Bell Pepper, sliced
1 tsp Garlic, minced
1 cup Celery stalk, chopped
1 tbsp Tomato Puree
½ tsp Cayenne Pepper
1 tsp Salt
3 cups Water
2 cups dried Navy Beans, drained and soaked
4 Garlic Cloves, sliced
1 handful Parsley, roughly chopped, to serve
1 cup Carrots, chopped into sticks
2 small Onions, chopped

DIRECTIONS

Sauté onions, celery, and garlic for about 3 minutes on SAUTÉ mode. Then, add the remaining ingredients, except for the parsley. Seal the lid, set on BEANS/CHILI for 20 minutes at High Pressure.

When ready, do a quick pressure release. Transfer to a serving bowl, sprinkle with parsley and serve.

Apple and Red Cabbage Vegetarian Dinner

Ready in about: 30 minutes | **Serves:** 4 | **Per serving:** Calories 139; Carbs 22g; Fat 4g; Protein 4g

INGREDIENTS

1 pound Red Cabbage, shredded
½ cup Red Wine
1 cup Apples, diced
1 cup Onions, diced
1 tsp Thyme
1 ½ cups Vegetable Stock
1 tbsp Coconut Oil
1 ½ tbsp Cornstarch Slurry
1 ½ tbsp Flour
Salt and Pepper, to taste
½ tsp Brown Sugar

DIRECTIONS

Melt oil on SAUTÉ mode, add onions and apples and cook for 5 minutes, until lightly browned.

Stir in the remaining ingredients, except the slurry. Cook for 20 minutes, and bring the mixture to a boil. Stir in the slurry and cook uncovered until thickened. Serve and enjoy!

Tomato and Kale "Rice"

Ready in about: 15 minutes | **Serves:** 4 | **Per serving:** Calories 68; Carbs 8g; Fat 4g; Protein 3g

INGREDIENTS

1 tbsp Oil
1 cup Veggie Broth
4 cups Cauliflower Rice, processed in a food processor
1 Large Tomato, chopped
½ cup Kale, chopped
1 tsp Cilantro, chopped
¼ tsp Pepper
¼ tsp Garlic Powder

DIRECTIONS

Heat the oil on SAUTÉ. Add the tomato, cauliflower, pepper, and garlic powder. Stir well to combine and cook for a minute or two. Pour the broth over and stir in the spinach.

Seal the lid, select PRESSURE COOK for 3 minutes, at High pressure. After you hear the beep, release the pressure quickly. Open the lid carefully, serve and enjoy!

Spicy Cannellini Bean Salad with Dates

Ready in: 35 minutes + chilling time | **Serves:** 12 | **Per serving:** Calories 195; Carbs 29g; Fat 3g; Protein 9g

INGREDIENTS

1 cup dry Cannellini Beans, soaked
1 cup fresh Dates, halved, pitted
2 ½ cups frozen Green peas, thawed
1 cup Scallions, chopped
1 cup Tomatoes, thinly sliced
3 Cloves Garlic, minced
1 tbsp Olive Oil
¼ cup White Wine Vinegar
¼ cup Tamari Sauce
2 tsp Chili Paste
Salt and Black Pepper, to taste
½ tsp Red Pepper flakes, for garnish

DIRECTIONS

To prepare the dressing, whisk tamari sauce, oil, vinegar, chili paste and garlic. Refrigerate overnight.

Place the beans in your pressure cooker and pour water to cover them. Seal the lid and switch the pressure release valve to close. Select BEANS/CHILI mode and cook for 25 minutes at High Pressure.

Once the cooking is complete, perform a quick pressure release. Drain the beans and transfer to a serving bowl. Add in the rest of the ingredients, and toss with the dressing until well coated.

Potato and Spinach Bowl

Ready in about: 15 minutes | **Serves:** 4 | **Per serving:** Calories 153; Carbs 15g; Fat 5g; Protein 4g

INGREDIENTS

1 Potato, peeled and cubed
1 Onion, chopped
2 cups Spinach
2 Garlic Cloves, minced
½ cup Veggie Broth
1 tsp Lemon Juice
1 tsp ground Ginger
½ tsp Cayenne Pepper
½ tbsp Olive Oil
¼ tsp Pepper

DIRECTIONS

Warm oil on SAUTÉ mode. When hot and sizzling, add the onion and cook for 2 minutes. Add the garlic, ginger, cayenne, and pepper, and cook for one more minute.

Add the sweet potatoes and cook for another minute. Pour the broth over and stir in the spinach. Seal the lid, select PRESSURE COOK for 4 minutes at High pressure. Release the pressure quickly.

Pears in Cranberry Sauce

Ready in about: 20 minutes | **Serves:** 4 | **Per serving:** Calories 133; Carbs 29g; Fat 0g; Protein 1g

INGREDIENTS

1 pound Pears, peeled, cored, and halved
2 ½ cups Cranberries
1 tsp Vanilla Paste
½ cup granulated Sugar

2 tsp Cornstarch
¼ tsp grated Nutmeg
½ tsp ground Cardamom
1 ½ cups Water

DIRECTIONS

Throw all ingredients, except for sugar and cornstarch, into your pressure cooker. Select PRESSURE COOK mode and cook for 10 minutes at High Pressure.

When ready, do a quick pressure release. Remove the pears with a spoon that has long narrow holes. Then, mash the berries with a heavy spoon. Combine the sugar and cornstarch with 2 tbsp of water.

Let simmer for 5 minutes on SAUTÉ, until it thickens. Serve the pears topped with cranberry sauce.

Green Minestrone Stew with Parmesan

Ready in about: 25 minutes | **Serves:** 4 | **Per serving:** Calories 313; Carbs 25g; Fat 21g; Protein 9g

INGREDIENTS

1 head Broccoli, chopped into small florets
2 Green Bell Peppers, thinly sliced
2 Celery stalks, chopped
1 tsp Garlic, minced
1 tsp Olive Oil

4 spring Onions, chopped
4 cups Vegetable Broth
1 bunch Kale, roughly chopped
2 tsp fresh Lime Juice
Freshly grated Parmesan cheese, to serve

DIRECTIONS

Heat the oil on SAUTÉ mode. Cook the spring onions and garlic until tender, for about 2 minutes.

Add the remaining ingredients, except for kale and Parmesan cheese. Seal the lid and switch the pressure release valve to close. Press SOUP/BROTH and cook for 10 minutes at High pressure.

Once the cooking is over, do a quick release. Add in the kale. Place the lid and cook for 12-15 minutes until tender, on SAUTÉ mode. Divide between 4 bowls and serve sprinkled with Parmesan cheese.

Savory Vegetarian Sandwiches

Ready in about: 35 minutes | **Serves:** 4 | **Per serving:** Calories 488; Carbs 62g; Fat 19g; Protein 28g

INGREDIENTS

1 tbsp Vegetable Oil
4 Vegetarian Sausages, sliced
1 Garlic Cloves, crushed
½ cup Tamari Sauce
2 Shallots, chopped
2 cups roasted Vegetable Stock

2 Bell Peppers, deveined and sliced
4 Burger Buns
1 cup freshly grated Cheddar Cheese
Salt and ground Black Pepper, to taste
2 ½ cups Water

DIRECTIONS

Heat oil on SAUTÉ and cook the garlic and shallots, until tender, for about 3 minutes. Stir in the sausages and cook for another 5 minutes. Add in the remaining ingredients, except for the buns and cheese.

Select PRESSURE COOK and cook for 15 minutes at High. Once ready, do a quick pressure release. Preheat oven to 460 degrees F. Divide prepared mixture among 4 burger buns and top with grated cheese.

Bake the sandwiches in the oven for 6-7 minutes, or until the cheese melts. Serve immediately!

Squash and Sweet Potato Lunch Soup

Ready in about: 30 minutes | **Serves:** 4 | **Per serving:** Calories 243; Carbs 33g; Fat 9g; Protein 7g

INGREDIENTS

2 cups Squash, cubed
2 cups Sweet Potatoes, cubed
2 tbsp Olive Oil
1 Onion, diced
1 tbsp Heavy Cream
3 cups Veggie Broth
A pinch of Thyme

DIRECTIONS

On SAUTÉ, warm the oil, and add the onions. Cook until soft, about 3 minutes. Stir in the potatoes and squash and cook for an additional minute, or until they begin to 'sweat'.

Pour the broth over and stir in the thyme. Seal the lid, choose PRESSURE COOK for 10 minutes at High. When done, do a natural pressure release, for about 10 minutes. Stir in the cream, and serve.

Broccoli and Chickpea Stew

Ready in about: 35 minutes | **Serves:** 4 | **Per serving:** Calories 415; Carbs 74g; Fat 8g; Protein 25g;

INGREDIENTS

12 ounces Chickpeas Beans, drained and soaked
1 bunch Broccoli rabe, chopped
½ head Red Cabbage, shredded
1 pound Zucchini, diced
2 Carrots, diced
2 Potatoes, diced
2 tbsp fresh Parsley, roughly chopped
2 Tomatoes, chopped
5 cups Vegetable Stock
1 tsp Fennel Seeds
½ tsp Salt
½ tsp ground Black Pepper
½ tsp Celery seeds

DIRECTIONS

Add all ingredients in the pressure cooker. Seal the lid, select MEAT/STEW and cook for 25 minutes at High Pressure. When ready, do a quick pressure release. Ladle in serving bowls to serve.

Potato & Leek Patties

Ready in about: 15 minutes | **Serves:** 3 | **Per serving:** Calories 265; Carbs 33g; Fat 11g; Protein 10g

INGREDIENTS

1 tbsp Olive Oil
4 ounces Leek, sliced
9 ounces Potatoes, boiled and mashed
½ cup Flour
¼ tsp Onion Powder
¼ tsp Paprika
¼ tsp Garlic Powder
A pinch of Pepper

DIRECTIONS

Place all ingredients, except the oil, in a bowl. Mix with your hands until well combined and shape the mixture into 6 small patties. Add olive oil to the pressure cooker and set to SAUTÉ.

When hot, add the patties and cook them for about 3 minutes on each side. Serve as desired.

Spicy Tofu Vegan Stew

Ready in about: 20 minutes | **Serves:** 4 | **Per serving:** Calories 355; Carbs 69g; Fat 3g; Protein 11g

INGREDIENTS

1 tsp Habanero Pepper, minced
2 cups Tofu, shredded or cubed
2 Bell Peppers, diced
2 ripe Tomatoes, finely chopped
2 White Onions, chopped
1 cup Parsnips, chopped
1 cup Green peas
⅓ cup Barbecue Sauce

2 Carrots, chopped
4 Sweet Potatoes, peeled and diced
1 tbsp Vegetable Oil
2 tbsp Ketchup
⅓ tsp Korean Gochugaru Chile Flakes
½ tsp Salt
½ tsp Black Pepper
1 cup Water

DIRECTIONS

Heat the oil on SAUTÉ mode, and cook the onions, carrots, parsnip, and peppers until soft, for about 5 minutes. Add the rest of the ingredients, and pour the water to cover the ingredients. Seal the lid, and cook for 10 minutes on PRESSURE COOK at High. Do a quick pressure release.

Smoked Tofu Bowl

Ready in about: 10 minutes | **Serves:** 6 | **Per serving:** Calories 387; Carbs 59g; Fat 9g; Protein 23g

INGREDIENTS

20 ounces Smoked Tofu, sliced
2 ½ tbsp Oyster Sauce
2 tbsp Mirin Wine
3 Garlic Cloves, minced
2 tsp Olive Oil
2 cups Vegetable Broth

1 Onion, chopped
3 cups cooked Wild Rice
2 tbsp fresh Chives, roughly chopped
Salt and Black Pepper, to taste
1-inch piece of fresh Ginger, grated

DIRECTIONS

Select SAUTÉ mode. Heat the oil and stir-fry the tofu cubes until lightly browned. In a blender, add in the remaining ingredients, except the rice. Blend until you obtain a smooth paste.

Transfer the mixture to the pressure cooker. Select PRESSURE COOK and cook for 2 minutes at High pressure. Do a quick pressure release. Serve on top of cooked rice to enjoy.

Pearl Barley and Butternut Winter Soup

Ready in about: 30 minutes | **Serves:** 6 | **Per serving:** Calories 335; Carbs 56g; Fat 6g; Protein 9g

INGREDIENTS

1 cup Pearl Barley, rinsed and drained
1 pound Buttenut Squash, cubed
1 tbsp Chili Pepper, V
½ cup Carrots, chopped
½ cup Parsnip, chopped
2 sticks Celery, diced

1 Turnip, chopped
3 tsp Olive Oil
1 ½ tsp Salt
6 cups Water
Salt and ground Black Pepper, to taste
½ tsp Cayenne Pepper

DIRECTIONS

Mix together barley, water, squash, celery, carrots, parsnip, turnip, and olive oil in your pressure cooker. Season with salt. Seal the lid, press SOUP/BROTH and cook for 25 minutes at High Pressure. Once ready, do a quick pressure release. Stir in cayenne pepper and ladle into bowls to serve.

Zucchini Coconut Burgers

Ready in about: 15 minutes | **Serves:** 4 | **Per serving:** Calories 235; Carbs 27g; Fat 7g; Protein 11g

INGREDIENTS

¼ cup Coconut Flakes, unsweetened
¼ cup Coconut Flour
½ cup Potatoes, mashed

1 large Zucchini, shredded
2 tbsp Olive Oil

DIRECTIONS

Heat the oil on SAUTÉ. Meanwhile, place all of the remaining ingredients in a bowl. Mix with your hands until fully incorporated and then shape the mixture into 4 equal patties.

When the oil becomes sizzling, add the patties and cook them for 3 minutes per side. For softer patties, add a few tbsp of water. Seal the lid, and cook for 1 minute at High pressure.

Once ready, let the pressure release naturally, for 5 minutes. Serve immediately.

Chickpea Bell Pepper Soup

Ready in about: 25 minutes | **Serves:** 4 | **Per serving:** Calories 289; Carbs 49g; Fat 10g; Protein 15g

INGREDIENTS

2 Red Bell Peppers, divined and chopped
6 ounces Chickpeas, soaked overnight
4 ½ cups Vegetable Stock
2 Shallots, thinly sliced
1 cup fresh Chives, thinly sliced

1 cup Sweet Potatoes, peeled and diced
3 tsp Olive Oil
½ tsp White Pepper
2 tbsp Tamari Sauce
2 tbsp Cider vinegar

DIRECTIONS

Heat oil on SAUTÉ and cook the shallots until translucent, for 2-3 minutes. Add the rest of the ingredients, except for the fresh chives.

Seal the lid, press SOUP/BROTH and cook for 20 minutes at High.

Once the cooking is complete, do a quick pressure release. Serve topped with freshly chopped chives.

Basil and Tomato "Pasta"

Ready in about: 12 minutes | **Serves:** 4 | **Per serving:** Calories 64; Carbs 12g; Fat 1g; Protein 4g

INGREDIENTS

½ cup Tomato Paste
4 cups Zoodles
¼ cup Water
2 Garlic Cloves, minced

¼ cup Veggie Broth
2 cups canned Tomatoes, diced
2 tbsp fresh Basil, chopped
1 tsp fresh Parsley, chopped

DIRECTIONS

Place all ingredients in your pressure cooker. Stir well to combine everything. Seal the lid, select PRESSURE COOK for 2 minutes, at High. Do a quick pressure release. Open the lid carefully, serve and enjoy!

Thyme-Flavored Fries

Ready in about: 13 minutes | **Serves:** 4 | **Per serving:** Calories 116; Carbs 24g; Fat 1g; Protein 2g

INGREDIENTS

1 pound Potatoes, cut into strips
1 tbsp dried Thyme
½ tsp Garlic Powder

1 tsp Olive Oil
1 cup Water

DIRECTIONS

Place the potatoes in a large bowl. Add thyme, olive oil, and garlic, and mix to coat them well.

Pour water into the pressure cooker. Arrange fries in a veggie steamer in a single layer. Seal the lid and cook for 3 minutes on PRESSURE COOK at High pressure. Do a quick release and serve.

Kale Chips with Garlic and Lime Juice

Ready in about: 15 minutes | **Serves:** 4 | **Per serving:** Calories 85; Carbs 8g; Fat 4g; Protein 2g

INGREDIENTS

1 pound Kale
½ cup Water
3 Garlic Cloves, minced

1 tbsp Olive Oil
2 tbsp Lime Juice

DIRECTIONS

Wash the kale and remove the stems. Heat the oil and cook garlic for a minute, or until fragrant, on SAUTÉ mode. Pack the kale well inside the cooker. Seal the lid.

Cook on STEAM mode for 6 minutes at High. Do a quick pressure release, and drizzle with lime juice.

Lime & Mint Zoodles

Ready in about: 10 minutes | **Serves:** 2 | **Per serving:** Calories 139; Carbs 73g; Fat 15g; Protein 4g

INGREDIENTS

2 Zucchini, spiralized
1 tsp Lime Zest
2 tbsp Lime Juice
2 tbsp Mint, chopped

2 tbsp Olive Oil
1 tsp Garlic, minced
¼ tsp Black Pepper

DIRECTIONS

Heat olive oil on SAUTÉ. When hot and sizzling, add garlic and lime zest, and cook for about 30 seconds. Add the rest of the ingredients, stir well to combine, and cook for only 2 minutes.

Divide the mixture among two serving bowls. Enjoy!

Cabbage, Beet & Apple Stew

Ready in about: 30 minutes | **Serves:** 4 | **Per serving:** Calories 156; Carbs 33g; Fat 2g; Protein 7g

INGREDIENTS

2 Carrots, chopped
½ Cabbage, chopped
1 Apple, diced

1 Onion, diced
1 tbsp grated Ginger
2 Beets, chopped

4 cups Veggie Broth
2 tbsp Parsley, chopped

½ tsp Garlic Salt
¼ tsp Pepper

DIRECTIONS

Place all ingredients in your pressure cooker. Stir well to combine everything and seal the lid. Hit the PRESSURE COOK, and set the cooking time to 20 minutes at High pressure.

When it goes off, do a quick pressure release. Pour into serving bowls and serve immediately.

Blueberry Oatmeal with Walnuts

Ready in about: 20 minutes | **Serves:** 2 | **Per serving:** Calories 340; Carbs 49g; Fat 12g; Protein 13g

INGREDIENTS

1 cup blueberries
1 ¼ cups Steel-cut oats
½ cup Walnut Milk
3 tbsp Walnuts, toasted and roughly chopped

1 cup Apricots, pitted and diced
1 tsp Vanilla Extract
½ tsp ground Cinnamon
1 ½ cups Water

DIRECTIONS

Place all ingredients, except for blueberries and walnuts, in your pressure cooker. Select PORRIDGE and seal the lid. Cook for 10 minutes at High Pressure. Release the pressure quickly.

Ladle the oatmeal between two serving bowls and top with blueberries and chopped walnuts.

Quick Coconut Moong Dhal

Ready in about: 20 minutes | **Serves:** 4 | **Per serving:** Calories 155; Carbs 27g; Fat 3g; Protein 12g

INGREDIENTS

1 cup Moong Dal
3 tsp Olive Oil
½ tsp Salt
1 tsp ground Turmeric
1 tbsp Cumin Seeds

½ tsp Cayenne Pepper
½ tsp ground Bay Leaves
¼ tsp Black Pepper, ground
3 cups Water
Fresh Cilantro leaves, yogurt, jalapeño slices, to garnish

DIRECTIONS

Put all ingredients in the cooker and seal the lid. Cook for 10 minutes on PRESSURE COOK at High. Do a quick pressure release. Serve garnished with fresh cilantro, jalapeño slices and coconut yogurt.

Mini Mac and Cheese

Ready in about: 17 minutes | **Serves:** 4 | **Per serving:** Calories 132; Carbs 15g; Fat 5g; Protein 7g

INGREDIENTS

8 ounces Whole-Wheat Macaroni
¾ cup Monterey Jack Cheese, shredded

2 cups Water

DIRECTIONS

Place the macaroni and water in your pressure cooker. Seal the lid and cook on RICE mode for 8 minutes at High. Do a quick pressure release, and drain the macaroni. Return to the pressure cooker. Stir in cheese, and cook on SAUTÉ for 30 seconds until melted. Divide between 4 small bowls, to serve

Beans & Grains Recipes

Kidney Beans with Bacon and Tomatoes

Ready in about: 35 minutes | **Serves:** 4 | **Per serving:** Calories 173; Carbs 6g; Fat 14g; Protein 6g

INGREDIENTS

2 cups Kidney Beans, soaked overnight
1 ½ cups Tomatoes, chopped
4 Bacon slices, diced
4 cups Water

½ cup Cumin
1 tsp Rosemary
Salt and Black Pepper, to taste

DIRECTIONS

Cook bacon on SAUTÉ until crispy, for about 3 minutes. Set aside. Add tomatoes, cumin, and rosemary, and cook for 2 minutes. Stir in the remaining ingredients and seal the lid.

Cook for 25 minutes on BEANS/CHILI mode at High. When ready, do a quick pressure release. Transfer to a bowl and stir in the bacon. Serve and enjoy!

Navy Beans with Ground Beef

Ready in about: 25 minutes | **Serves:** 8 | **Per serving:** Calories 196; Carbs 6g; Fat 11g; Protein 18g

INGREDIENTS

2 pounds canned Navy Beans
1 pound mixed Ground Beef
½ cup Cheddar Cheese, shredded
1 tsp Garlic, minced

2 tbsp Onion, chopped
1 tbsp Olive Oil
3 cups Water
Salt and Black Pepper, to taste

DIRECTIONS

Heat oil on SAUTÉ mode, add onion and garlic and cook for 2 minutes, until soft and fragrant. Add meat and cook until browned, for a few minutes. Stir the remaining ingredients.

Seal the lid, and cook for 10 minutes on PRESSURE COOK at High. Do a quick release.

Curried Chickpeas

Ready in about: 40 minutes | **Serves:** 8 | **Per serving:** Calories 341; Carbs 53g; Fat 8g; Protein 16g

INGREDIENTS

3 cups Chickpeas, soaked and rinsed
2 Tomatoes, chopped
2 Onions, chopped
2 tbsp Curry Powder
2 tbsp Oil

2 tsp Garlic, minced
½ tsp Cumin
2 tsp Chipotle Powder
Salt and Black Pepper, to taste
Water, as needed

DIRECTIONS

Place the chickpeas, salt, pepper, and 1 tbsp oil in the pressure cooker. Cover with water and seal the lid. Cook for 30 minutes on BEANS/CHILI mode at High pressure.

When ready, do a quick pressure release. Stir in the remaining ingredients. Cook for 5 more minutes, on SAUTÉ mode, with the lid off. Serve and enjoy!

Mixed Bean Italian Sausage Chili

Ready in about: 35 minutes | **Serves:** 8 | **Per serving:** Calories 335; Carbs 47g; Fat 10g; Protein 18g

INGREDIENTS

4 Italian Sausages, sliced
1 ½ cups Black Beans, soaked, drained and rinsed
1 ½ cups Pinto Beans, soaked, drained and rinsed
2 Red Bell Peppers, deveined and thinly sliced
4 cups Chicken Broth
2 Tomatoes, chopped
2 tbsp Ketchup
3 tsp Vegetable Oil
2 Carrots, chopped into sticks
1 tsp Chili Pepper, minced
½ tsp ground Black Pepper
½ tsp Sea Salt, to taste
1 cup Green Onions, chopped
3 Cloves Garlic, minced
1 Bay Leaf

DIRECTIONS

Heat oil on SAUTÉ. Add in sausage and brown for 3-5 minutes. Stir in the onions and garlic and keep stirring for another 2-3 minutes, until tender.

Add in the remaining ingredients, and cook for 20 minutes at High pressure. Do a quick pressure release.

Navy Bean Dip

Ready in about: 35 minutes | **Serves:** 12 | **Per serving:** Calories 103; Carbs 11g; Fat 2g; Protein 3g

INGREDIENTS

¼ cup Jalapenos, seeded and chopped
3 cups navy Beans, soaked and rinsed
2 Red Onions, peeled and chopped
2 ripe Tomatoes, chopped
2 tbsp Cilantro, chopped
2 tbsp Olive Oil
2 tbsp lime juice
Salt and Black Pepper, to taste
6 cups Water
Pita crackers, to serve

DIRECTIONS

Add beans with 6 cups of water in your pressure cooker. Seal the lid and select BEANS/CHILI mode for 30 minutes at High Pressure. Once the cooking is complete, do a quick pressure release.

Transfer to a bowl and add the rest of the ingredients. Puree cooled mixture with an immersion blender until smooth, working in batches and serve with pita crackers.

Cannellini Beans Chili

Ready in about: 25 minutes | **Serves:** 4 | **Per serving:** Calories 261; Carbs 41g; Fat 9g; Protein 6g

INGREDIENTS

2 cups Cannellini Beans, soaked overnight
1 cup Red Onions, chopped
4 ½ cups Water
1 cup canned Corn, drained
½ cup Cilantro, chopped
1 tsp Cumin
1 tsp Chili Powder
1 tsp Garlic, minced
Salt and Pepper, to taste
2 tbsp Olive Oil
2 Tomatoes, chopped

DIRECTIONS

On SAUTÉ, heat oil and cook onion, garlic, cumin, and chili powder for 3 minutes, stirring frequently. Pour in water, and add tomatoes and beans. Seal the lid, and set to BEANS/CHILI for 30 minutes at High. Do a quick release. Adjust the seasoning. Ladle into bowls and serve garnished with corn.

Ham and Parmesan Grits

Ready in about: 30 minutes | **Serves:** 6 | **Per serving:** Calories 296; Carbs 9g; Fat 21g; Protein 17g

INGREDIENTS

1 cup Quick-Cooking Grits
1 cup grated Parmesan Cheese
10 ounces cooked Ham, diced
2 Eggs, whisked
½ Butter Stick
1 Shallot, chopped
1 tsp Paprika
Salt and Pepper, to taste
3 cups Water

DIRECTIONS

Melt the butter, and brown the ham on SAUTÉ mode. Stir in the shallots and spices and cook for 2 minutes. Add the grits and pour the water.

Seal the lid, and cook for 8 minutes on RICE mode, at High. Do a quick pressure release, and stir in the parmesan and eggs. Seal again, and cook for 3 minutes at High. Do a quick release and serve.

Black Bean and Mushroom Spread

Ready in about: 25 minutes | **Serves:** 6 | **Per serving:** Calories 256; Carbs 43g; Fat 3g; Protein 16g

INGREDIENTS

2 cups Black Beans, soaked and rinsed
1 cup Porcini Mushrooms, sliced
1 cup Red Onions, chopped
2 ½ cups Water
2 cups Beef Broth
1 ½ tsp Paprika
1 tbsp Butter
1 tsp Rosemary
½ tsp Cumin
Salt and Black Pepper

DIRECTIONS

Melt butter and sauté the onions for a few minutes, until soft, on SAUTÉ mode. Add mushrooms and cook for 3 more minutes, until tender. Stir in the remaining ingredients and seal the lid.

Cook on BEANS/CHILI for 25 minutes at High. When ready, do a quick pressure release. Drain and transfer to a food processor. Pulse until smooth.

Farmer's Meal

Ready in about: 20 minutes | **Serves:** 4 | **Per serving:** Calories 215; Carbs 3g; Fat 7g; Protein 16g

INGREDIENTS

½ cup Barley
½ pound cooked Ham, chopped
1 cup Mushrooms, sliced
1 cup Bell Peppers, chopped
2 tbsp Butter
2 Green Onions, chopped
2 cups Veggie Stock
1 tsp Ginger, minced
¼ cup Celery, chopped
Salt and Pepper, to taste

DIRECTIONS

Melt the butter on SAUTÉ mode, add the onions and cook for 3 minutes, until soft. Stir in mushrooms, celery, and bell peppers, and cook for 3 more minutes, until tender.

Add ham and ginger and cook for 1 minute. Stir in the remaining ingredients. Seal the lid and cook on RICE for 10 minutes at High. When cooking is over, release the pressure quickly.

Butter Bean and Kale Stew

Ready in about: 30 minutes | **Serves:** 6 | **Per serving:** Calories 394; Carbs 57g; Fat 8g; Protein 18g

INGREDIENTS

2 cups Butter Beans, soaked overnight
1 cup Spinach
2 cups Vegetable Stock
2 Cloves Garlic, peeled and smashed
2 tbsp Olive Oil
2 Shallots, chopped

1 can Tomatoes, crushed
¼ tsp ground Black Pepper
2 sprigs fresh Rosemary, finely chopped
1 tsp Salt
4 cups Water

DIRECTIONS

Place butter beans in the pressure cooker and pour the water. Seal the lid, select PRESSURE COOK, at High Pressure for 15 minutes. Do a quick pressure release. Drain and rinse beans under cold water.

Discard cooking liquid, and set aside. Warm the oil on SAUTÉ mode and cook shallots and garlic for 3 minutes. Add in the tomatoes, stock, and rinsed beans; season to taste. Seal the lid and set to High.

Cook for 10 minutes. Quick release the pressure. Stir in kale and rosemary, and cook until kale wilts.

Mushroom and Parmesan Barley

Ready in about: 45 minutes | **Serves:** 4 | **Per serving:** Calories 385; Carbs 48g; Fat 16g; Protein 16g

INGREDIENTS

3 cups Chicken Broth
1 cup Barley
½ cup Parmesan Cheese, grated
1 pound Mushrooms, sliced

1 Onion, chopped
3 tbsp Olive Oil
2 tbsp Thyme
1 tsp Garlic, minced

DIRECTIONS

Heat oil in on SAUTÉ. Stir in the onions and cook for 2 minutes, until soft. Add garlic and cook for 1 more, until fragrant. Stir in the mushrooms and cook for 4 more minutes, until soft.

Stir in the remaining ingredients, except the cheese. Seal the lid, and cook for 8 minutes on RICE at High pressure. Do a natural release, for 10 minutes. Stir in the parmesan, and serve immediately.

Tasty Three-Bean Stew

Ready in about: 30 minutes | **Serves:** 6 | **Per serving:** Calories 455; Carbs 73g; Fat 13g; Protein 19g

INGREDIENTS

½ cup Pinto Beans, soaked overnight
½ cup Black Beans, soaked overnight
½ cup Cannellini Beans, soaked overnight
2 Bell Peppers, deveined and chopped
2 tbsp Olive Oil
2 Onions, chopped

1 (14 oz) can Tomatoes, crushed
1 tbsp Garlic paste
Sea Salt and freshly ground Black Pepper, to taste
4 cups Water
1 Avocado, sliced, to serve

DIRECTIONS

Add the water, beans, oil, bell peppers, tomatoes, garlic paste, and onions to the pressure cooker. Season to taste. Seal the lid. Select BEANS/CHILI mode and cook for 25 minutes at High pressure.

Once the cooking is over, do a quick pressure release. Serve topped with avocado slices.

Simple Cornbread

Ready in about: 40 minutes | **Serves:** 4 | **Per serving:** Calories 423; Carbs 41g; Fat 21g; Protein 12g

INGREDIENTS

1 ¼ cup Cornmeal
1 cup Buttermilk
½ Butter Stick, melted
2 Eggs, beaten
½ cup Water
½ tsp Salt
1 tsp Baking Powder

DIRECTIONS

Combine the dry ingredients in one bowl. Whisk the wet ones in another bowl. Gently stir in the wet ingredients into the dry ingredients. Transfer the mixture into a greased baking dish.

Pour water in your pressure cooker and lower the trivet. Place the dish on top of the trivet, and seal the lid. Cook on SOUP/BROTH for 30 minutes at High pressure. Do a quick release.

Prawns in Moong Dal

Ready in about: 25 minutes | **Serves:** 6 | **Per Serving:** Calories 255; Carbs 41g; Fat 3g; Protein 32g

INGREDIENTS

2 ½ cups Moong Dal
1 pound Tiger Prawns, frozen
1 cup Leeks, chopped
½ tbsp Miso paste
2 Bell Peppers, stemmed, cored, and chopped
3 ½ cups Vegetable Stock
2 tbsp Grapeseed Oil
2 ripe Plum Tomatoes, chopped
1 tsp Molasses
1 tsp Sea Salt
¼ tsp ground Black Pepper
½ tsp Cumin powder

DIRECTIONS

Heat oil on SAUTÉ, and stir-fry the prawns, leeks and peppers for 4 minutes. Set the prawns aside. Add the rest of the ingredients, seal the lid, and cook on BEANS/CHILI for 15 minutes at High.

Once the cooking is over, do a quick pressure release. Add in the prawns and serve immediately.

Herby White Bean and Corn Dip

Ready in about: 30 minutes | **Serves:** 12 | **Per serving:** Calories 150; Carbs 19g; Fat 5g; Protein 8g

INGREDIENTS

1 cup fresh Corn Kernels
5 cups Water
1 pound White Beans, rinsed and drained
1 cup Onion, finely chopped
½ tsp Celery seeds
4 Garlic Cloves, minced
2 tbsp Vegetable Oil
½ tsp Sea Salt
¼ tsp ground Black Pepper
½ tsp Cumin Seeds
1 cup mild Picante sauce
1 Garlic Clove, crushed

DIRECTIONS

Place the beans and pour water into the pressure cooker. Seal the lid, select BEANS/CHILI and cook for 25 minutes at High. Meanwhile, in a saucepan, cook the remaining ingredients for about 5 minutes.

Once the cooking is complete, do a quick pressure release. Add in the sautéed mixture. Give it a good stir and blend the mixture in a blender or a food processor, in batches.

Delicious Yellow Split Lentil Beef Stew

Ready in about: 30 minutes | **Serves:** 4 | **Per serving:** Calories 343; Carbs 45g; Fat 5g; Protein 21g

INGREDIENTS

1 ½ cups Yellow Split Lentils, rinsed
½ pound Beef Stew Meat, cubed
1 cup Scallions, chopped
2 Garlic Cloves, minced
4 Potatoes, peeled and diced
1 cup Carrots, chopped

3 tsp Vegetable Oil
1 cup Celery, chopped
5 cups Chicken Stock
Sea Salt and Black Pepper, to taste
1 tsp Saffron

DIRECTIONS

Heat oil on SAUTÉ, and cook scallions and garlic for 2 minutes. Add meat and cook for another 5 minutes, until slightly browned. Add the remaining ingredients, seal the lid and set on PRESSURE COOK.

Cook for 20 minutes at High pressure. When ready, do a quick pressure release. Serve immediately.

Celery and Cheese Chickpea Stew

Ready in about: 30 minutes | **Serves:** 4 | **Per serving:** Calories 355; Carbs 48g; Fat 9g; Protein 18g

INGREDIENTS

2 cups Chickpeas, soaked 1 fennel bulb, chopped
½ cup Parmesan cheese, finely grated
½ cup Scallions, chopped
3 tsp Olive Oil

3 Cloves Garlic, minced
Salt and ground Black Pepper
4 cups Water

DIRECTIONS

Select SAUTÉ and heat the oil. Add in the garlic, fennel, scallions and sauté until tender. Then, add in the remaining ingredients, except for the cheese.

Seal the lid, press PRESSURE COOK and cook for 20 minutes at High pressure. Once the cooking is done, do a quick pressure release. Serve topped with grated Parmesan cheese.

Meatless Lasagna

Ready in about: 1 hour | **Serves:** 6 | **Per serving:** Calories 325; Carbs 29g; Fat 19g; Protein 11g

INGREDIENTS

1 ¼ cups Mushrooms, thinly sliced
1 ½ jars Pasta Sauce
1 tsp Cayenne Pepper
2 tsp dried Basil
1 tsp dried Rosemary
1 tsp Red Pepper flakes

½ tsp dried Oregano
½ tsp Sea Salt
1 ⅓ cups Cream Cheese
½ tsp ground Black Pepper
1 ½ packages pre-baked Lasagne Noodles

DIRECTIONS

Place two lasagne shells at the bottom of a baking dish. Spread the pasta sauce. Add a layer of cream cheese on top. Arrange sliced fresh mushrooms over the cheese layer.

Sprinkle with spices and herbs. Repeat the layering until you have used all ingredients.

Place a trivet and pour 1 cup of water. Lower the dish onto the trivet. Seal the lid and cook for 45 minutes at High pressure on PRESSURE COOK. Do a quick pressure release, and serve immediately.

Banana and Fig Millet

Ready in about: 20 minutes | **Serves:** 6 | **Per serving:** Calories 363; Carbs 53g; Fat 8g; Protein 9g

INGREDIENTS

2 cups Millet
1 cup Milk
2 Bananas, sliced
¼ cup dried Figs, chopped
½ tsp Vanilla
½ tsp Cinnamon
2 tbsp Coconut Oil
2 cups Water
A pinch of Salt

DIRECTIONS

Combine all ingredients, except the bananas, in your pressure cooker.

Seal the lid, and cook for 10 minutes on PRESSURE COOK mode at High pressure. When ready, let the pressure drop naturally, for about 10 minutes. Serve topped with banana slices.

Parsley Pureed Navy Beans

Ready in about: 25 minutes | **Serves:** 6 | **Per serving:** Calories 302; Carbs 45g; Fat 2g; Protein 18g

INGREDIENTS

1 ½ cups Water
1 ½ tsp Garlic powder
1 cup Red Onions, peeled and chopped
2 ¼ cups dry Pinto Beans, soaked
3 tsp Vegetable Oil
¼ tsp Black Pepper
1 tsp Chipotle powder
¼ tsp Red Pepper
½ tsp Sea Salt
½ cup fresh Cilantro, roughly chopped

DIRECTIONS

Heat the oil on SAUTÉ mode. Cook the onions, cilantro, garlic, and chipotle powders, for about 2-3 minutes. Add in the beans and the water. Season with salt, black and red pepper.

Seal the lid, select BEANS/CHILI mode and cook for 20 minutes at High pressure.

Do a quick release. Puree the beans using a potato masher. Season with black pepper and salt.

Mexican-Style Black Bean and Avocado Salad

Ready in about: 35 minutes | **Serves:** 4 | **Per serving:** Calories 485; Carbs 62g; Fat 29g; Protein 19g

INGREDIENTS

1 tsp Garlic, smashed
2 Avocados, diced
½ tsp freshly cracked Black Pepper
1 tsp Salt
2 tbsp Wine Vinegar
½ cup fresh Cilantro, chopped
1 tsp dried Dill Weed
¼ tsp hot Pepper Sauce
¼ tsp Chili powder
1 tbsp ground Cumin
½ cup Olive Oil
2 cups Black Beans, soaked overnight
1 ½ cups Water
1 Lime, juiced
1 cup Red Onions, peeled and coarsely chopped

DIRECTIONS

Pour water and add black beans in the pressure cooker. Select BEANS/CHILI mode and cook for 25 minutes at High Pressure. Do a quick pressure release, and drain the beans.

Add in the remaining ingredients. Serve chilled with diced avocado.

Bean and Bacon Dip

Ready in about: 30 minutes | **Serves:** 12 | **Per serving:** Calories 105; Carbs 12g; Fat 4g; Protein 5g

INGREDIENTS

20 ounces frozen Lima Beans
4 Bacon slices, cooked and crumbled
3 tsp Butter, melted

½ tsp Cayenne Pepper
Salt and Black Pepper, to taste
Water, as needed

DIRECTIONS

Place the beans in the cooker and cover with water. Seal the lid and cook on BEANS/CHILI mode for 25 minutes at High pressure When ready, do a quick pressure release.

Transfer to a food processor along with the remaining ingredients. Process until smooth.

Apricot and Raisin Oatmeal

Ready in about: 15 minutes | **Serves:** 4 | **Per serving:** Calories 325; Carbs 78g; Fat 4g; Protein 8g

INGREDIENTS

2 ¼ cups Water
1 ½ cups Steel Cut Oats
1 ½ cups Almond Milk
A handful of Raisins

8 Apricots, chopped
1 tsp Vanilla Paste
¾ cup Brown Sugar

DIRECTIONS

Combine all ingredients in your pressure cooker. Set it to RICE mode, seal the lid, and cook for 8 minutes, at High pressure. Once cooking is over, do a quick pressure release.

Cinnamon Bulgur with Pecans

Ready in about: 20 minutes | **Serves:** 8 | **Per serving:** Calories 105; Carbs 21g; Fat 2g; Protein 2g

INGREDIENTS

2 cups Bulgur Wheat
¼ cup Pecans, chopped
½ tsp Cloves
1 tsp Cinnamon

¼ tsp Nutmeg
½ cup Honey
6 cups Water

DIRECTIONS

Place all ingredients in your pressure cooker. Stir to combine well. Seal the lid and cook on PRESSURE COOK mode for 15 minutes at High. When ready, do a quick pressure release.

Peach Quinoa Pudding

Ready in about: 15 minutes | **Serves:** 4 | **Per serving:** Calories 456; Carbs 76g; Fat 10g; Protein 16g

INGREDIENTS

2 cups Quinoa
2 Peaches, diced
2 tbsp Raisins
2 cups Milk
2 tsp Peanut Oil

½ tsp Cardamom
2 cups Water
A pinch of Nutmeg
A pinch of Ground Star Anise
2 tbsp Honey

DIRECTIONS

Combine all ingredients, except peaches and honey, in the pressure cooker. Seal the lid and cook on RICE for 10 minutes, at High. Quick-release the pressure, and stir in the peaches. Drizzled with honey.

Mushroom and Farro Beans

Ready in about: 25 minutes | **Serves:** 4 | **Per serving:** Calories 408; Carbs 75g; Fat 3g; Protein 23g

INGREDIENTS

1 ¼ cups Navy Beans
¾ cup Farro
2 ½ cups Mushrooms, sliced
4 Green Onions, chopped

1 tsp Garlic, minced
½ Jalapeno, minced
1 cup Tomatoes, diced
3 cups Chicken Broth

DIRECTIONS

Combine all ingredients in your pressure cooker. Seal the lid and cook on BEANS/CHILI mode for 25 minutes at High pressure. When ready, do a quick pressure release.

Pear and Almond Oatmeal

Ready in about: 15 minutes | **Serves:** 4 | **Per serving:** Calories 180; Carbs 42g; Fat 5g; Protein 8g

INGREDIENTS

½ cup Almonds, chopped
1 ½ cups Oats
½ cup Milk
2 ½ cups Water

2 Pears, sliced
1 tbsp Maple Syrup
2 tsp Butter
½ tsp Vanilla

DIRECTIONS

Place all ingredients, except the pears, in the pressure cooker. Seal the lid and cook for 8 minutes on RICE mode at High. Do a quick pressure release. Top with pears, to serve.

Lemony Oats with Chia Seeds

Ready in about: 15 minutes | **Serves:** 4 | **Per serving:** Calories 360; Carbs 59g; Fat 16g; Protein 13g

INGREDIENTS

1 ½ cups Lemon Juice
1 ½ cups Oats
½ cup Chia Seeds
3 tbsp Brown Sugar

1 tbsp Honey
A pinch of Salt
1 tbsp Butter
¼ tsp Lemon Zest

DIRECTIONS

Melt the butter on SAUTÉ mode for 3 minutes.

Stir in the remaining ingredients and seal the lid. Cook for 8 minutes on RICE mode, at High.

When ready, do a quick pressure release.

Pearl Barley with Mushrooms

Ready in about: 25 minutes | **Serves:** 4 | **Per serving:** Calories 265; Carbs 41g; Fat 1g; Protein 19g

INGREDIENTS

½ tbsp Shallot powder
1 tsp Jalapeno Pepper, finely minced
1 tbsp Garlic, smashed
¾ cup Pearl Barley
1 ¼ cups dried navy Beans

4 Green Onions, chopped
1 cup Tomatoes, diced
2 cups Mushrooms, thinly sliced
2 cups Vegetable Broth

DIRECTIONS

In the pressure cooker, add all ingredients, except for the tomatoes. Select BEANS/CHILI mode and cook for 25 minutes at High pressure. Do a quick pressure release. Stir in the diced tomatoes, and serve.

Rosemary Goat Cheese Barley

Ready in about: 30 minutes | **Serves:** 6 | **Per serving:** Calories 570; Carbs 53g; Fat 31g; Protein 21g

INGREDIENTS

2 cups Barley
6 cups Stock
1 Butter Stick, melted
1 cup Spring Onions, chopped

½ cup Goat Cheese
¼ tsp Black Pepper
½ tsp Salt
2 tsp Rosemary

DIRECTIONS

Melt butter on SAUTÉ. Add onions and cook until soft, for about 3 minutes.

Stir in the remaining ingredients, except the cheese.

Seal the lid and cook for 15 minutes on PRESSURE COOK at High pressure.

When ready, do a quick pressure release. Stir in the goat cheese and serve.

Mouth-Watering Lima Beans

Ready in about: 20 minutes | **Serves:** 6 | **Per serving:** Calories 95; Carbs 9g; Fat; 2g Protein 3g

INGREDIENTS

2 tsp Olive Oil
2 cups Lima Beans, soaked and rinsed
2 Cloves Garlic, finely minced
½ tsp ground Black Pepper

½ tsp ground Bay Leaf
½ tsp Salt
4 cups Water

DIRECTIONS

Put all ingredients in the pressure cooker. Select PRESSURE COOK mode, and cook for 15 minutes at High pressure. Once done, do a quick pressure release. Discard bay leaf and serve hot.

African Lentil Dip

Ready in about: 15 minutes | **Serves:** 12 | **Per serving:** Calories 185; Carbs 19g; Fat 7g; Protein 12g

INGREDIENTS

2 cups dry Green Lentils, rinsed
½ tsp Dukkah
3 Garlic Cloves, minced
¼ cup Tomato Paste
2 tbsp tahini
2 tbsp Vegetable Oil
1 tsp Maple Syrup
½ tsp ground Black Pepper
1 tsp Salt
1 tsp dry Thyme, minced
¼ tsp Cardamom
4 cups Water

DIRECTIONS

Pour 4 cups water, and add lentils to the pressure cooker. Cook on PRESSURE COOK for 5 minutes at High.

Allow for a natural pressure release, for 10 minutes.

Stir in the remaining ingredients, and serve.

Quinoa Pilaf with Cherries

Ready in about: 20 minutes | **Serves:** 4 | **Per serving:** Calories 281; Carbs 44g; Fat 7g; Protein 11g

INGREDIENTS

1 ½ cups Quinoa
½ cup Almonds, sliced
¼ cup Cherries, chopped
1 Celery Stalk, chopped
½ Onion, chopped
14 ounces Chicken Broth
¼ cup Water
1 tbsp Butter

DIRECTIONS

Melt the butter on SAUTÉ mode, and cook the onions for 2 minutes, until translucent.

Add celery and cook for 2 more, until soft. Stir in the remaining ingredients.

Seal the lid and cook for 8 minutes on RICE at High.

Release the pressure quickly and serve.

Cheesy Chicken Quinoa

Ready in about: 20 minutes | **Serves:** 4 | **Per serving:** Calories 484; Carbs 47g; Fat 20g; Protein 29g

INGREDIENTS

1 ½ cups Quinoa
2 ½ cups Chicken Broth
½ cup Cheddar Cheese, shredded
1 cup Chicken Breasts, cooked and shredded
1 cup Sour Cream
¼ cup Parmesan Cheese, grated
Salt and Black Pepper, to taste

DIRECTIONS

Combine quinoa and broth in pressure cooker. Seal the lid and cook on RICE for 8 minutes, at High. Do a quick pressure release. Stir in the remaining ingredients. Cook for 3 minutes, on SAUTÉ, lid off.

Rice & Pasta Recipes

Colorful Risotto

Ready in about: 40 minutes | **Serves:** 6 | **Per serving:** Calories 324; Carbs 58g; Fat 5g; Protein 11g

INGREDIENTS

2 cups Brown Rice
4 cups Veggie Broth
½ cup Carrots, chopped
1 Yellow Bell Pepper, chopped
1 Green Bell Pepper, chopped

2 Tomatoes, chopped
1 Red Onion, chopped
3 tsp Oil
1 cups Green Peas
Salt and Pepper, to taste

DIRECTIONS

Heat oil on SAUTÉ mode, add the onions and cook for a few minutes, until soft. Add carrots and peppers and cook for 2 more minutes. Stir in the remaining ingredients.

Seal the lid and cook for 20 minutes at High pressure. Do a quick pressure release.

Rice Pilaf with Chicken

Ready in about: 40 minutes | **Serves:** 8 | **Per serving:** Calories 341; Carbs 41g; Fat 9g; Protein 21g

INGREDIENTS

2 cups Rice
2 Chicken Breasts, diced
1 tsp Garlic, minced
1 Onion, chopped
2 Bell Peppers, chopped

1 tbsp Oil
4 cups Chicken Broth
1 tsp Rosemary
Salt and Pepper, to taste

DIRECTIONS

Heat oil on SAUTÉ mode, and cook the onions for 2 minutes, until translucent. Stir in garlic and cook for 1 more minute, until fragrant. Add peppers and cook for 2 minutes, until soft

Stir in the remaining ingredients. Seal the lid and cook for 25 minutes on POULTRY mode at High. When cooking is over, do a quick pressure release. Serve and enjoy!

Apple and Apricot Wild Rice

Ready in about: 30 minutes | **Serves:** 8 | **Per serving:** Calories 246; Carbs 50g; Fat 3g; Protein 8g

INGREDIENTS

2 cups Wild Rice
¼ cup Maple Syrup
½ cup dried Apricots, chopped
1 ½ cups Apple Juice
½ cup Milk

3 Egg Yolks
¼ tsp ground Ginger
½ tsp Cinnamon
A pinch of Salt
4 cups Water

DIRECTIONS

Combine all ingredients, except the apricots, in your pressure cooker. Seal the lid and cook on POULTRY mode for 25 minutes at High. Do a quick pressure release. Stir in the apricots, serve and enjoy!

Spinach Vermouth Risotto

Ready in about: 20 minutes | **Serves:** 4 | **Per serving:** Calories 327; Carbs 44g; Fat 8g; Protein 10g

INGREDIENTS

1 cup Mushrooms, sliced
2 cups Spinach, chopped
½ cup Vermouth
1 cup Rice
1 Zucchini, sliced

½ cup Parmesan Cheese, shredded
1 Shallot, chopped
1 tsp Garlic, minced
1 tbsp Oil
2 cups Chicken Stock

DIRECTIONS

Heat oil on SAUTÉ mode. Cook the shallot and garlic for 2 minutes, until translucent and fragrant. Add mushrooms and cook for 3 more minutes, until soft.

Stir in the remaining ingredients, except the cheese. Seal the lid, and cook for 8 minutes on RICE mode, at High. When done, do a quick release. Stir in the cheese, and serve warm.

Shrimp Risotto

Ready in about: 20 minutes | **Serves:** 4 | **Per serving:** Calories 476; Carbs 59g; Fat 12g; Protein 32g

INGREDIENTS

1 pound Shrimp, peeled and deveined
1 ½ cups White Rice
1 tbsp Oil
3 tbsp Butter
3 cups Fish Stock

2 tsp Garlic, minced
2 Shallots, chopped
¼ cup White Wine
Salt and Pepper, to taste

DIRECTIONS

Heat oil on SAUTÉ mode, and cook onion and garlic for 3 minutes, until soft. Add shrimp and cook for 3 minutes, until lightly browned. Stir in the remaining ingredients and seal the lid.

Cook for 8 minutes on RICE mode at High. When ready, do a quick pressure release.

Spring Pearl Barley Salad

Ready in about: 25 minutes | **Serves:** 4 | **Per serving:** Calories 350; Fat 9g; Carbs 62g; Protein 9g

INGREDIENTS

¼ cups Pearl Barley, rinsed and drained
½ cup Onion, thinly sliced
½ cup Kalamata Olives, pitted and sliced
1 tbsp Olive Oil
2 Bell Peppers, thinly sliced
1 cup grape Tomatoes, diced
2 tbsp Vinegar

½ cup Goat Cheese, crumbled to serve
½ tsp Sea Salt
1 tsp dried Basil
½ tsp dried Oregano
½ tsp ground Black Pepper
4 cups Water

DIRECTIONS

Select RICE mode, and add the barley, water and salt. Seal the lid and cook for 15 minutes at High. When ready, do a quick pressure release and open the lid. Transfer the barley to a bowl to let cool.

Stir in slowly the remaining ingredients. Season to taste and enjoy.

Fresh Tagliatelle Pasta Bolognese

Ready in about: 20 minutes | **Serves:** 6 | **Per serving:** Calories 523; Carbs 56g; Fat 23g; Protein 31g

INGREDIENTS

2 tsp Butter
20 ounces Tagliatelle
1 ½ pounds mixed Ground Meat
1 ½ pounds Tomato Pasta Sauce
1 tsp Oregano
1 cup Onions, chopped
2 tsp Garlic, minced
6 ounces Bacon, diced
½ cup White Wine
1 cup Heavy Cream
1 cup Parmesan cheese grated
Water, as needed
Salt and Pepper, to taste

DIRECTIONS

Melt the butter on SAUTÉ mode, and cook the onions and garlic for 3 minutes, until soft and fragrant. Add meat and cook until browned, for a few minutes.

Stir in the remaining ingredients, except for the heavy cream and Parmesan cheese. Pour in water to cover entirely. Seal the lid and cook for 10 minutes on PRESSURE COOK at High pressure.

When ready, do a quick release. Stir in heavy cream and serve with grated parmesan cheese.

Fennel Jasmine Rice

Ready in about: 15 minutes | **Serves:** 4 | **Per serving:** Calories 241; Carbs 34g; Fat 14g; Protein 10g

INGREDIENTS

1 ½ cups Jasmine Rice
1 cup Fennel Bulb, chopped
2 Spring Onions, chopped
1 cup Parsnips, chopped
1 Carrot, chopped
2 cups Chicken Stock
1 cup Water
1 tsp Sage
1 tbsp Oil
Salt and Pepper, to taste

DIRECTIONS

Heat oil on SAUTÉ mode, and cook the onions until soft, for 2-3 minutes. Add parsnip, carrots, and fennel and cook for 2 more minutes, until soft. Stir in the remaining ingredients.

Seal the lid and cook for 10 minutes on RICE, at High. When ready, do a quick release.

Simple Mushroom Risotto

Ready in about: 15 minutes | **Serves:** 4 | **Per serving:** Calories 254; Carbs 26g; Fat 16g; Protein 15g

INGREDIENTS

1 ½ cups Arborio Rice
½ cup dried Chanterelle Mushrooms, soaked, drained, and chopped
½ cup Parmesan Cheese, grated
¼ cup Onion, chopped
1 tsp Garlic, minced
4 cups Chicken Stock
1 ½ cups Water
1 tbsp Butter
¼ tsp Salt
¼ tsp White Pepper

DIRECTIONS

Melt butter and cook onion and garlic for 2 minutes, until soft and fragrant, on SAUTÉ. Add in the remaining ingredients. Seal the lid and cook for 10 minutes on RICE at High. Do a quick pressure release.

Creamy Coconut Rice Pudding

Ready in about: 20 minutes | **Serves:** 6 | **Per serving:** Calories 362; Carbs 57g; Fat 8g; Protein 11g

INGREDIENTS

2 cups White Rice
½ cup Raisins
2 Eggs plus 1 Egg yolk, at room temperature
8 ounces Milk
¼ cup Sugar
3 tsp Coconut Oil

¼ tsp ground Cinnamon
½ tbsp Vanilla Extract
¼ tsp Kosher Salt
¼ tsp ground Cardamom
8 ounces Water

DIRECTIONS

In the pressure cooker, add the oil, water, milk, rice, sugar, cinnamon, vanilla, salt, and cardamom. Press RICE and cook for 8 minutes at High pressure.

Once the cooking is complete, perform a quick pressure release. Add the whisked eggs and raisins. Select SAUTÉ and cook with the lid off until the mixture boils. Serve warm.

Simple Saucy Jasmine Rice

Ready in about: 15 minutes | **Serves:** 4 | **Per serving:** Calories 299; Carbs 62g; Fat 3g; Protein 7g

INGREDIENTS

1 ½ cups Jasmine Rice
1 cup Celery, chopped
2 spring Onions, sliced
1 Carrot, trimmed and chopped
3 tsp Olive Oil

1 tsp dried Sage
¼ tsp ground Black Pepper
1 tsp Salt
2 cups stock
1 cup Water

DIRECTIONS

Select SAUTÉ and heat the oil. Add in the onions and cook until translucent. Stir in the carrots and celery and keep stirring for another 2-3 minutes. Add in the remaining ingredients.

Select RICE and cook for 10 minutes at High. When ready, do a quick pressure release.

Ziti Pork Meatballs

Ready in about: 25 minutes | **Serves:** 4 | **Per serving:** Calories 421; Carbs 25g; Fat 23g; Protein 28g

INGREDIENTS

¾ pound Ground Pork
1 box Ziti Pasta
2 Tomatoes, chopped
1 cup Veggie Stock
3 tsp Oil
2 cups Cauliflower Florets

2 Bell Peppers, chopped
½ cup Cider
1 cup Water
1 Red Onion, chopped
½ tbsp Basil

DIRECTIONS

Combine pork and basil and shape the mixture into 4-5 meatballs. Heat the oil on SAUTÉ. Cook meatballs until browned. Set aside. Cook onions, cauliflowers, and peppers for a few minutes, until soft.

Stir in the remaining ingredients, including the meatballs. Seal the lid and cook for 20 minutes on MEAT/STEW at High. When done, quick release the pressure.

Pizza Pasta

Ready in about: 30 minutes | **Serves:** 6 | **Per serving:** Calories 491; Carbs 38g; Fat 23g; Protein 35g

INGREDIENTS

1 pound Pasta
16 ounces Pasta Sauce
8 ounces Pizza Sauce
1 pound Italian Sausage
4 ounces Pepperoni

8 ounces Mozzarella Cheese, shredded
3 ½ cups Water
1 tbsp Olive Oil
1 tsp Garlic, minced

DIRECTIONS

Heat oil on SAUTÉ mode. Cook the sausage and garlic for a few minutes, until lightly browned. Stir in the remaining ingredients, except the cheese and half of the pepperoni.

Seal the lid and cook for 8 minutes on RICE mode at High pressure. When it goes off, do a quick pressure release. Stir in the cheese and pepperoni. Serve immediately.

Delicious Quinoa Pilaf with Almonds

Ready in about: 20 minutes | **Serves:** 6 | **Per serving:** Calories 305; Carbs 47g; Fat 8g; Protein 9g

INGREDIENTS

1 ½ cups Quinoa
2 tsp Butter
5 cups Chicken Stock
2 White Onions, finely chopped

2 Carrots, trimmed and chopped
Sea Salt and Black Pepper, to taste
4 tbsp flaked Almonds, toasted

DIRECTIONS

Select SAUTÉ mode and melt the butter. Cook the onions for about 3 minutes, until tender. Add in the carrots and keep cooking for 4 minutes more. Stir in the remaining ingredients, except for the almonds.

Select RICE mode and cook for 8 minutes at High Pressure. Do a quick pressure release. Arrange the pilaf on a serving platter and fluff the quinoa with a fork. Serve scattered with toasted almonds.

Cheese Tortellini with Broccoli and Turkey

Ready in about: 30 minutes | **Serves:** 6 | **Per serving:** Calories 395; Carbs 9g; Fat 23g; Protein 35g

INGREDIENTS

3 Bacon Slices, chopped
1 ½ pounds Turkey Breasts, diced
3 cups Broccoli Florets
8 ounces Cheese Tortellini
¼ cup Heavy Cream
¼ cup Half and Half

2 cups Chicken Stock
1 Onion, chopped
1 Carrot, chopped
1 tbsp chopped Parsley
Salt and Pepper, to taste

DIRECTIONS

Cook the bacon on SAUTÉ mode until crispy. Add onions and garlic and cook for 2 minutes, until sweaty Add turkey and cook until no longer pink, for a few minutes.

Stir in the remaining ingredients, except heavy cream. Seal the lid, and cook for 8 minutes on RICE mode at High pressure. When ready, release the pressure quickly. Stir in the heavy cream and serve.

Chili and Cheesy Beef Pasta

Ready in about: 15 minutes | **Serves:** 6 | **Per serving:** Calories 346; Carbs 29g; Fat 14g; Protein 26g

INGREDIENTS

1 pound Ground Beef
2 Scallions, chopped
3 cups Fusilli Pasta, cooked
1 tbsp Butter
½ cup Cheddar Cheese, grated

1 tsp Garlic, minced
2 cups Mild Salsa
½ cup Tomato Puree
1 tbsp Chili Powder
Water, as needed

DIRECTIONS

Melt the butter on SAUTÉ mode, and cook scallions for 3 minutes, until soft. Stir in the garlic and cook for one minute, until fragrant. Add beef and cook until browned, for a few minutes.

Stir in salsa, tomato paste, and spices. Seal the lid and cook for 8 minutes on RICE at High. Do a quick pressure release, and stir in cheese and pasta. Cook uncovered for 2 minutes, until well incorporated.

Rice Custard with Hazelnuts

Ready in about: 30 minutes | **Serves:** 3 | **Per serving:** Calories 444; Carbs 78g; Fat 10g; Protein 11g

INGREDIENTS

1 cup Rice
4 tbsp Hazelnuts, chopped
1 tsp Vanilla Paste
1 Egg plus 1 Yolk
½ cup Sultanas

½ tsp Anise Seed
1 cup Milk
¼ cup Sugar
½ tsp Hazelnut Extract
1 ½ cups Water

DIRECTIONS

Pour 1 ½ cups water in the pressure cooker, and lower the trivet.

Mix together all ingredients in a baking dish. Place the dish inside the pressure cooker and cover with foil. Seal the lid and cook on BEANS/CHILI for 25 minutes at High. Release the pressure quickly.

Spaghetti with Meatballs

Ready in about: 30 minutes | **Serves:** 6 | **Per serving:** Calories 306; Carbs 16g; Fat 13g; Protein 27g

INGREDIENTS

10 ounces Noodles
2 Eggs
1 pound Ground Beef
¼ cup Breadcrumbs
½ small Red Onion, grated

1 Egg
1 jar Spaghetti Sauce
½ tsp Garlic, minced
Water as needed

DIRECTIONS

Combine the beef, crumbs, garlic, onion, and egg, in a bowl. Mix with hands. Shape the mixture into about 6 meatballs. Add the sauce and spaghetti in your pressure cooker.

Pour enough water to cover. Add the meatballs and seal the lid. Cook at High pressure for 14 minutes. When ready, release the pressure naturally, for 10 minutes.

Bulgur and Potato Soup

Ready in about: 30 minutes | **Serves:** 4 | **Per serving:** Calories 355; Carbs 65g; Fat 10g; Protein 11g

INGREDIENTS

¾ cup Bulgur
4 Potatoes, peeled and diced
1 Carrot, diced
1 tsp Garlic paste
1 Celery stalk, chopped
½ cup White Onions, chopped
3 tsp coconut oil
4 ½ cups Chicken Stock
½ tsp dried Thyme
¼ tsp ground Black Pepper
1 tsp Red Pepper, flakes
½ tsp Sea Salt

DIRECTIONS

Add all ingredients to the pressure cooker. Select SOUP/BROTH and seal the lid.

Cook for 30 minutes at High pressure.

Once done, use a natural pressure release, for 10 minutes.

Lemony Rice with Veggies

Ready in about: 15 minutes | **Serves:** 4 | **Per serving:** Calories 213; Carbs 34g; Fat 7g; Protein 13g

INGREDIENTS

1 cup Rice
½ cup Onions, chopped
1 cup Broccoli Florets, frozen
1 cup Carrots, sliced
1 cup Peas
1 tbsp Oil
2 tsp Lemon Zest
¼ cup Lemon Juice
2 cups Veggie Stock

DIRECTIONS

Heat oil on SAUTÉ, and cook the onions for 2 minutes, until soft. Stir the remaining ingredients.

Seal the lid and cook for 10 minutes on RICE at High pressure.

Do a quick pressure release. Serve and enjoy!

Sausage Penne

Ready in about: 20 minutes | **Serves:** 6 | **Per serving:** Calories 413; Carbs 48g; Fat 18g; Protein 21g

INGREDIENTS

18 ounces Penne Pasta
16 ounces Sausage
2 cups Tomato Paste
1 tbsp Olive Oil
2 tsp Garlic, minced
1 tsp Oregano
¼ cup Parmesan Cheese, grated
Water, as needed

DIRECTIONS

Heat oil on SAUTÉ mode. Add sausage, cook until browned while crumbling. Add garlic and cook for 1 minute.

Stir in the remaining ingredients, except Parmesan and oregano.

Cover with water, seal the lid, and cook for 10 minutes on PRESSURE COOK at High. Release the pressure quickly.

To serve, top with freshly grated Parmesan cheese and sprinkle with dry oregano.

Pineapple and Honey Risotto

Ready in about: 15 minutes | **Serves:** 6 | **Per serving:** Calories 374; Carbs 78g; Fat 4g; Protein 5g

INGREDIENTS

2 cups White Rice
½ cup Honey
1 cup Pineapple, crushed

3 cups Water
2 tbsp Butter
½ tsp Vanilla

DIRECTIONS

Place the rice, juice, water, butter, and vanilla in your pressure cooker.

Seal the lid and cook for 8 minutes on RICE at High.

Release the pressure quickly. Stir in the pineapple and drizzle with honey.

Buckwheat Breakfast Porridge with Figs

Ready in about: 20 minutes | **Serves:** 6 | **Per serving:** Calories 415; Carbs 58g; Fat 19g; Protein 11g

INGREDIENTS

1 cup Buckwheat Groats
¼ cup dried Figs, chopped
2 Bananas, sliced
1 cup Almond Milk
2 tbsp Coconut Oil

½ tsp Vanilla Extract
½ tsp Cinnamon
¼ tsp ground Nutmeg
½ tsp Kosher Salt
2 cups Water

DIRECTIONS

Rinse buckwheat groats under cold water and drain them through a colander. Add buckwheat groats, figs, vanilla, coconut oil, cinnamon, nutmeg, salt to your pressure cooker. Pour in the milk and water.

Seal the lid, select PORRIDGE and cook for 15 minutes at High pressure.

When ready, do a quick pressure release. Carefully open the lid.

Top with sliced bananas and serve in a bowl.

Bacon and Cheese Pasta

Ready in about: 10 minutes | **Serves:** 6 | **Per serving:** Calories 437; Carbs 72g; Fat 12g; Protein 13g

INGREDIENTS

16 ounces Dry Rigatoni Pasta
1 cup chopped Onions
1 cup diced Bacon
2 ½ cups Tomato Puree
1 tsp Sage

1 tsp Thyme
½ cup Cheddar Cheese, grated
Water, as needed
Salt to taste
Freshly chopped basil, to garnish

DIRECTIONS

Fry the bacon on SAUTÉ mode, until brown and crispy, for about 3 minutes. Add the onions and cook for a few minutes, until soft. Stir in rigatoni pasta, tomato puree, sage, thyme, and salt. Add enough water to cover them.

Seal the lid and cook for 6 minutes at High pressure. When ready, release the pressure quickly.

Stir in the freshly grated Cheddar cheese and serve topped with fresh basil.

Chicken Enchilada Pasta

Ready in about: 20 minutes | **Serves:** 6 | **Per serving:** Calories 567; Carbs 49g; Fat 25g; Protein 31g

INGREDIENTS

2 Chicken Breasts, diced
3 cups dry Pasta
10 ounces canned Tomatoes
20 ounces canned Enchilada Sauce
1 ¼ cups Water

1 cup diced Onion
1 tsp Garlic, minced
1 tsp Taco Seasoning
1 tbsp Olive Oil
2 cups Cheddar Cheese, shredded

DIRECTIONS

Heat oil on SAUTÉ, and cook the onions until soft, for about 3 minutes. Stir in the remaining ingredients, except the cheese. Seal the lid and cook for 8 minutes at High pressure.

Quick-release the pressure. Stir in cheese and cook for 2 minutes, lid off, on SAUTÉ, until melted.

Noodles with Tuna

Ready in about: 20 minutes | **Serves:** 2 | **Per serving:** Calories 461; Carbs 17g; Fat 29g; Protein 37g

INGREDIENTS

8 ounces Egg Noodles, uncooked
1 can diced Tomatoes
1 can Tuna Flakes, drained
½ cup Red Onion, chopped
1 ¼ cups Water

1 jar Artichoke, marinated and chopped
1 tbsp Olive Oil
1 tsp Parsley
½ cup Feta Cheese, crumbled

DIRECTIONS

Heat oil on SAUTÉ, and cook the onions for a few minutes, until translucent. Stir in the remaining ingredients, except cheese. Seal the lid and cook for 4 minutes at High pressure.

When ready, release the pressure quickly. Stir in the feta cheese and serve and enjoy..

Soups and Stews

Chicken & Pancetta Noodle Soup

Ready in about: 35 minutes | **Serves:** 8 | **Per serving:** Calories 419; Carbs 15g; Fat 19g; Protein 34g

INGREDIENTS

5 oz dry Egg Noodles
4 Chicken Breasts, skinless and boneless
1 large White Onion, chopped
8 Pancetta Slices, chopped
4 cloves Garlic, minced
Salt and Black Pepper to taste

2 medium Carrots, sliced
2 cups sliced Celery
½ cup chopped Parsley
1 ½ tsp Dried Thyme
8 cups Chicken Broth

DIRECTIONS

Select SAUTÉ mode at High. Cook the pancetta for 5 minutes until brown and crispy. Add the onion and garlic, and cook for 3 more minutes. Then, transfer the pancetta mixture with a slotted spoon to a plate and set aside.

Remove the grease from the pot. Pour the pancetta mixture back into the pot and add chicken breasts, noodles, carrots, celery, chicken broth, thyme, salt, and pepper. Seal the lid, select MANUAL at High pressure for 5 minutes.

Once the timer has ended, do a quick pressure release. Remove the chicken onto a plate. Shred it with two forks and add it back to the soup. Stir well with a wooden spoon. Adjust the seasoning, and dish the soup into serving bowls. Sprinkle with cheddar cheese and serve with a side of bread.

Beef Soup with Tacos Topping

Ready in about: 30 minutes | **Serves:** 8 | **Per serving:** Calories 498; Carbs 21g; Fat 26g; Protein 47g

INGREDIENTS

2 tbsp Olive Oil
6 Green Bell pepper, diced
2 medium Yellow Onion, chopped
3 lb Ground Beef, grass fed
Salt and Black Pepper to taste
3 tbsp Chili Powder
2 tbsp Cumin Powder
2 tsp Paprika

1 tsp Garlic Powder
1 tsp Cinnamon
1 tsp Onion Powder
6 cups chopped Tomatoes
½ cup chopped Green Chilies
3 cups Bone Broth
3 cups Milk

Topping:
Chopped Jalapenos, Sliced Avocados, Chopped Cilantro, Chopped Green Onions, Lime Juice

DIRECTIONS

Select SAUTÉ mode at High, heat the oil. Add the yellow onion and green peppers. Sauté them until soft, for about 5 minutes. Add the ground beef, stir the ingredients, and cook for about 8 minutes until the beef browns.

Next, sitr in the chili powder, cumin powder, black pepper, paprika, cinnamon, garlic powder, onion powder, and jalapenos. Top with tomatoes, milk, and broth, and stir. Seal the lid and select SOUP at High for 20 minutes.

Once the timer has ended, do a quick pressure release. Keep in Warm mode. Season with salt and pepper. Dish the taco soup into serving bowls and add the toppings. Serve warm with a side of tortillas.

Ham and Pea Soup

Ready in about: 40 minutes | **Serves:** 6 | **Per serving:** Calories 276; Carbs 46g; Fat 1g; Protein 19g

INGREDIENTS

1 Onion, diced
1 pound Split Peas, dried
2 Carrots, diced
8 cups Water
2 Celery Stalks, diced
1 pound Ham Chunks
1 ½ tsp dried Thyme

DIRECTIONS

Put all ingredients in your pressure cooker. Seal the lid, and select SOUP/BROTH at High pressure. Adjust the time to 20 minutes. When ready, do a quick pressure release.

Taste and adjust the seasoning. If you don't like the density, cook for an additional 10 minutes.

Tortellini Minestrone Soup

Ready in about: 20 minutes | **Serves:** 6 | **Per serving:** Calories 245; Carbs 34g; Fat 9g; Protein 7g

INGREDIENTS

1 Onion, diced
2 Carrots, diced
1 tbsp Garlic, minced
2 tbsp Olive Oil
4 cups Veggie Broth
24 ounces Jarred Spaghetti Sauce
1 tsp Sugar
2 Celery Stalks, sliced
¼ tsp Black Pepper
1 ½ tsp Italian Seasoning
14 ounces canned diced Tomatoes
8 ounces dry Cheese Tortellini

DIRECTIONS

Heat olive oil on SAUTÉ. Add onions, garlic, celery, and carrots, and cook until soft, about 3 minutes.

Stir in the rest of the ingredients. Seal the lid, and set to PRESSURE COOK for 15 minutes at High pressure. When ready, do a quick pressure release. Adjust the seasoning and serve hot.

Chicken Enchilada Soup

Ready in about: 40 minutes | **Serves:** 8 | **Per serving:** Calories 397; Carbs 46g; Fat 5g; Protein 45g

INGREDIENTS

8 cups Butternut Squash, cubed
1 pound Chicken Breasts, boneless and skinless
8 ounces canned Tomato Soup
2 tsp Cumin
1 Onion, chopped
3 ½ ounces canned Chillies, chopped
2 tsp Taco Seasoning
2 tsp Salt
3 Russet Potatoes, quartered
3 Garlic Cloves, minced
4 cups Chicken Broth
30 ounces canned Cannellini Beans
1 Red Bell Pepper, chopped

DIRECTIONS

Add all ingredients and stir to combine well. Select MEAT/STEW mode; and the time to 25 minutes. Lock the lid; turn the pressure valve to "closed" position.

When it beeps, press CANCEL and do a quick pressure release. Remove the chicken from the cooker to a bowl. With a hand blender, puree the soup until smooth. Shred the chicken with two forks and return to the soup. Adjust the seasoning and serve.

Fall Pumpkin and Cauliflower Soup

Ready in about: 35 minutes | **Serves:** 4 | **Per serving:** Calories 183; Carbs 25g; Fat 5g; Protein 10g

INGREDIENTS

2 tsp Olive Oil
1 large White Onion, chopped
4 cloves Garlic, minced
1 (2 pounds) Pumpkin, peeled, seeded, and cubed
2 heads Cauliflower, cut in florets

3 cups Chicken Broth
3 tsp Paprika
Salt and Black Pepper to taste
1 cup Milk, full fat

Topping:
Grated Cheddar Cheese, Crumbled Bacon, Chopped Chives, Pumpkin Seeds

DIRECTIONS

Select SAUTÉ at High. Heat olive oil, add the onion and sauté it for about 3 minutes, until soft. Then, add the garlic and cook until fragrant, for about 2 minutes. Stir in pumpkin, cauliflower, broth, paprika, pepper, and salt.

Seal the lid, select MANUAL mode at High pressure for 10 minutes. Once the timer has ended, do a quick pressure release. Top the ingredients with the milk and use a stick blender to puree them.

Adjust the seasoning, stir, and dish the soup into serving bowls. Add the toppings on the soup and serve warm.

Cream of Broccoli Soup

Ready in about: 25 minutes | **Serves:** 6 | **Per serving:** Calories 523; Carbs 12g; Fat 39g; Protein 17g

INGREDIENTS

3 cups Heavy Cream
3 cups Vegetable Broth
4 tbsp Butter
4 tbsp All-purpose Flour
4 cups chopped Broccoli Florets, only the bushy tops
1 medium Red Onion, chopped

3 cloves Garlic, minced
1 tsp Italian Seasoning
Salt and Black Pepper to taste
1 ½ oz Cream Cheese
1 ½ cups grated Yellow and White Cheddar Cheese + extra for topping

DIRECTIONS

Select SAUTÉ mode at High, and melt the butter. Add flour and use a spoon to stir until it clumps up. Gradually stir in the heavy cream until white sauce forms. Fetch out the butter sauce into a bowl and set aside.

Press Cancel, and stir in onions, garlic, broth, broccoli, Italian seasoning, and cream cheese. Seal the lid and select MANUAL at High pressure for 15 minutes. Once the timer has ended, do a quick pressure release.

Keep the pot in Warm mode and stir in butter sauce and cheddar cheese, salt, and pepper, until the cheese melts. Dish the soup into serving bowls, top it with extra cheese, and serve.

Vegetables and Beef Brisket Stew

Ready in about: 70 minutes | **Serves:** 4 | **Per serving:** Calories 487; Carbs 41g; Fat 16g; Protein 47g

INGREDIENTS

2 lb Brisket, cut into 2-inch pieces
4 cups Beef Broth
Salt and Black Pepper to taste
1 tbsp Dijon Mustard

1 tbsp Olive Oil
1 lb small Potato, quartered
¼ lb Carrots, cut in 2-inch pieces
1 large Red Onion, quartered

3 cloves Garlic, minced
1 Bay Leaf
2 fresh Thyme sprigs

2 tbsp Cornstarch
3 tbsp chopped Cilantro to garnish

DIRECTIONS

Pour the beef broth, cornstarch, mustard, ½ teaspoon salt, and ½ teaspoon pepper in a bowl. Whisk them and set aside. Season the beef strips with salt and pepper. Select SAUTÉ mode at High.

Add olive oil, once heated include the beef strips and cook until brown, for about 8 minutes.

Flip the strips halfway through cooking. Add potato, carrots, onion, garlic, thyme, mustard mixture, and bay leaf. Stir once more. Seal the lid, select MANUAL mode at High pressure for 45 minutes. Do a quick pressure release.

Stir the stew and remove the bay leaf. Season with salt and pepper.

Smoked Sausage and Seafood Stew

Ready in about: 40 minutes | **Serves:** 8 | **Per serving:** Calories 465; Carbs 39g; Fat 21g; Protein 35g

INGREDIENTS

1 lb Halibut, skinless and cut into 1-inch pieces
1 lb medium Shrimp, peeled and deveined
2 lb Mussels, debearded and scrubbed
2 (16 oz) Clam Juice
6 cups Water
2 (8 oz) Smoked Sausage, sliced
1 cup White Wine
Salt and Black Pepper to taste

4 tbsp Olive Oil
4 cloves Garlic, minced
2 small Fennel Bulb, chopped
4 small Leeks, sliced
A little pinch Saffron
2 Bay Leaves
2 (28 oz) can Diced Tomatoes
4 tbsp chopped Parsley

DIRECTIONS

Select SAUTÉ at High. Warm the oil, and cook sausages, fennel, and leeks, for 5 minutes stirring occasionally. Stir in garlic, saffron, and bay leaf, and wine, and cook for 2 minutes. Add tomatoes, clam juice, water, mussels, halibut, and shrimp. se the spoon to cover them with the sauce but don't stir. Seal the lid.

Select MANUAL at High pressure for 15 minutes. Once the timer has ended, do a quick pressure release. Remove and discard the bay leaf. Add parsley, adjust the seasoning, and stir. Serve with a side of garlic bread.

Pepperoni and Vegetable Stew

Ready in about: 35 minutes | **Serves:** 4 | **Per serving:** Calories 435; Carbs 34g; Fat 31g; Protein 15g

INGREDIENTS

3 tbsp Olive Oil
2 large White Onions, chopped
8 oz Pepperoni, sliced
2 Eggplants, cut in half moons
2 cups Vegetable Broth
2 cloves Garlic, minced

¾ lb Brussels Sprouts, halved
Salt and Black Pepper to taste
1 ½ lb Tomatoes, chopped
3 Zucchinis, quartered
¾ lb Green Beans

DIRECTIONS

Select SAUTÉ mode at High. Warm 1 tbsp of oil, stir in onions, garlic, and pepperoni. Cook for 8 minutes. Sit in the remaining oil, eggplants, Brussel sprouts, tomatoes, zucchinis, beans, broth, salt, and pepper. Seal the lid.

Select MANUAL mode at High pressure for 15 minutes. Once the timer has stopped, do a quick pressure release. Dish the stew into a serving bowl and serve with a side of braised bamboo shoots.

Creamy Chicken Stew with Mushrooms & Spinach

Ready in about: 55 minutes | **Serves:** 4 | **Per serving:** Calories 456; Carbs 22g; Fat 26g; Protein 42g

INGREDIENTS

4 Chicken Breasts, diced
1 ¼ lb White Button Mushrooms, halved
3 tbsp Olive Oil
1 large Onion, sliced
5 cloves Garlic, minced
Salt and Black Pepper to taste
1 ¼ tsp Cornstarch

½ cup Spinach, chopped
1 Bay Leaf
1 ½ cups Chicken Stock
1 tsp Dijon Mustard
1 ½ cup Sour Cream
3 tbsp Chopped Parsley

DIRECTIONS

Select SAUTÉ mode at High. Heat the olive oil, and sauté onion for 3 minutes. Stir in mushrooms, chicken, garlic, bay leaf, salt, pepper, mustard, and broth. Seal the lid, select MANUAL mode at High pressure for 15 minutes. Once the timer has ended, do a natural release for 5 minutes, then a quick pressure release to let the remaining steam out. Select SAUTÉ again. Stir the stew, remove the bay leaf, and scoop some of the liquid into a bowl.

Add the cornstarch and mix until completely lump free. Pour the liquid into the sauce, stir, and thicken the sauce to your desired consistency. Top with sour cream, stir the sauce, and hit Warm mode. After 4 minutes, dish the sauce into serving bowls and garnish with chopped parsley. Serve with steamed green peas.

White Beans and Easy Chicken Chili

Ready in about: 40 minutes | **Serves:** 4 | **Per serving:** Calories 535; Carbs 15g; Fat 33g; Protein 48g

INGREDIENTS

3 Chicken Breasts, cubed
3 cups Chicken Broth
1 tbsp Butter
1 White Onion, chopped
Salt and Black Pepper

2 (14.5 ounce) cans White beans, drained and rinsed
1 tsp Cumin Powder
1 tsp dried Oregano
½ cup heavy Whipping Cream
1 cup Sour Cream

DIRECTIONS

Select SAUTÉ mode at High. Melt the butter, and stir in the onion and chicken. Cook for 6 minutes, until lightly browned. Stir in the cannellini beans, cumin powder, oregano, salt, and pepper. Stir in the broth, and sel the lid.

Select MANUAL mode at High pressure for 10 minutes. Once the timer has ended, do a quick pressure release, after 10 minutes. Stir in the whipping and sour creams. Dish the sauce into serving bowls.

Spicy Beef Chili with Worcestershire Sauce

Ready in about: 40 minutes | **Serves:** 4 | **Per serving:** Calories 437; Carbs 15g; Fat 19g; Protein 38g

INGREDIENTS

2 lb Ground Beef
2 tbsp Olive Oil
1 large Red Bell Pepper, seeded and chopped
1 large Yellow Bell Pepper, seeded and chopped
1 White Onion, Chopped
2 cups Chopped Tomatoes
2 cups Beef Broth
2 Carrots, cut in little bits

2 tsp Onion Powder
2 tsp Garlic Powder
5 tsp Chili Powder
2 tbsp Worcestershire Sauce
2 tsp Paprika
½ tsp Cumin Powder
2 tbsp chopped Parsley
Salt and Black Pepper to taste

DIRECTIONS

Select SAUTÉ mode at High, heat oil and add ground beef. Cook until browned, stirring occasionally, for about 8 minutes. Mix in the remaining ingredients. Seal the lid and cook on MANUAL at High pressure for 20 minutes. Do a quick pressure release. Dish it into serving bowls. Serve with some crackers.

Chipotle Chile sin Carne

Ready in about: 30 minutes | **Serves:** 4 | **Per serving:** Calories 387; Carbs 42g; Fat 26g; Protein 18g

INGREDIENTS

4 Celery Stalks, chopped
2 (15 oz) cans Diced Tomatoes
1 tbsp Olive Oil
3 Carrots, chopped
2 cloves Garlic, minced
2 tsp Smoked Paprika
2 Green Bell Pepper, diced
½ cup Water

1 tbsp Cumin Powder
1 Sweet Onion, chopped
2 cups Tomato Sauce
1.5 oz Dark Chocolate, chopped
1 small Chipotle, minced
1 ½ cups raw Walnuts, chopped + extra to garnish
Salt and Pepper, to taste
Chopped Cilantro to garnish

DIRECTIONS

Heat oil, and add onion, celery, and carrots. Sauté for 4 minutes on SAUTÉ. Add garlic, cumin, and paprika. Stir and cook the sauce for 2 minutes. Stir in peppers, tomatoes, tomato sauce, chipotle, water, and walnuts.

Seal the lid, select MANUAL mode at High pressure for 15 minutes. Once the timer has ended, do a quick pressure release, and open the lid. Stir in chocolate until it melts. Season with salt and pepper. Dish the chili into a serving bowl, garnish with the remaining walnuts and cilantro. Serve with noodles.

Pork Roast Green Chili

Ready in about: 70 minutes | **Serves:** 6 | **Per serving:** Calories 410; Carbs 16g; Fat 18g; Protein 38g

INGREDIENTS

1 ½ lb Pork Roast, cut into 1-inch cubes
1 lb Tomatillos, husks removed
2 tbsp Olive Oil, divided into 2
1 bulb Garlic, tail sliced off
2 Green Chilies
3 cups Chicken Broth
1 Green Bell Pepper, seeded and roughly chopped

Salt and Pepper, to taste
½ tsp Cumin Powder
1 tsp dried Oregano
1 Bay Leaf
1 bunch Cilantro, chopped and divided into 2
2 Potatoes, peeled and cut into ½-inch cubes

DIRECTIONS

Preheat an oven to 450 F. Put the garlic bulb on a baking tray and drizzle with olive oil. Add bell peppers, onion, green chilies, and tomatillos on the baking tray in a single layer. Tuck the tray in the oven and roast the veggies and spices for 25 minutes. Then, remove them from the oven to let cool.

Peel the garlic with a knife and place it in a blender. Add the green bell pepper, tomatillos, onion, and green chilies to the blender. Pulse for a few minutes not to be smooth but slightly chunky.

On the pressure cooker, select SAUTÉ mode. Heat the remaining oil. Season the pork with salt and pepper. Brown the pork in the oil, for about 5 minutes. Stir in oregano, cumin, bay leaf, green sauce, potatoes, and broth.

Seal the lid, and select MANUAL mode on High pressure for 35 minutes. Do a natural pressure release for 10 minutes. Remove and discard bay leaf, stir half of the cilantro, adjust with salt and pepper. Dish the chili into serving bowls and garnish with the remaining cilantro. Serve topped with a side of chips or crusted bread.

Mushroom and Beef Stew

Ready in about: 25 minutes | **Serves:** 4 | **Per serving:** Calories 527; Carbs 50g; Fat 18g; Protein 45g

INGREDIENTS

2 tbsp Canola Oil
1 tsp dried Parsley
1 Onion, chopped
1 ½ pound Beef, cut into pieces
4 Red Potatoes, cut into chunks
4 Carrots, cut into chunks
8 Button Mushrooms, sliced
10 ounces Golden Mushroom Soup
12 ounces Water

DIRECTIONS

Set to SAUTÉ and heat oil. Cook the meat in until browned, 5-6 minutes per side. Stir in the remaining ingredients. Lock the lid, turn the pressure valve to "closed" position and set at High for 20 minutes.

When it beeps, press CANCEL and do a quick pressure release. Serve warm and enjoy.

Pomodoro Soup

Ready in about: 25 minutes | **Serves:** 8 | **Per serving:** Calories 314; Carbs 16g; Fat 23g; Protein 11g

INGREDIENTS

3 pounds Tomatoes, peeled and quartered
1 Carrot, diced
1 Onion, diced
¼ cup Fresh Basil
1 cup Half & Half
1 tbsp Tomato Paste
3 tbsp Butter
½ tsp Salt
½ tsp Pepper
4 cups Chicken Broth
½ cup Parmesan Cheese, grated
1 tsp Garlic, minced

DIRECTIONS

Melt the butter on SAUTÉ mode, and cook the onions, celery, garlic, and carrots until soft, for about 4 minutes. Stir in the remaining ingredients, except the cream and cheese.

Seal the lid, select SOUP/BROTH mode, and cook for 25 minutes at High pressure. When it goes off, do a quick pressure release. Stir in half & half and freshly grated Parmesan cheese.

Skim and Fast Miso and Tofu Soup

Ready in about: 12 minutes | **Serves:** 4 | **Per serving:** Calories 94; Carbs 4g; Fat 2g; Protein 4g

INGREDIENTS

4 cups Water
½ cup Corn
2 tbsp Miso Paste
1 Onion, sliced
1 tsp Wakame Flakes
1 cup Silken Tofu, cubed
2 Celery Stalks, chopped
2 Carrots, chopped
Soy Sauce, to taste

DIRECTIONS

Add all ingredients, except for miso paste and soy sauce. Seal the lid, select PRESSURE COOK for 7 minutes at High pressure. Do a quick pressure release. Mix the miso paste with one cup of broth.

Stir it into the soup. Add some soy sauce and stir. Ladle to serving bowls and serve.

Navy Bean and Ham Shank Soup

Ready in about: 8 hours 30 minutes | **Serves:** 12 | **Per serving:** Calories 427, Carbs 49g, Fat 34g, Protein 36g

INGREDIENTS

½ cup Vegetable Oil
4 cups dried Navy Beans
3 pounds Ham Shank
2 Onions, chopped
4 Carrots, sliced
½ cup minced Green Pepper

3 Quarts Water
2 cups Tomato Sauce
4 Celery Stalks, chopped
2 Garlic Cloves, minced
Salt and Pepper, to taste

DIRECTIONS

Soak the beans in water overnight. Drain and discard water. Heat oil on SAUTÉ and cook onion, garlic, carrots, celery, salt, and pepper for 4-5 minutes, until tender. Stir in the remaining ingredients.

Seal the lid and cook on BEANS/CHILI for 25 minutes at High. Do a quick pressure release, and serve.

Lentil Soup

Ready in about: 30 minutes | **Serves:** 4 | **Per serving:** Calories 259; Carbs 35g; Fat 8g; Protein 13g

INGREDIENTS

4 Garlic Cloves, minced
1 tsp Cumin
4 cups Veggie Broth
½ Onion, chopped
2 Celery Stalks, chopped

2 Carrots, chopped
1 cup dry Lentils
2 Bay Leaves
2 tbsp Olive Oil
Salt and Pepper, to taste

DIRECTIONS

Heat the olive oil and sweat onions, garlic, and carrots for 3-4 minutes, on SAUTÉ mode. Add celery and sauté for one more minute. Stir in the remaining ingredients. Seal the lid.

Set to BEANS/CHILI mode and adjust the timer to 25 minutes. When it beeps, press CANCEL and do a natural release, for 10 minutes. Season with salt and pepper, and serve warm.

Irish Lamb Stew

Ready in about: 25 minutes | **Serves:** 4 | **Per serving:** Calories 321; Carbs 29g; Fat 11g; Protein 25g

INGREDIENTS

1 pound Lamb, cut into pieces
1 Onion, sliced
2 tbsp Cornstarch or Arrowroot
1 ½ tbsp Olive Oil

2 Sweet Potatoes, cut into cubes
3 Carrots, chopped
2 ½ cups Veggie Broth
½ tsp dried Thyme

DIRECTIONS

Season lamb with salt and pepper. On SAUTÉ mode, heat olive oil and sear the lamb until browned on all sides, about 4-5 minute. Add all remaining ingredients, except for the cornstarch, and stir well to combine. Close the lid, turn the steaming vent clockwise to seal.

Cook on High Pressure for 18 minutes. When ready, do a quick pressure release. Whisk the cornstarch with a little bit of water and stir it into the stew. Cook on SAUTÉ for 3 more minutes, lid off. Serve hot.

Pressure Cooked Chili

Ready in about: 45 minutes | **Serves:** 4 | **Per serving:** Calories 388; Carbs 15g; Fat 27g; Protein 22g

INGREDIENTS

1 pound Ground Beef
½ cup Beef Broth
1 Onion, diced
1 tbsp Olive Oil
28 ounces canned Tomatoes, undrained

½ tbsp Cumin
1 ½ tbsp Chili Powder
1 tsp Garlic Powder
2 tbsp Tomato Paste

DIRECTIONS

On SAUTÉ, heat the oil and sauté the beef until browned, for about 4-5 minutes. Add onion, cumin, chili, garlic, tomato paste, and cook for 3-4 more minutes. Stir in tomatoes and beef broth.

Seal the lid, set to BEANS/CHILI and cook for 30 minutes. Do a quick pressure release, and serve hot.

Pumpkin, Corn and Chicken Chowder

Ready in about: 15 minutes | **Serves:** 4 | **Per serving:** Calories 314; Carbs 17g; Fat 21g; Protein 15g

INGREDIENTS

2 Chicken Breasts
2 cups Corn, canned or frozen
1 Onion, diced
¼ tsp Pepper
½ cup Half & Half
15 ounces Pumpkin Puree
2 cups Chicken Broth

½ tsp dried Oregano
1 Garlic Clove, minced
A pinch of Nutmeg
A pinch of Red Pepper Flakes
2 Potatoes, cubed
2 tbsp Butter

DIRECTIONS

Melt butter on SAUTÉ, and stir-fry onion, for 2-3 minutes. Stir in garlic and cook for an additional minute. Add in pumpkin puree, broth, potatoes, chicken, and all the seasonings.

Close the lid, turn the steaming vent clockwise to seal. Cook for 10 minutes at High pressure. When it beeps, do a quick pressure release. Stir in the half & half and corn, and serve.

Spicy Beef and Potato Soup

Ready in about: 25 minutes | **Serves:** 8 | **Per serving:** Calories 242; Carbs 27g; Fat 9g; Protein 14g

INGREDIENTS

1 pound Ground Beef
4 cups Water
24 ounces Tomato Sauce
2 cups Fresh Corn
1 tsp Salt

4 cups cubed Potatoes
1 Onion, chopped
½ tsp Hot Pepper Sauce
1 ½ tsp Black Pepper
3 tbsp Vegetable Oil

DIRECTIONS

Heat the oil on SAUTÉ mode, and brown the beef for about 3-4 minutes. Add onions and cook for 2 more minutes. Stir in the remaining ingredients, and seal the lid.

Cook on PRESSURE COOK mode, at High pressure for 12 minutes. Once the cooking is over, press CANCEL and do a quick pressure release, by turning the valve to "open" position.

Creamy Curried Cauliflower Soup

Ready in about: 35 minutes | **Serves:** 4 | **Per serving:** Calories 115; Carbs 20g; Fat 3g; Protein 3g

INGREDIENTS

1 Cauliflower Head, chopped
1 tbsp Curry Powder
½ tsp Turmeric Powder
1 Sweet Potato, diced
1 Onion, diced

1 Carrot, diced
1 cup Coconut Milk
2 cups Veggie Broth
½ tbsp Coconut Oil

DIRECTIONS

Melt the coconut oil on SAUTÉ, and cook onion and carrot until tender, 3-4 minutes. Season with salt and pepper. Add the rest of the ingredients, except milk, and stir to combine well.

Seal the lid, set to PRESSURE COOK mode for 20 minutes at High pressure.

When it beeps, press CANCEL and do a quick pressure release, by turning the valve to "open" position. Blend the soup with immersion blender until smooth, and garnish with coconut milk to serve.

Spanish-Style Chorizo and Broccoli Soup

Ready in about: 15 minutes | **Serves:** 6 | **Per serving:** Calories 205; Carbs 6g; Fat 10g; Protein 13g

INGREDIENTS

3 Spanish Chorizo, chopped
2 cups Broccoli, torn into pieces
½ lb. Zucchini, sliced
½ tsp Sugar
1 Red Onion, chopped
½ tsp dry Basil
1 tsp Red Pepper flakes, crushed

½ tsp dried Oregano
3 tsp Olive Oil
¼ cup sour cream
2 Cloves Garlic, peeled and minced
6 ½ cups Vegetable Broth
Salt and ground Black Pepper, to taste

DIRECTIONS

Select SAUTÉ and heat the oil for a few minutes, then sauté the chorizo, garlic and onion. Cook the chorizo until brown. Add the remaining ingredients, except the sour cream.

Seal the lid and cook for 5 minutes on PRESSURE COOK at High Pressure. Once cooking is complete, release the pressure quickly. Remove the lid and add the sour cream, stir and serve.

Fish and Seafood Recipes

Garlicky Mackerel and Vegetables Parcels

Ready in: 25 minutes + 2h marinating | **Serves:** 6 | **Per serving:** Calories 291; Carbs 15g; Fat 16g; Protein 15

INGREDIENTS

3 large Whole Mackerel, cut into 2 pieces
1 pound Asparagus, trimmed
1 Carrot, cut into sticks
1 Celery stalk, cut into sticks
½ cup Butter, at room temperature
6 medium Tomatoes, quartered
1 large Brown Onion, sliced thinly

1 Orange Bell Pepper, seeded and cut into sticks
Salt and Black Pepper to taste
2 ½ tbsp Pernod
3 cloves Garlic, minced
2 Lemons, cut into wedges
1 ½ cups Water

DIRECTIONS

Cut 6 pieces of parchment paper a little longer and wider than a piece of fish. Cut 6 pieces of foil slightly longer than the parchment papers. Lay the foil wraps on a flat surface and place each parchment paper on each foil.

In a bowl, mix tomatoes, onions, garlic, bell pepper, pernod, butter, asparagus, carrot, celery, salt, and pepper.

Place each fish piece on the layer of parchment and foil wraps. Spoon the vegetable mixture on each fish. Then, wrap the fish and refrigerate these fish packets, to marinate, for 2 hours. Remove the fish onto a flat surface.

Pour the water in the cooker, and fit the trivet at the bottom of the pot. Put the packets on the trivet. Seal the lid and select STEAM mode at High pressure for 5 minutes. Once the timer has ended, do a quick pressure release.

Remove the trivet with the fish packets onto a flat surface. Carefully open the foil and using a spatula, transfer the fish with vegetables to serving plates. Serve with a side of the lemon wedges.

Sea Bass Stew

Ready in about: 25 minutes | **Serves:** 4 | **Per serving:** Calories 390; Carbs 17g; Fat 18g; Protein 37g

INGREDIENTS

1 Red Onion, diced
4 tbsp Olive Oil
½ cup Chicken Broth
1 cup Clam Juice
½ pound Potatoes, peeled and cubed
2 ½ cups Water

14 ounces canned diced Tomatoes
1 ½ pounds Sea Bass Fillets, chopped
1 tsp, minced, Garlic
2 tbsp chopped Dill
2 tbsp Lemon Juice
Salt and Pepper, to taste

DIRECTIONS

Heat half of the oil on SAUTÉ mode. Add the onions and cook for 3 minutes. Add the garlic and sauté for a minute. Pour the broth over and deglaze the bottom of the pot.

Stir in the tomatoes, potatoes, water, and clam juice. Seal the lid, select PRESSURE COOK mode, and set the cooking time to 5 minutes at High pressure.

When the timer goes off, do a quick pressure release. Add the sea bass pieces. Seal the lid again and cook on PRESSURE COOK for another 5 minutes, at High.

When ready, do a quick pressure release, and open the lid. Press the SAUTÉ button. Stir in the remaining ingredients along with the rest of the oil, and cook for 3 more minutes, lid off.

Ladle into serving bowls immediately, and enjoy!

Power Greens with Lemony Monf Fish

Ready in about: 25 minutes | **Serves:** 4 | **Per serving:** Calories 271; Carbs 20g; Fat 11g; Protein 12g

INGREDIENTS

2 tbsp Olive Oil
4 (8 oz) Monk Fish Fillets, cut in 2 pieces each
½ cup chopped Green Beans
2 cloves Garlic, sliced
1 cup Kale Leaves

½ lb Baby Bok Choy, stems removed and chopped largely
1 Lemon, zested and juiced
Lemon Wedges to serve
Salt and White Pepper to taste

DIRECTIONS

Select SAUTÉ mode at High. Pour in the coconut oil, garlic, red chili, and green beans. Stir fry for 5 minutes. Add the kale leaves, and cook them to wilt, for about 3 minutes. Meanwhile, place the fish on a plate and season with salt, white pepper, and lemon zest. After, remove the green beans and kale to a plate and set aside.

Back to the pot, add the olive oil and fish. Brown the fish on each side, for about 2 minutes, and add the bok choy.

Pour the lemon juice over the fish and gently stir. Cook for 2 minutes and then turn off the pressure cooker. Spoon the fish with bok choy over the green beans and kale. Serve with a side of lemon wedges.

Steamed Salmon Filets with Paprika-Lemon Sauce

Ready in about: 10 minutes | **Serves:** 4 | **Per serving:** Calories 542; Carbs 7g; Fat 31g; Protein 62g

INGREDIENTS

4 (5 oz) Salmon Filets
1 cup Water
Salt and Black Pepper to taste
2 tsp Cumin Powder
1 ½ tsp Paprika
2 tbsp chopped Parsley

2 tbsp Olive Oil
2 tbsp Hot Water
1 tbsp Maple Syrup
2 cloves Garlic, minced
1 Lime, juiced

DIRECTIONS

In a bowl, mix cumin, paprika, parsley, olive oil, hot water, maple syrup, garlic, and lime juice.

Pour the water in the pressure cooker, and fit the steamer rack in it. Season the salmon with pepper and salt; place on the steamer rack in the pot. Seal the lid, and select STEAM mode on High pressure for 5 minutes.

Once the timer has ended, do a quick pressure release. Use a set of tongs to transfer the salmon to a serving plate and drizzle the lime sauce all over it. Serve with steamed swiss chard.

Mediterranean Salmon

Ready in about: 15 minutes | **Serves:** 4 | **Per serving:** Calories 431 Carbs 6g; Fat 31g; Protein 42g

INGREDIENTS

4 Salmon Fillets
2 tbsp Olive Oil
1 Rosemary Sprig

1 cup Cherry Tomatoes
15 ounces Asparagus
1 cup Water

DIRECTIONS

Pour in water and insert the rack. Place the salmon on top, sprinkle with rosemary, and arrange the asparagus on top. Seal the lid and cook on STEAM mode for 3 minutes at High.

Do a quick release, add cherry tomatoes, and cook for 2 minutes, on SAUTÉ. Drizzled with oil, to serve.

Alaskan Cod with Fennel and Beans

Ready in about: 25 minutes | **Serves:** 4 | **Per serving:** Calories 294; Carbs 26g; Fat 14g; Protein 15g

INGREDIENTS

2 (18 oz) Alaskan Cod, cut into 4 pieces each
4 tbsp Olive Oil
2 cloves Garlic, minced
2 small Onions, chopped
½ cup Olive Brine
3 cups Chicken Broth
Salt and Black Pepper to taste

½ cup Tomato Puree
1 head Fennel, quartered
1 cup Pinto Beans, soaked, drained and rinsed
1 cup Green Olives, pitted and crushed
½ cup Basil Leaves
Lemon Slices to garnish

DIRECTIONS

Select SAUTÉ mode at High. Warm the olive oil and stir-fy the garlic and onion, until soft and fragrant. Pour in the broth and tomato puree. Let simmer for about 3 minutes. Add the fennel, olives, beans, salt, and pepper.

Seal the lid and select MANUAL mode at High pressure for 20 minutes. Once the timer has stopped, do a quick pressure release. Transfer the beans to a plate with a slotted spoon. Season the broth with salt and pepper.

Add the cod pieces to the cooker. Seal the lid again, and select STEAM mode on Low pressure for 3 minutes. Do a quick pressure release. Remove the cod to soup bowls, top with beans and basil leaves, and pour the broth over.

Deliciously Sweet and Spicy Mahi Mahi

Ready in about: 10 minutes | **Serves:** 4 | **Per serving:** Calories 291; Carbs 20g; Fat 12g; Protein 23g

INGREDIENTS

4 Mahi Mahi Fillets, fresh
4 cloves Garlic, minced
1 ¼-inch Ginger, grated
Salt and Black Pepper
2 tbsp Chili Powder

1 tbsp Sriracha Sauce
1 ½ tbsp Maple Syrup
1 Lime, juiced
1 cup Water

DIRECTIONS

Place mahi mahi on a plate and season with salt and pepper on both sides. In a bowl, mix in garlic, ginger, chili powder, sriracha sauce, maple syrup, and lime juice. With a brush, apply the hot sauce mixture on the fillet.

Then, pour the water in the cooker, and fit the trivet at the bottom. Put the fillets on the trivet. Seal the lid, select Steam mode at High pressure for 5 minutes. Once the timer has ended, do a quick pressure release.

Use a set of tongs to remove the mahi mahi onto serving plates. Serve with steamed or braised asparagus.

Party Crab Legs

Ready in about: 20 minutes | **Serves:** 4 | **Per serving:** Calories 263; Carbs 37g; Fat 10g; Protein 7g

INGREDIENTS

1 ½ pounds Crab Legs
2 tbsp Butter, melted

1 cup Veggie Broth
½ cup White Wine

DIRECTIONS

Pour broth and wine into the pressure cooker. Place crab legs in the steaming basket. Seal the lid and cook for 5 minutes at High pressure. When ready, do a quick release, and serve drizzled with butter.

Salmon with Broccoli and Potatoes

Ready in about: 8 minutes | Serve: 1 | **Per serving:** Calories 432; Carbs 19g; Fat 15g; Protein 35g

INGREDIENTS

4-ounce Salmon Fillet
4 New Potatoes
4 ounces Broccoli Florets

2 tsp Olive Oil
Salt and Pepper, to taste
1 ½ cups Water

DIRECTIONS

Pour water and lower the rack. Season the potatoes with salt and pepper, and place them on top of the rack. Drizzle half of the oil over. Seal the lid, select the PRESSURE COOK for 2 minutes at High pressure.

When the timer goes off, release the pressure quickly. Season the broccoli and salmon with salt and pepper. Arrange the broccoli on top of the potatoes and top with the salmon fillet.

Drizzle them with the remaining olive oil. Seal the lid and cook on PRESSURE COOK for 3 more minutes at High. Do a quick pressure release, and serve hot.

Veggie Noodle Salmon

Ready in about: 15 minutes | **Serves:** 4 | **Per serving:** Calories 313; Carbs 12g; Fat 13g; Protein 40g

INGREDIENTS

4 Trut Fillets
2 tsp Olive Oil
1 large Carrot, peeled and spiralized
2 Large Potatoes, peeled and spiralized
1 Zucchini, peeled and spiralized

1 cup Water
1 Thyme Sprig
¼ tsp Pepper
¼ tsp Salt

DIRECTIONS

Pour the water and add thyme sprig. Arrange the noodles inside the steaming basket and top with the salmon. Season with salt and pepper, and drizzle with oil.

Place the basket inside the cooker. Seal the lid, press STEAM, and set to 5 minutes at High. When the timer goes off, do a quick pressure release. Serve immediately and enjoy.

Crab Cakes

Ready in about: 14 minutes | **Serves:** 2 | **Per serving:** Calories 321; Carbs 11g; Fat 8g; Protein 19g

INGREDIENTS

1 cup Crab Meat
¼ cup Black Olives, chopped
1 Carrot, shredded
½ cup Potatoes, boiled and mashed
¼ cup Flour

¼ cup Onion, grated
1 ½ cup canned Tomatoes, diced
1 tbsp Olive Oil
½ cup Chicken Broth

DIRECTIONS

Place crab meat, carrots, olives, flour, potatoes, and onion, in a bowl. Mix with hands until fully incorporated. Shape the mixture into two patties. Heat olive oil on SAUTÉ.

When hot and sizzling, add the crab cakes and cook for a minute. Flip them over and cook for another minute. Pour tomatoes and broth over and seal the lid. Select PRESSURE COOK mode and set the cooking time to 2 minutes at High pressure. When the timer goes off, do a quick pressure release and serve immediately.

Tilapia Chowder

Ready in about: 25 minutes | **Serves:** 4 | **Per serving:** Calories 320; Carbs 14g; Fat 16g; Protein 25g

INGREDIENTS

1 ½ cups Water
1 cup Milk
1 cup Potatoes, peeled and chopped
½ pounds Tilapia, chopped
½ cups chopped Celery
½ cup Chicken Stock
¾ cup diced Onion
¼ tsp Salt
¼ tsp Pepper
¼ tsp Onion Powder
1 tbsp Cornstarch mixed with 1 ½ tbsp Water

DIRECTIONS

Combine everything, except for the cornstarch mixture, in your pressure cooker. Seal the lid, select PRESSURE COOK and set the timer to 10 minutes at High pressure. When the timer goes off, do a quick pressure release.

Set to SAUTÉ. Stir in the cornstarch mixture and cook for about 5 minutes, or until the chowder is thickened. Serve immediately!

Shrimp and Egg Risotto

Ready in about: 30 minutes | **Serves:** 6 | **Per serving:** Calories 221; Carbs 22g; Fat 10g; Protein 13g

INGREDIENTS

4 cups Water
4 Garlic Cloves, minced
2 Eggs, beaten
½ tsp Ginger, grated
3 tbsp Sesame Oil
1 tbsp Butter
¼ tsp Cayenne Pepper
1 ½ cups frozen Peas
2 cups Brown Rice Arborio
¼ cup White Wine
1 cup chopped Onion
12 ounces peeled and pre-cooked Shrimp, thawed
3 tbsp Half & Half
¼ cup Parmesan cheese, grated

DIRECTIONS

Warm oil and scramble the eggs, stirring constantly, about 4-5 minutes, on SAUTÉ. Transfer to a plate. Melt butter and cook the onions, garlic, and rice for 4 minutes, until translucent.

Stir in the ginger, cayenne pepper, wine, peas, water, salt, and black pepper. Seal the lid, set to MEAT/STEW mode and adjust the time to 15 minutes at High.

Once the cooking is over, do a quick pressure release. Stir in the shrimp, parmesan cheese, cream, and eggs and let them heat for a couple of seconds with the lid off, on SAUTÉ mode.

Buttery and Lemony Dill Clams

Ready in about: 10 minutes | **Serves:** 4 | **Per serving:** Calories 123; Carbs 12g; Fat 2g; Protein 15g

INGREDIENTS

28 Scrubbed Clams
1 tbsp minced Dill
1 ¼ cups Water
½ cup White Wine
3 tbsp Lemon Juice
2 tbsp Brown Sugar
1 tsp Garlic, minced

DIRECTIONS

Combine all ingredients in the pressure cooker and add the clams inside. Seal the lid and cook at High pressure for 5 minutes. When ready, release the pressure quickly.

White Wine Steamed Mussels

Ready in about: 15 minutes | **Serves:** 4 | **Per serving:** Calories 211; Carbs 12g; Fat 5g; Protein 28g

INGREDIENTS

1 Onion, chopped
2 pounds Mussels, cleaned
1 cup White Wine
1 Garlic Clove, crushed
½ cup Water

DIRECTIONS

Heat oil on SAUTÉ mode, and cook the onion and garlic for 3 minutes, until soft and fragrant. Pour wine and cook for 1 more minute, constantly stirring.

Tumble the mussels into the steaming basket. Insert trivet in the cooker and lower the basket onto the trivet, and seal the lid. Cook for 3 minutes on STEAM mode at High.

When ready, let the pressure drop naturally, for about 10 minutes. Arrange the mussels on a serving platter. Spoon the cooking juices over and serve.

Prawns and Fish Kabobs

Ready in about: 15 minutes | **Serves:** 4 | **Per serving:** Calories 369; Carbs 22g; Fat 15g; Protein 40g

INGREDIENTS

1 lb Tuna Fillets, cubed
1 lb King Prawns, peeled and deveined
1 tbsp Salt
½ Onion, diced
1 Red Bell Pepper, diced 1 tsp lemon zest
1 packet dry Ranch dressing mix
1 cup Water

DIRECTIONS

In a large bowl, and mix the fish and shrimp. Sprinkle with some salt. Toss to spread the salt over the ingredients and leave aside for 5 minutes for decent flavoring.

Use wooden skewers to prick the fish and the shrimp by separating with bell pepper and slices of onion. Take the steel pot of your pressure cooker to mix water with the dressing.

Wait for the dressing mix to dissolve. Then, insert the trivet in the same pot. Lay the sewers over the pot crosswise. Seal the lid, set on PRESSURE COOK for about 4 minutes at High.

When ready, do a quick release. Remove the lid so the skewers can rest and cool down.

Almond-Crusted Tilapia

Ready in about: 10 minutes | **Serves:** 4 | **Per serving:** Calories 327; Carbs 4g; Fat 15g; Protein 46g

INGREDIENTS

4 Tilapia Fillets
⅔ cup sliced Almonds
1 cup Water
2 tbsp Dijon Mustard
1 tsp Olive Oil
¼ tsp Black Pepper

DIRECTIONS

Pour water into inner pot of pressure cooker and place a trivet in water. Mix olive oil, pepper, and mustard in a small bowl. Brush the fish fillets with the mustard mixture on all sides.

Coat the fish in almonds slices. Arrange the fish fillets on top of the trivet. Seal the lid, select STEAM and adjust the time to 10 minutes at High. When done, do a quick pressure release.

Lobster and Gruyere Pasta

Ready in about: 25 minutes | **Serves:** 4 | **Per serving:** Calories 441; Carbs 44g; Fat 15g; Protein 28g

INGREDIENTS

6 cups Water
1 tbsp Flour
8 ounces dried Ziti
1 cup Half & Half
1 tbsp Tarragon, chopped

¾ cup Gruyere Cheese, shredded
3 Lobster Tails, about 6 oz each
½ cup White Wine
½ tsp Pepper
1 tbsp Worcestershire Sauce

DIRECTIONS

Pour in water and add the lobster tails and ziti. Seal the lid, set to STEAM for 10 minutes at High. Once the cooking is over, do a quick pressure release. Drain the pasta and set aside.

Remove the meat from the tails, chop it, and stir into the bowl with pasta. Mix in the rest of the ingredients, set on SAUTÉ, and cook until the sauce thickens, then stir in pasta and lobster.

Clams in White Wine

Ready in about: 17 minutes | **Serves:** 4 | **Per serving:** Calories 224; Carbs 6g; Fat 14g; Protein 16g

INGREDIENTS

¼ cup White Wine
2 cups Veggie Broth
¼ cup Basil, chopped
¼ cup Olive Oil

2 ½ pounds Clams
2 tbsp Lemon Juice
2 Garlic Cloves, minced

DIRECTIONS

Heat the olive oil, add garlic and cook for one minute, until fragrant, on SAUTÉ mode. Pour wine, broth, and add basil, lemon juice. Bring the mixture to a boil and let cook for one minute.

Add your steaming basket, and place the clams inside. Seal the lid, and set to PRESSURE COOK mode and adjust the time to 6 minutes at High. Wait 5 minutes before releasing the pressure quickly.

Remove the clams to a bowl, discard any that did not open. Drizzle with the cooking juices to serve.

Fancy Shrimp Scampi with Soy Sauce

Ready in about: 45 minutes | **Serves:** 4 | **Per serving:** Calories 183; Carbs 4g; Fat 8g; Protein 24g

INGREDIENTS

2 tbsp Butter
1 tbsp Parmesan Cheese, grated
2 Shallots, chopped
¼ cup White Wine
1 tsp Garlic, minced
2 tbsp Lemon Juice

1 pound Shrimp, peeled and deveined
For the dip Sauce:
2 tbsp Soy Sauce
1 tbsp chopped chives
½ tbsp Olive Oil

DIRECTIONS

Melt butter on SAUTÉ, and cook the shallots until soft. Add garlic and cook for 1 more minute. Stir in wine and cook for another minute. Add the remaining ingredients and stir to combine.

Seal the lid and cook for 2 minutes, at High pressure. When ready, release the pressure quickly. Serve on a platter with dipping sauce on the side.

Tuna and Pea Cheesy Noodles

Ready in about: 17 minutes | **Serves:** 4 | **Per serving:** Calories 430; Carbs 42g; Fat 22g; Protein 18g

INGREDIENTS

1 can Tuna, drained
3 cups Water
4 ounces Cheddar Cheese, grated
16 ounces Egg Noodles

¼ cup Breadcrumbs
1 cup Frozen Peas
28 ounces canned Mushroom Soup

DIRECTIONS

Place the water and noodles in your pressure cooker. Stir in soup, tuna, and frozen peas.

Seal the lid, and cook for 5 minutes on at High pressure. When ready, do a quick pressure release. Stir in the cheese. Transfer to a baking dish; sprinkle with breadcrumbs on top.

Insert a baking dish in your cooker, seal the lid, and cook 3 minutes on STEAM mode at High.

Wrapped Fish and Potatoes

Ready in about: 15 minutes | **Serves:** 4 | **Per serving:** Calories 310; Carbs 9g; Fat 14g; Protein 30g

INGREDIENTS

4 Cod Fillets
4 Thyme Sprigs
2 Medium Potatoes, sliced
1 Lemon, sliced thinly

1 Onion, sliced
A Handful of Fresh Parsley
2 cups Water
2 tbsp Olive Oil

DIRECTIONS

Place each cod fillet onto a parchment paper. Divide the potatoes, thyme, parsley, onion, and lemon between the 4 parchment papers.

Drizzle each of them with ½ tbsp of olive oil and mix with your hands to coat everything. Wrap the fish with the parchment paper. Wrap each of the 'packets' in aluminum foil.

Pour the water in your pressure cooker and insert a steam rack. Place the packets inside. Seal the lid and cook for about 5 minutes on STEAM at High. When ready, do a quick release and serve.

Lemon Sauce Salmon

Ready in about: 10 minutes | **Serves:** 4 | **Per serving:** Calories 493; Carbs 6g; Fat 31g; Protein 41g

INGREDIENTS

4 Salmon Fillets
1 tbsp Honey
½ tsp Cumin
1 tbsp Hot Water
1 tbsp Olive Oil

1 tsp Smoked Paprika
1 tbsp chopped Fresh Parsley
¼ cup Lemon Juice
1 cup of Water

DIRECTIONS

Pour the water inside your Pressure cooker. Place the salmon fillets on the rack. Seal the lid and cook for 3 minutes on STEAM at High pressure. Whisk together the remaining ingredients, to form a sauce.

Once cooking is over, release the pressure quickly, and drizzle the sauce over the salmon. Seal the lid again, and cook for 3 more minutes on STEAM at High. Do a quick release and serve hot.

Creamy Crabmeat

Ready in about: 12 minutes | **Serves:** 4 | **Per serving:** Calories 450; Carbs 13g; Fat 10g; Protein 40g

INGREDIENTS

¼ cup Butter
1 small Red Onion, chopped
1 pound Lump Crabmeat
½ Celery Stalk, chopped

½ cup Heavy Cream
½ cup Chicken Broth
Salt and Pepper, to taste

DIRECTIONS

Season the crabmeat with some salt and pepper to taste. Melt the butter and cook the celery for a minute, on SAUTÉ mode. Add onions and cook for another 3 minutes, or until soft.

Place the crabmeat and stir in the broth. Seal the lid, set to STEAM for 10 minutes at High pressure. Once the cooking is over, do a quick pressure release. Season with salt and pepper, if needed.

Cod in a Tomato Sauce

Ready in about: 15 minutes | **Serves:** 4 | **Per serving:** Calories 251; Carbs 3g; Fat 5g; Protein 45g

INGREDIENTS

4 Cod Fillets about 7-ounce each
2 cups Tomatoes, chopped
1 cup Water

1 tbsp Olive Oil
Salt and Pepper, to taste
¼ tsp Garlic Powder

DIRECTIONS

Place the tomatoes in a baking dish and crush them with a fork. Sprinkle with salt, pepper, and garlic powder. Season the cod with salt and pepper and place it over the tomatoes.

Drizzle the olive oil over the fish and tomatoes. Place the dish in your Pressure cooker. Seal the lid and set on STEAM for 5 minutes at High pressure. When ready, release naturally, for 5 minutes.

Squid and Peas

Ready in about: 30 minutes | **Serves:** 4 | **Per serving:** Calories 177; Carbs 18g; Fat 2g; Protein 22g

INGREDIENTS

1 pound Squid, cleaned and chopped
1 pound Green Peas
1 Onion, chopped
½ pound canned Tomatoes

1 tbsp White Wine
Salt and Black Pepper, to taste
Cooking Spray, to grease
Water, as needed

DIRECTIONS

Coat the pressure cooker with cooking spray and cook the onions for 3 minutes, until soft.

Add squid and cook for another 3 minutes, stirring occasionally. Add in the remaining ingredients, and give it a good stir. Add water, enough to cover everything, and seal the lid.

Cook at High pressure for 20 minutes. Once ready, do a natural pressure release, for 10 minutes.

Glazed Orange Salmon

Ready in about: 25 minutes | **Serves:** 4 | **Per serving:** Calories 449; Carbs 4g; Fat 17g; Protein 65g

INGREDIENTS

4 Salmon Filets
2 tsp Orange Zest
3 tbsp Orange Juice
1 tbsp Olive Oil

1 tsp Ginger, minced
1 cup White Wine
Salt and Pepper, to taste

DIRECTIONS

Whisk in everything, except the salmon, in the pressure cooker. Then, add salmon and seal the lid. Cook on STEAM and cook for 7 minutes at High pressure. When ready, release the pressure quickly.

Scallops and Mussels Cauliflower Paella

Ready in about: 17 minutes | **Serves:** 4 | **Per serving:** Calories 155; Carbs 11g; Fat 4g; Protein 7g

INGREDIENTS

2 Bell Peppers, diced
1 tbsp Coconut Oil
1 cup Scallops
2 cups Mussels

1 Onion, diced
2 cups ground Cauliflower
2 cups Fish Stock
A pinch of Saffron

DIRECTIONS

Melt the coconut oil, add onions and bell peppers and cook for about 4 minutes, on SAUTÉ. Stir in scallops and saffron and cook for another 2 minutes. Add in the remaining ingredients.

Seal the lid, and set to STEAM mode for 15 minutes at High. When ready, do a quick release.

Snacks and Appetizers

Chili Hash Browns

Ready in about: 20 minutes | **Serves:** 4 | **Per serving:** Calories 161; Carbs 18g; Fat 8g; Protein 2g

INGREDIENTS

1 pound Potatoes, peeled and grated
1 tsp Chili Powder
¼ tsp Smoked Paprika
¼ tsp Black Pepper
½ tsp Sea Salt
1 ½ tbsp Olive Oil

DIRECTIONS

Heat the oil on SAUTÉ mode, and add the potatoes. Season with spices and stir to combine. Press them with a spatula and cook for about 5 minutes.

Flip over, and cook for 5 more minutes. Divide the hash browns between 4 plates, to serve

Cheese and Prosciutto Eggs

Ready in about: 10 minutes | **Serves:** 4 | **Per serving:** Calories 457; Carbs 5g; Fat 34g; Protein 31g

INGREDIENTS

8 Eggs
8 Prosciutto Slices
4 Swiss Cheese Slices
4 tbsp Spring Onions, chopped
2 tbsp Parsley, chopped
2 tbsp Butter
1 ½ cups Water

DIRECTIONS

Pour 1 ½ cups water in the pressure cooker and lower the trivet. Coat 4 ramekins with butter. Break 2 eggs into each ramekin and top with the spring onions.

Place 2 prosciutto slice over the onions and top with ½ slice of cheese. Sprinkle with parsley. Cover the ramekins with foil and place them in the pressure cooker.

Seal the lid and cook for 8 minutes on RICE, at High. Use a natural release, for 10 minutes, and serve

Porcini and Sesame Dip

Ready in about: 15 minutes | **Serves:** 8 | **Per serving:** Calories 195; Carbs 19g; Fat 8g; Protein 5g

INGREDIENTS

2 pounds Porcini Mushrooms, sliced
2 tbsp Sesame Paste
3 tbsp Sesame Seeds
1 tbsp Lemon Juice
2 tsp Garlic, minced
2 tbsp Olive Oil
1 cup Water

DIRECTIONS

Heat the oil on SAUTÉ mode. Add the garlic and mushrooms and cook for a minute. Pour in the water and seal the lid. Set on PRESSURE COOK for 4 minutes at High. Do a quick pressure release.

Drain the mushrooms and garlic. Transfer to a food processor. Add the lemon juice, olive oil, salt, pepper, and sesame paste. Process until smooth, and stir in the sesame seeds. Serve and enjoy!

Nutty Carrot Sticks

Ready in about: 15 minutes | **Serves:** 8 | **Per serving:** Calories 163; Carbs 17g; Fat 10g; Protein 2g

INGREDIENTS

¼ cup Olive Oil
3 ½ cups Water
3 pounds Carrots, peeled and cut into matchsticks
¼ cup chopped Nuts by choice

2 tbsp Balsamic Vinegar
1 tbsp Orange Juice
2 tsp Lemon Juice
½ tsp Onion Powder

DIRECTIONS

Combine the water and carrots in your pressure cooker. Seal the lid, select PRESSURE COOK, and set the timer to 5 minutes at High. When it goes off, do a quick pressure release.

Drain the carrots and place in a bowl. Whisk together vinegar, orange juice, lemon juice, onion powder, and olive oil. Pour mixture over the carrots and toss to coat well. Sprinkle over the nuts, to serve.

Lemony Cippolini Onions

Ready in about: 15 minutes | **Serves:** 6 | **Per serving:** Calories 130; Carbs 21g; Fat 1g; Protein 3g

INGREDIENTS

1 ½ pounds Cipppolini Onions, peeled
2 tbsp Lemon Juice
3 tbsp Olive Oil
½ tsp Rosemary, chopped

2 Bay Leaves
1 cup Water
1 tsp Lemon Zest
Salt and Pepper, to taste

DIRECTIONS

Combine water, onions, and bay leaves in your pressure cooker. Seal the lid, press PRESSURE COOK, and set the timer to 6 minutes at High. When it goes off, do a quick release.

Drain the onions and transfer to a cutting board. Cut into quarters. Whisk together the remaining ingredients and pour over the onions.

Party Duck Bites

Ready in about: 30 minutes | **Serves:** 6 | **Per serving:** Calories 400; Carbs 5g; Fat 23g; Protein 31g

INGREDIENTS

1 ½ pounds Duck Legs
½ cup Maple Syrup
½ cup Tomato Puree

1 ½ cups Water
2 tsp Basil
Salt and Pepper, to taste

SAUCE:

½ cup Sour Cream
½ cup chopped Parsley
¼ cup Olive Oil

2 tbsp Lemon Juice
2 Jalapeños, chopped
1 Garlic Clove

DIRECTIONS

Pour the water in the pressure cooker and place the duck a baking pan. In a bowl combine all of the duck ingredients and pour over the meat. Put the baking pan on the inserted rack. Seal the lid.

Cook on MEAT/STEW for 20 minutes at High. Release the pressure naturally, for 10 minutes. Pulse all sauce ingredients in a food processor and transfer to a serving bowl. Serve duck bites with the sauce.

Pico de Gallo with Carrots

Ready in about: 70 minutes | **Serves:** 4 | **Per serving:** Calories 85; Carbs 12g; Fat 4g; Protein 2g

INGREDIENTS

1 cup Onions, chopped
1 cup Carrots, chopped
2 cups Tomatoes, chopped
½ cup Bell Peppers, chopped
2 tbsp Cilantro, chopped
1 tsp Garlic, minced

¼ cup Lime Juice
½ cup Water
1 Jalapeño, deseed and minced
1 tbsp Olive Oil
½ tsp Sea Salt
¼ tsp Black Pepper

DIRECTIONS

Heat oil on SAUTÉ, add onions, peppers, and carrots, and cook for 4 minutes. Add the tomatoes and cook for 3 minutes. Stir in the garlic and sauté for another minute.

Transfer to a bowl and let cool for about 15 minutes. Stir in the remaining ingredients. Cover the bowl with a plastic wrap and refrigerate for about 45 minutes before serving.

Christmas Egg Custard

Ready in about: 20 minutes | **Serves:** 4 | **Per serving:** Calories 314; Carbs 17g; Fat 25g; Protein 6g

INGREDIENTS

1 Egg plus 2 Yolks
1 ½ cups Milk
2 cups Heavy Cream
½ tsp Rum Extract

¾ cup Sugar
1 tsp Anise Seeds
1 ½ cups Water

DIRECTIONS

Beat eggs and yolks in a bowl. Beat in the milk, rum, and heavy cream. Whisk in star anise and sugar. Divide the mixture between 4 ramekins. Pour 1½ cups of water in the cooker.

Place the ramekins inside onto an inserted trivet. Seal the lid and cook for 10 minutes at High pressure. Once cooking is complete, release the pressure naturally, for 5 minutes, and serve.

Paprika Potato Slices

Ready in about: 15 minutes | **Serves:** 4 | **Per serving:** Calories 183; Carbs 29g; Fat 7g; Protein 3g

INGREDIENTS

4 Potatoes, peeled and sliced
½ tsp Smoked Paprika
Salt and Pepper, to taste

1 tbsp Olive Oil
Water, as needed

DIRECTIONS

Place the potato slices in the pressure cooker and pour enough water to cover them. Seal the lid, select PRESSURE COOK and set the timer to 2 minutes at High pressure. Release the pressure quickly.

Drain the potatoes and discard the water. Transfer the potatoes to a bowl. Wipe clean the cooker. Press SAUTÉ, and add heat oil. Sprinkle the potatoes with paprika, salt, and pepper, and toss to combine.

Be careful not to break them. When the oil is hot, add the potatoes and cook for about a minute per side.

Buttery Beets

Ready in about: 30 minutes | **Serves:** 4 | **Per serving:** Calories 185; Carbs 19g; Fat 11g; Protein 3g

INGREDIENTS

1 tbsp Olive Oil
1 pound Beets, peeled and sliced
½ tsp Garlic Salt
4 tbsp Butter, melted
1 tsp dried Basil
1 cup Chicken Broth

DIRECTIONS

Add the beets and pour broth in your pressure cooker. Seal the lid and cook on BEANS/CHILI mode for 25 minutes at High. When ready, do a quick pressure release.

Drain the liquid and drizzle the beets with olive oil. Cook for 5 minutes, on SAUTÉ, lid off. Stir in garlic salt and basil, and cook for 2 more minutes. Serve drizzled with the melted butter.

Ricotta and Cheddar Veggie Appetizer

Ready in about: 30 minutes | **Serves:** 6 | **Per serving:** Calories 259; Carbs 22g; Fat 15g; Protein 10g

INGREDIENTS

1 cup Cheddar Cheese, grated
½ cup Ricotta Cheese
1 ½ pounds Potatoes, diced
1 cup Broccoli Florets
½ cup Carrots, chopped
¾ tsp Paprika
½ tsp Cumin Powder
2 cups Water
2 tbsp Oil
1 tsp Salt

DIRECTIONS

Combine the water, potatoes, carrots, and broccoli, in your pressure cooker. Seal the lid and cook on MEAT/STEW mode for 20 minutes at High. Release the pressure quickly.

Drain the veggies and place in a food processor. Add the remaining ingredients and process until smooth. Chill until ready to serve.

Appetizer Meatballs

Ready in about: 25 minutes | **Serves:** 8 | **Per serving:** Calories 202; Carbs 10g; Fat 15g; Protein 11g

INGREDIENTS

½ pound Ground Pork
½ pound Ground Beef
½ cup Grape Jelly
1 tbsp Mustard
1 cup diced Onions
2/3 cup Breadcrumbs
1 ½ tbsp Cornstarch
¼ cup Sugar
¼ cup Chili Sauce
Salt and Pepper, to taste
1 ½ cups Water

DIRECTIONS

Combine meat, breadcrumbs, and onion in a large bowl. Season with salt and pepper.

Form small meatballs out of the mixture. Coat the pressure cooker with cooking spray and cook the meatballs on SAUTÉ, until lightly browned. Transfer to a plate.

Whisk together the remaining ingredients in the pressure cooker. Seal the lid and cook on PRESSURE COOK, at High, for 17 minutes. Release the pressure naturally, for 10 minutes.

Southern Chicken Dip

Ready in about: 30 minutes | **Serves:** 12 | **Per serving:** Calories 188; Carbs 5g; Fat 13g; Protein 12g

INGREDIENTS

1 pound Chicken Breasts, cut into cubes
3 Bacon Slices, chopped
1 cup Cheddar Cheese, shredded
½ cup Sour Cream
½ cup Salsa
1 Onion, diced
¼ cup Ketchup
½ cup Cilantro, minced

2 tbsp Olive Oil
½ cup Chicken Broth
3 Garlic Cloves
½ tsp Onion Powder
1 tbsp Flour
½ tsp Cumin
½ tsp Cayenne Pepper
1 tsp Chili Powder

DIRECTIONS

Heat oil and brown the bacon in your cooker on SAUTÉ. Add onions, cilantro, and garlic. Cook for 3 minutes, until translucent and fragrant. Stir in the chicken, salsa, broth, and spices.

Seal the lid and cook for 20 minutes on MEAT/STEW at High. When ready, quick release the pressure. Whisk in flour and cook for a few more minutes, until thickened, lid off, on SAUTÉ.

Transfer to a food processor, and add cheddar and sour cream. Pulse until smooth. Serve with crackers.

Potato and Bacon Snack

Ready in about: 25 minutes | **Serves:** 4 | **Per serving:** Calories 214; Carbs 21g; Fat 12g; Protein 7g

INGREDIENTS

1 pound Potatoes
4 Bacon Slices, chopped
1 tsp Garlic Salt
¼ tsp Pepper

4 tbsp Sour Cream
¼ cup Chicken Broth
1 ½ cups Water

DIRECTIONS

Combine the water and potatoes in the pressure cooker. Seal the lid and cook on POULTRY mode for 15 minutes at High. When ready, do a quick pressure release and drain the potatoes.

Dice the potatoes and transfer them to a bowl. In the pressure cooker, add the bacon slices and cook until crisp on SAUTÉ, lid off. Remove bacon to the potatoes bowl and stir to combine.

In a separate bowl, whisk together cream, broth, and spices. Drizzle the potatoes to serve.

Spicy Homemade Peanuts

Ready in about: 50 minutes | **Serves:** 16 | **Per serving:** Calories 211; Carbs 15g; Fat 13g; Protein 11g

INGREDIENTS

2 ¼ cups Peanuts, raw
1 tsp Chili Powder
¼ cup Sea Salt

½ tsp Garlic Powder
4 quarts Water

DIRECTIONS

Place peanuts in your pressure cooker, and pour in water. Seal the lid and cook on PRESSURE COOK for 40 minutes at High. Do a quick release. Sprinkle with spices and discard any remaining liquid, to serve.

Mini Beefy Cabbage Rolls

Ready in about: 35 minutes | **Serves:** 15 | **Per serving:** Calories 185; Carbs 17g; Fat 8g; Protein 11g

INGREDIENTS

1 Cabbage, leaves separated
1 pound Ground Beef
1 Red Bell Pepper, chopped
1 cup Rice
1 cup Beef Broth
3 cups Water

2 tbsp Lemon Juice
1 Onion, diced
½ cup Olive Oil
1 tsp Fennel Seeds
Salt and Pepper, to taste

DIRECTIONS

Pour 1 cup of water and place the cabbage leaves in the pressure cooker. Seal the lid and cook on STEAM mode for 3 minutes, at High. When ready, release the pressure quickly.

Remove the leaves to an ice bath, to cool. In a bowl, combine the remaining ingredients, except water and broth. Divide this mixture between the cabbage leaves.

Roll them up and return them to the pressure cooker. Pour in water and broth. Seal the lid and cook for 15 minutes at High pressure. Do a quick release. Serve with yogurt optional.

Buttery Potato Sticks

Ready in about: 20 minutes | **Serves:** 6 | **Per serving:** Calories 130; Carbs 27g; Fat 1g; Protein 3g

INGREDIENTS

2 pounds Potatoes, cut into sticks
1 tsp Salt
½ tsp Paprika

¼ tsp Pepper
1 ½ cups Water
1 tbsp Butter, melted

DIRECTIONS

Place all ingredients, except butter, in your ´pressure cooker. Seal the lid and cook for 10 minutes on PRESSURE COOK, at High. Release the pressure quickly. Drain the liquid and drizzle with butter.

Salmon Bites

Ready in about: 15 minutes | **Serves:** 4 | **Per serving:** Calories 327; Carbs 12g; Fat 18g; Protein 25g

INGREDIENTS

1 can Salmon, flaked
1 Spring Onion, minced
1 cup Breadcrumbs
½ cup Cream Cheese
1 tbsp Parsley, chopped

¼ tsp Salt
¼ tsp Black Pepper
1 tbsp Butter
½ cup Tomato Sauce
1 cup Water

DIRECTIONS

Combine the first 7 ingredients in a bowl. Mix well with hands and make 4 balls out of the mixture. Melt the butter in the Pressure cooker on SAUTÉ mode.

Add the balls and cook until golden on all sides, for about 3 – 5 minutes, lid off. Remove to a baking dish, that fits in your pressure cooker, and pour the tomato sauce over.

Pour the water in and lower the trivet. Place baking dish on top of the trivet, inside the cooker. Seal the lid, and cook for 5 minutes at High. Use a naturally pressure release, for 10 minutes.

Agave Carrot Sticks

Ready in about: 10 minutes | **Serves:** 4 | **Per serving:** Calories 145; Carbs 16g; Fat 8g; Protein 2g

INGREDIENTS

1 pound Carrots, sliced into sticks
½ Stick Butter, melted
2 tbsp Agave Nectar

2 cups Water
½ tsp Cinnamon
A pinch of Salt

DIRECTIONS

Place the carrot sticks in your pressure cooker. Pour in the water. Seal the lid and cook on STEAM mode for 5 minutes at High. When ready, release the pressure quickly.

Whisk together the remaining ingredients and coat the carrots with this mixture, and serve.

Cheesy Fingerling Potato Rounds

Ready in about: 20 minutes | **Serves:** 4 | **Per serving:** Calories 331; Carbs 30g; Fat 18g; Protein 13g

INGREDIENTS

1 ½ pounds Fingerling Potatoes, sliced
1 cup Gorgonzola Cheese, crumbled
4 tbsp Butter

½ cup Vegetable Broth
½ tsp Cayenne Pepper
½ tsp Salt

DIRECTIONS

Melt butter on SAUTÉ mode, and add the potato slices, broth, salt, and pepper. Seal the lid and cook for 10 minutes at High pressure. When ready, do a quick pressure release.

Serve the potatoes immediately, topped with crumbled blue cheese.

Kale Hummus

Ready in about: 25 minutes | **Serves:** 10 | **Per serving:** Calories 206; Carbs 27g; Fat 8g; Protein 10g

INGREDIENTS

2 cups Chickpeas
2 cups Kale, chopped
3 tbsp Tahini
1 cup Green Onions, minced

4 ½ cups Water
½ tsp Salt
¼ tsp Pepper
2 tbsp Olive Oil

DIRECTIONS

Combine the chickpeas and water in your pressure cooker. Seal the lid and cook on BEANS/CHILI mode for 25 minutes at High pressure. When ready, release the pressure quickly.

Drain the chickpeas and place in a food processor. Add the remaining ingredients. Blend until smooth.

Balsamic Carrots

Ready in about: 15 minutes | **Serves:** 4 | **Per serving:** Calories 185; Carbs 12g; Fat 11g; Protein 2g

INGREDIENTS

1 pound Baby Carrots
3 tbsp Balsamic Vinegar
½ tsp Pepper
3 tbsp Thyme, chopped
½ tsp Sea Salt

¼ cup Olive Oil
1 tbsp Sunflower Seeds, chopped
Water, as needed

DIRECTIONS

Place the carrots inside the pressure cooker, and add water to cover them. Seal the lid, select PRESSURE COOK, and set the timer to 8 minutes at High pressure. When ready, release the pressure quickly.

Drain the carrots, and place in a bowl. Discard water from the cooker, and wipe clean. Set on SAUTÉ and add in the carrots. Add the rest of the ingredients and toss to coat well. Cook for about 3 minutes.

Tahini, Carrot, and Spinach "Hummus"

Ready in about: 15 minutes | **Serves:** 6 | **Per serving:** Calories 173; Carbs 17g; Fat 6g; Protein 4g

INGREDIENTS

3 cups chopped Carrots
3 tbsp Tahini
2 cups chopped Spinach
1 Garlic Clove, crushed

2 tbsp Lemon Juice
2 tbsp Olive Oil
2 cups Water
Salt and Pepper, to taste

DIRECTIONS

Combine carrots and water in the cooker. Seal the lid, select PRESSURE COOK, and set the timer to 4 minutes at High pressure. When it goes off, release the pressure quickly, and drain the carrots.

Transfer to a food processor. Add the remaining ingredients, and pulse until smooth and creamy.

Colby Cheese and Pancetta Frittata

Ready in about: 30 minutes | **Serves:** 4 | **Per serving:** Calories 325; Carbs 4g; Fat 24g; Protein 22g

INGREDIENTS

6 Eggs, beaten
½ cup grated Colby Cheese
6 Pancetta Slices, cooked and crumbled
3 tbsp Sour Cream

½ tsp Onion Powder
2 tsp Butter, melted
¼ tsp Pepper
1 ½ cups Water

DIRECTIONS

Pour the water in your pressure cooker and lower the trivet. Whisk the remaining ingredients in a baking dish. Place the dish on top of the trivet, inside the cooker.

Seal the lid and cook on MEAT/STEW for 20 minutes at High. Release the pressure quickly, and serve.

Eggs de Provence

Ready in about: 20 minutes | **Serves:** 8 | **Per serving:** Calories 331; Carbs 3g; Fat 29g; Protein 10g

INGREDIENTS

8 Eggs
1 cup Heavy Cream
2 Shallots, chopped
1 cup Bacon de Provence, cooked and crumbled

1 ½ cups chopped Kale
1 tbsp Herbs de Provence
Salt and Black Pepper, to taste
1 ½ cups + 4 tbsp Water

DIRECTIONS

Whisk the eggs with water and cream in a baking dish. Stir in shallots, bacon, kale, and herbs. Season with salt and pepper. Cover with a piece of foil. Pour 1 ½ cups of water in the pressure cooker.

Lower the trivet, and place the dish on top. Seal the lid and cook on RICE for 15 minutes at High. When ready, do a quick release.

Pressure Cooked Eggplant Dip

Ready in about: 20 minutes | **Serves:** 8 | **Per serving:** Calories 84; Carbs 9g; Fat 5g; Protein 2g

INGREDIENTS

2 Eggplants, diced
1 cup Water
¼ cup chopped Cilantro
2 Garlic Cloves

1 ½ tbsp Sesame Paste
2 tbsp Olive Oil
½ tsp Pepper
½ tsp Salt

DIRECTIONS

Add water and eggplants in your cooker. Seal the lid, set on STEAM for 10 minutes at High. Release the pressure quickly. Drain and transfer the drained eggplants to a food processor. Add the remaining ingredients, and process until smooth.

Garlicky Pepper and Tomato Appetizer

Ready in about: 15 minutes | **Serves:** 4 | **Per serving:** Calories 123; Carbs 12g; Fat 7g; Protein 3g

INGREDIENTS

1 pounds Bell Peppers, cut into strips
2 Large Tomatoes, chopped
1 cup Tomato Sauce
½ cup Chicken Broth

1 tbsp Garlic, minced
2 tbsp chopped Parsley
1 tbsp Olive Oil
Salt and Pepper

DIRECTIONS

Heat oil on SAUTÉ, add the peppers and cook for 2-3 minutes. Add garlic and sauté for 1 minute. Stir in the remaining ingredients, and seal the lid. Cook at High pressure for 6 minutes. Do a quick release.

Spicy Sweet Potato Cubes

Ready in about: 15 minutes | **Serves:** 6 | **Per serving:** Calories 191; Carbs 38g; Fat 3g; Protein 4g

INGREDIENTS

6 Large Sweet Potatoes, cubed
2 tbsp Butter, melted
1 tsp Chili Powder
¼ tsp Black Pepper
½ tsp Salt

¼ tsp Cayenne Pepper
¼ tsp Turmeric Powder
1 tbsp freshly Parmesan Cheese, grated
1 ½ cups Water

DIRECTIONS

Pour the water in your pressure cooker. Place the potatoes in the steamer basket. Seal the lid and cook on PRESSURE COOK for 10 minutes at High. When ready, do a quick release. Sprinkle the potatoes with spices, drizzle with butter, and top with grated parmesan.

Pea and Avocado Dip

Ready in about: 25 minutes | **Serves:** 4 | **Per serving:** Calories 123; Carbs 15g; Fat 8g; Protein 5g

INGREDIENTS

1 ½ cups dried Green Peas
1 tbsp Lime Juice
1 Avocado, peeled and deseeded

¼ tsp Pepper
1 Garlic Clove, peeled
2 cups Water

DIRECTIONS

Combine the water and peas in the pressure cooker. Seal the lid and turn clockwise to seal. Select the PRESSURE COOK mode, set the timer to 16 minutes at High pressure.

When the timer goes off, release the pressure quickly. Drain the peas and transfer them to a food processor. Add the remaining ingredients, and pulse until smooth and creamy.

Turmeric Potato Sticks

Ready in about: 15 minutes | Serve: 1 | **Per serving:** Calories 140; Carbs 16g; Fat 4g; Protein 1g

INGREDIENTS

1 Potato, peeled and cut into sticks
1 tbsp Olive Oil
¼ tsp Pepper
¼ tsp Sea Salt
1 tsp Turmeric
1 ½ cups Water

DIRECTIONS

Combine water and potato sticks in the pressure cooker. Seal the lid, press PRESSURE COOK and set the timer to 5 minutes at High. When ready, do a quick pressure release. Drain the potatoes.

Discard the water, and wipe the cooker clean. Set to SAUTÉ and heat the oil. When hot, add potato sticks and sprinkle with turmeric, salt, and pepper. Sauté for 5 minutes, flipping once. Serve and enjoy!

Three-Cheese Small Macaroni Cups

Ready in about: 15 minutes | **Serves:** 8 | **Per serving:** Calories 224; Carbs 25g; Fat 9g; Protein 11g

INGREDIENTS

½ pound Elbow Macaroni
2 cups Water
4 ounces Cheddar Cheese, shredded
4 ounces Monterey Jack Cheese, shredded
¼ cup Parmesan Cheese, shredded
2 tbsp Butter
½ can Evaporated Milk
Salt and Black Pepper, to taste

DIRECTIONS

Add the water, butter, macaroni, salt, and pepper, in the cooker. Seal the lid and cook for 8 minutes on RICE mode at High. When ready, do a quick pressure release and stir in milk and cheeses. Seal the lid again, and cook for a minute at High. When done, do a quick pressure release. Divide between 8 cups.

Turnip and Sultana Dip with Pecans

Ready in about: 10 minutes | **Serves:** 4 | **Per serving:** Calories 273; Carbs 45g; Fat 10g; Protein 5g

INGREDIENTS

1 cup Water
2 pounds Turnips, peeled and chopped
½ cup Sultanas
1 tbsp Vinegar
1 tbsp Olive Oil
¼ tsp Sea Salt
¼ tsp Black Pepper

DIRECTIONS

Heat oil on SAUTÉ, and cook turnips, until softened, for about 3 minutes. Stir in sultanas and water. Seal the lid, select the PRESSURE COOK mode for 2 minutes at High pressure. Do a quick release.

Drain turnips and sultanas, and place in a food processor. Add some of the cooking water in, to make it creamier. Add vinegar, salt, and pepper, and pulse until smooth. Serve topped with chopped pecans.

Blue Cheese and Bacon Polenta Squares

Ready in about: 80 minutes | **Serves:** 6 | **Per serving:** Calories 271; Carbs 19g; Fat 17g; Protein 11g

INGREDIENTS

2 cups Polenta
6 Bacon Slices, cooked and crumbles
1 Onion, chopped
2 ounces Blue Cheese, crumbled
2 tsp Rosemary
1 tsp Thyme
4 cups Beef Stock
1 tbsp Oil
½ tsp Garlic, minced
Salt and Black Pepper, to taste

DIRECTIONS

Heat oil and cook the onions until soft, on SAUTÉ mode. Add garlic and cook for another minute, until fragrant. Stir in thyme, rosemary, stock, polenta. Season with salt and pepper.

Seal the lid and cook for 10 minutes at High pressure. Release the pressure quickly. Stir in the cheese and bacon. Place in a lined baking pan and refrigerate for 1 hour. Cut into squares to serve.

Barbecue Wings

Ready in about: 15 minutes | **Serves:** 4 | **Per serving:** Calories 140; Carbs 2g; Fat 3g; Protein 19g

INGREDIENTS

12 Chicken Wings
¼ cup Barbecue Sauce
1 cup of Water

DIRECTIONS

Place chicken wings and water in your pressure cooker. Seal the lid. Cook for 5 minutes on PRESSURE COOK at High. When ready, do a quick release. Rinse under cold water and pat wings dry.

Remove the liquid from the pot. Return the wings to the pressure cooker and pour in barbecue sauce. Mix with hands to coat them well. Cook on SAUTÉ, lid off, on all sides, until sticky. Serve hot.

Chili Sriracha Eggs

Ready in about: 20 minutes | **Serves:** 6 | **Per serving:** Calories 156; Carbs 3g; Fat 11g; Protein 10g

INGREDIENTS

6 Eggs
½ tsp Chili Powder
1 ½ tbsp Sour Cream
1 tbsp Mayonnaise
A pinch of Black Pepper
1 tsp Sriracha
1 tbsp grated Parmesan Cheese
2 cups Water, enough to cover the Eggs

DIRECTIONS

Combine the eggs and water in the pressure cooker. Seal the lid and cook on RICE for 8 minutes at High. Do a quick pressure release, and remove eggs to cold water, let cool for a few minutes, and peel.

Meanwhile, in a bowl, whisk together the sour cream, mayonnaise, black pepper, chili powder, and sriracha. Cut the eggs in half and top with the mixture. To serve, sprinkle with Parmesan cheese.

Salty and Peppery Potato Snack

Ready in about: 20 minutes | **Serves:** 6 | **Per serving:** Calories 213; Carbs 43g; Fat 5g; Protein 3g

INGREDIENTS

2 pounds Potatoes
1 tsp Sea Salt
1 tsp Pepper
2 tbsp Olive Oil
1 ½ cups Water

DIRECTIONS

Pour water in the cooker and lower the trivet. Wash and peel the potatoes, and place each of them on a piece of aluminum foil. Season with salt and pepper, and drizzle with olive oil.

Wrap them in foil and place the wraps on top of the trivet. Seal the lid, select PRESSURE COOK mode and set the timer to 11 minutes at High pressure. After the beep, do a quick pressure release.

Place the potatoes on your kitchen counter. Unwrap gently, chop or slice them to your liking, and enjoy.

Jalapeno and Pineapple Salsa

Ready in about: 65 minutes | **Serves:** 6 | **Per serving:** Calories 41; Carbs 8g; Fat 1g; Protein 0

INGREDIENTS

1 cup Red Onions, diced
2 cups Pineapple, diced
¼ cup Cilantro, chopped
3 Jalapenos, minced
¼ tsp Garlic Powder
2 tbsp Lime Juice
¼ tsp Sea Salt
1 tbsp Olive Oil

DIRECTIONS

Heat oil on SAUTÉ, add the onions and cook until softened, for about 3 minutes. Then, stir in jalapenos, pineapple, and garlic powder, and cook just for 1-2 minutes. Transfer to a bowl.

In a small bowl, whisk together lime juice, pepper, and salt. Pour over the pineapples and coat to combine. Stir in the cilantro. Let sit at room temperature for about 15 minutes.

Cover the bowl with a plastic wrap. Refrigerate for 45 minutes before serving.

Breakfast & Brunch Recipes

Poached Eggs with Feta and Tomatoes

Ready in about: 10 minutes | **Serves:** 4 | **Per serving:** Calories 125; Carbs 8g; Fat 7g; Protein 6g

INGREDIENTS

4 large Eggs
2 cups Water
2 large Cherry Tomatoes, halved crosswise
Salt and Black Pepper to taste

1 tsp chopped Fresh Herbs, of your choice
½ cup Feta cheese, crumbled
4 slices toasted Bread

DIRECTIONS

Pour the water in and fit a trivet at the center of the pot. Grease the ramekins with the cooking spray and crack each egg into them. Place the ramekins on the trivet. Seal the lid, and select STEAM mode for 3 minutes at High.

Do a quick pressure release. Remove ramekins onto a flat surface. In serving plates, toss the eggs in the ramekin over on each bread slice, top with the feta cheese and cherry tomatoes, and garnish with chopped herbs.

Classic Sunday Big Pancakes

Ready in about: 30 minutes | **Serves:** 6 | **Per serving:** Calories 432; Carbs 58g; Fat 16g; Protein 11g

INGREDIENTS

3 cups All-purpose Flour
¾ cup Sugar
5 Eggs
¼ cup Olive Oil

¼ cup Sparkling Water
¼ tsp Salt
1 ½ tsp Baking Soda

To Serve:
2 tbsp Maple Syrup

A dollop of Whipped Cream

DIRECTIONS

Start by pouring the flour, sugar, eggs, olive oil, sparkling water, salt, and baking soda into the food processor and blend them until smooth. Pour the batter in the pressure cooker, and let it sit in there for 15 minutes.

Seal the lid, and select MANUAL mode at Low pressure for 15 minutes. Once the timer goes off, quick-release the pressure. Stick in a toothpick, and once it comes out clean, the pancake is done.

Gently run a spatula around the pancake to let loose any sticking. Then, slide the pancakes into a serving plate. Top with the whipped cream and drizzle the maple syrup over it to serve.

Easy Softboiled Eggs

Ready in about: 10 minutes | **Serves:** 8 | **Per serving:** Calories 130; Carbs 1g; Fat 9g; Protein 9g

INGREDIENTS

8 Eggs

1 cup of Water

DIRECTIONS

Pour the water into the pressure cooker and add in the eggs. Seal the lid, and cook on EGG mode for 4 minutes at High pressure. When ready, do a quick pressure release by moving the handle from Prepare an ice bath and drop the eggs in, to ease the peeling.

Sweet Potato & Carrot Egg Casserole

Ready in about: 15 minutes | **Serves:** 4 | **Per serving:** Calories 220; Carbs 17g; Fat 7g; Protein 6g

INGREDIENTS

8 Eggs
½ cup Milk
2 cups Sweet Potatoes, shredded
1 cup Carrots, shredded
½ tbsp Olive Oil

½ tsp dried Parsley
¼ tsp Pepper
¼ tsp Paprika
¼ tsp Garlic Powder

DIRECTIONS

Heat the olive oil on SAUTÉ mode. When hot and sizzling, add the carrots and sweet potatoes. Add the herbs and spices, stir well to combine, and cook the veggies for about 2-3 minutes.

Meanwhile, beat together the eggs and almond milk in a bowl. Pour the mixture over the carrots and stir to incorporate well. Seal the lid, hit PRESSURE COOK for 7 minutes at High.

When ready, do a quick pressure release and open the lid carefully. Serve and enjoy!

Whole Hog Omelet

Ready in about: 40 minutes | **Serves:** 6 | **Per serving:** Calories 489; Carbs 38g; Fat 2g; Protein 32g

INGREDIENTS

6 Eggs, beaten
1 cup Cheddar Cheese, shredded
½ cup Ham, diced
1 cup ground Sausage
4 Bacon Slices, cooked and crumbled

½ cup Milk
2 Green Onions, chopped
Salt and Pepper, to taste
1 ½ cups Water

DIRECTIONS

Whisk all the ingredients together, in a bowl. Transfer to a baking dish. Pour 1 ½ cups water in your pressure cooker and lower the trivet. Place the dish on top of the trivet.

Seal the lid and cook for 20 minutes on MEAT/STEW at High. When done, do a quick release.

Onion and Tomato Eggs

Ready in about: 20 minutes | **Serves:** 2 | **Per serving:** Calories 380; Carbs 13g; Fat 16g; Protein 15g

INGREDIENTS

4 Eggs
1 Tomato, chopped
1 Red Onion, diced
¼ tsp Garlic Powder

A pinch of Cayenne Pepper
A pinch of Black Pepper
1 ½ cups Water

DIRECTIONS

Pour the water into the pressure cooker and lower the trivet. Grease a baking dish with some cooking spray. Beat the eggs along with the garlic powder, cayenne, and black pepper.

Add tomatoes and onions; stir to combine. Pour the mixture into the greased baking dish. Place the baking dish on top of the trivet and seal the lid. Cook at High pressure for 8 minutes.

After the beep, do a quick pressure release. Remove the baking dish from the pot, and serve.

Cheesy Sausage and Egg Bundt Cake

Ready in about: 25 minutes | **Serves:** 6 | **Per serving:** Calories 381; Carbs 14g; Fat 26g; Protein 25g

INGREDIENTS

8 Eggs, cracked into a bowl
8 oz Breakfast Sausage, chopped
3 Bacon Slices, chopped
1 large Green Bell Pepper, chopped
1 large Red Bell Pepper, chopped
1 cup chopped Green Onion

1 cup grated Cheddar Cheese
1 tsp Red Chili Flakes
Salt and Black Pepper to taste
½ cup Milk
4 slices Bread, cut into ½-inch cubes
2 cups Water

DIRECTIONS

Whisk the eggs, sausage, bacon slices, green bell pepper, red bell pepper, green onion, chili flakes, cheddar cheese, salt, pepper, and milk in a bowl. Grease the bundt pan with cooking spray and pour in the egg mixture.

After, drop the bread slices in the egg mixture all around while using a spoon to push them into the mixture. Pour water in the cooker, and fit the trivet at the center of the pot. Place bundt pan on the trivet and seal the lid.

Select STEAM mode at High for 8 minutes. Once the timer goes off, do a quick pressure release. Use a napkin to gently remove the bundt pan onto a flat surface. Run a knife around the egg in the bundt pan, place a serving plate on the bundt pan, and then, turn the egg bundt over. Cut into slices, and serve with sauce of your choice.

Banana and Cinnamon French Toast

Ready in about: 50 minutes | **Serves:** 6 | **Per serving:** Calories 313; Carbs 39g; Fat 15g; Protein 8g

INGREDIENTS

1 ½ tsp Cinnamon
¼ tsp Vanilla Extract
6 Bread Slices, cubed
4 Bananas, sliced
2 tbsp Brown Sugar
1 tbsp White Sugar

½ cup Milk
¼ cup Pecans, chopped
3 Eggs
¼ cup Cream Cheese, softened
2 tbsp cold and sliced Butter
¾ cup Water

DIRECTIONS

Grease a baking dish and arrange half of the bread cubes. Top with half of the banana slices. Sprinkle with half of the brown sugar. Spread cream cheese over the bananas.

Arrange the rest of the bread cubes and banana slices on top. Sprinkle with brown sugar and top with pecans. Top with butter slices. In a bowl, whisk together eggs, white sugar, milk, cinnamon, and vanilla.

Pour the mixture into the baking dish. Place the trivet inside the cooker and pour the water. Lower the baking dish onto the trivet. Cook on MEAT/STEW for 30 minutes at High. Do a quick pressure release.

Carrot & Pecan Muffins

Ready in about: 30 minutes | **Serves:** 8 | **Per serving:** Calories 265; Carbs 6g; Fat 25g; Protein 6g

INGREDIENTS

¼ cup Coconut Oil
½ cup Milk
½ cup Pecans, chopped
1 tsp Apple Pie Spice
1 cup Carrots, shredded

3 Eggs
½ cup Pure & Organic Applesauce
1 cup ground Almonds
1 ½ cups Water

DIRECTIONS

Pour the water into the Pressure cooker and lower the trivet. Place the coconut oil, milk, eggs, applesauce, almonds, and apple pie spice, in a large mixing bowl.

Beat the mixture well with an electric mixer, until it becomes fluffy. Fold in the carrots and pecans. Pour the batter into 8 silicone muffin cups and arrange them on top of the trivet.

Seal the lid, and cook on PRESSURE COOK mode at High pressure for 15 minutes. When it goes off, do a quick pressure release. Remove the muffins, and wait for a few minutes before serving.

Pear-Coconut Porridge with Walnuts

Ready in about: 8 minutes | Serve: 1 | **Per serving:** Calories 568; Carbs 38g; Fat 48g; Protein 9g

INGREDIENTS

½ cup ground Walnuts
1 ounce Coconut Flakes

1 Pear, diced
½ cup Coconut Milk

DIRECTIONS

Place all ingredients in your pressure cooker and stir well to combine. Seal the lid, and cook on PRESSURE COOK for 3 minutes at High. Do a quick pressure release, and serve in a bowl.

Almond & Gala Apple Porridge

Ready in about: 8 minutes | Serve: 1 | **Per serving:** Calories 445; Carbs 40g; Fat 18g; Protein 4g

INGREDIENTS

½ cup Almond Milk
3 tbsp ground Almonds
1 Gala Apple, grated
1 tbsp Almond Butter

2 tbsp Flaxseed
A pinch of Cinnamon
¼ tsp Vanilla Extract

DIRECTIONS

Place all ingredients in your pressure cooker. Give the mixture a good stir to combine the ingredients well. Seal the lid, and cook on High pressure for 5 minutes. When ready, release the pressure quickly. Stir well and transfer the mixture to a serving bowl.

Eggs & Smoked Salmon

Ready in about: 8 minutes | Serves: 2 | **Per serving:** Calories 240; Carbs 2g; Fat 17g; Protein 19g

INGREDIENTS

2 slices Smoked Salmon
2 Eggs
1 tsp Cilantro, chopped

A pinch of Paprika
A pinch of Pepper
1 cup Water

DIRECTIONS

Pour the water into the pressure cooker and lower the trivet. Grease 4 ramekins with cooking spray or olive oil.

Place a slice of smoked salmon at the bottom of each ramekin. Crack an egg on top of the salmon. Season with pepper and paprika and sprinkle with the cilantro.

Arrange the ramekins on top of the trivet and seal the lid. Set at High pressure for 5 minutes. When the timer goes off, release the pressure quickly.

Bell Pepper & Onion Frittata

Ready in about: 15 minutes | **Serves:** 2 | **Per serving:** Calories 241; Carbs 6g; Fat 16g; Protein 15g

INGREDIENTS

3 Eggs
¼ cup Bell Pepper, diced
¼ cup Onion, diced
2 tbsp Milk

¼ tsp Garlic Powder
A pinch of Turmeric Powder
1 ½ cups Water

DIRECTIONS

Pour water into the pressure cooker and lower the trivet. Grease a small baking dish with cooking spray. In a bowl, beat eggs along with milk, turmeric, and garlic powder.

Add onions and bell peppers and stir well to combine. Pour the mixture into the greased baking dish and place it on top of the trivet. Seal the lid, select PRESSURE COOK and cook for 8 minutes at High. After the timer goes off, release the pressure quickly. Serve and enjoy!

Cheese and Thyme Cremini Oats

Ready in about: 20 minutes | **Serves:** 4 | **Per Serving:** Calories 266; Carbs 31g; Fat 12g; Protein 9g

INGREDIENTS

8 ounces Cremini Mushrooms, sliced
2 cups Chicken Broth
½ Onion, diced
2 tbsp Butter
1 cup Steel-Cut Oats

½ cup Cheddar Cheese, grated
2 sprigs Thyme
½ cup Water
1 Garlic Clove, minced
Salt and Pepper to taste

DIRECTIONS

On SAUTÉ mode, melt the butter and stir-fry onion and mushrooms for 3 minutes, until soft. Add garlic and cook for 1 minute. Stir in oats and cook for another minute.

Pour in water, broth, oats, and mix in thyme sprigs. Season with salt and pepper. Seal the lid, and set on PORRIDGE for 20 minutes. Quick release the pressure. Remove to serving bowls and sprinkle with grated cheddar to serve.

Kale, Tomato & Carrot Quiche

Ready in about: 30 minutes | **Serves:** 4 | **Per serving:** Calories 170; Carbs 7g; Fat 10g; Protein 13g

INGREDIENTS

1 Carrot, shredded
1 Tomato, chopped
½ cup Kale, chopped
¼ cup Milk
¼ Onion, diced
½ Bell Pepper, diced

1 tsp Basil
A pinch of Pepper
¼ tsp Paprika
8 Eggs
1 ½ cups Water

DIRECTIONS

Pour the water into your pressure cooker and lower the trivet. Place the eggs, milk, pepper, basil, and paprika, in a large bowl. Whisk until well combined and smooth. Add the veggies to the mixture and stir well to combine.

Grease a baking dish with some cooking spray and pour in the egg and veggie into it. Place the baking dish on top of the trivet. Seal the lid, and cook on High pressure for 20 minutes. Do a natural pressure release, for about 10 minutes. Remove quiche from the cooker, and serve!

Bacon and Colby Cheese Grits

Ready in about: 20 minutes | **Serves:** 4 | **Per serving:** Calories 280; Carbs 8g; Fat 21g; Protein 14g

INGREDIENTS

3 slices smoked Bacon, diced
1 ½ cups grated Gruyères Cheese
1 cup ground Grits
2 tsp Butter

Salt and Black Pepper
½ cup Water
½ cup Milk

DIRECTIONS

Select SAUTÉ at High and fry the bacon until crispy, for about 5 minutes. Set aside. Add the grits, butter, milk, water, salt, and pepper to the pot and stir using a spoon. Seal the lid and select MANUAL at High for 10 minutes.

Once the timer has ended, do a quick pressure release again. Immediately add the cheddar cheese and give the pudding a good stir. Dish the cheesy grits into serving bowls and spoon over the crisped bacon.

Herby Pork Breakfast Biscuits

Ready in about: 30 minutes | **Serves:** 8 | **Per serving:** Calories 445; Carbs 31g; Fat 22g; Protein 26g

INGREDIENTS

1 ½ pounds Ground Pork
8 Biscuits
¾ cup Apple Cider
1 ½ cups Milk
½ cup Flour
3 tsp Butter

½ cup Onions, chopped
1 tsp Garlic, minced
1 tsp Thyme
1 tsp Rosemary
Salt and Pepper, to taste

DIRECTIONS

Melt butter SAUTÉ mode, add the pork and cook until browned. Add onions and garlic and cook for another 1-2 minutes, until soft. Stir in the cider, thyme, and rosemary. Seal the lid and cook for 20 minutes on MEAT/STEW mode at High.

When ready, release the pressure quickly. Whisk together the flour and milk, and pour in over the pork. Seal the lid. Cook at High pressure for 5 minutes. Release the pressure quickly, and serve over biscuits.

Cheddar and Eggs Hash Bake

Ready in about: 10 minutes | **Serves:** 4 | **Per serving:** Calories 459; Carbs 42g; Fat 20g; Protein 27g

INGREDIENTS

6 small Potatoes, shredded
6 Large Eggs, beaten
½ cup Water

1 cup Cheddar Cheese, shredded
1 cup Ham, diced
Cooking spray, to grease

DIRECTIONS

Grease with some cooking spray the inner pot of your pressure cooker and set to SAUTÉ mode.

Add the shredded potatoes and cook until lightly browned, for 5-6 minutes. Pour in the water.

Meanwhile, in a bowl, mix the ham, cheese, and eggs, and add to the pressure cooker. Stir to combine well. Seal the lid and set to PRESSURE COOK for 10 minutes.

It will take a few minutes before pressure is built inside the cooker. Do a quick pressure release.

Cheesy Eggs in Hollandaise Sauce

Ready in about: 12 minutes | **Serves:** 4 | **Per Serving:** Calories 231; Carbs 9g; Fat 13g; Protein 15g

INGREDIENTS

4 Bread Slices, roughly chopped
4 Eggs
½ cup Arugula, chopped
4 slices Mozzarella Cheese
1 cup Water
1 ½ Ounces Hollandaise Sauce

DIRECTIONS

Place the steamer basket in the cooker and pour water. Divide the bread pieces in between 4 ramekins.

In a bowl, whisk the eggs and mix with arugula. Divide this mixture among the ramekins. Cover them with aluminum foil and place them in the steamer basket. Select PRESSURE COOK mode, and adjust the time to 8 minutes.

Lock the lid and turn the valve to close. It will take a few minutes before pressure is built inside the cooker. When cooking is over, do a quick pressure release. Remove the ramekins from the cooker and discard the foil. Top with a slice of mozzarella and some hollandaise sauce.

Egg and Beef Green Casserole

Ready in about: 40 minutes | **Serves:** 4 | **Per serving:** Calories 422; Carbs 13g; Fat 30g; Protein 24g

INGREDIENTS

8 ounces Ground Beef
6 Eggs, beaten
¾ cup Leeks, Sliced
¾ cup Kale, chopped
1 Sweet Potato, peeled and shredded
1 Garlic Clove, minced
1 tbsp Olive Oil
A pinch of Pepper
1 ½ cups Water
Cooking spray, to grease

DIRECTIONS

Grease a baking dish with cooking spray and set aside. Melt the oil on SAUTÉ. Add the leeks and cook for about 2 minutes. Add the garlic and cook for about 30 seconds.

Add the beef and cook for a few more minutes, until browned. Transfer to a bowl. Add the remaining ingredients and stir well to combine. Pour the water and lower the trivet.

Pour the egg and beef mixture into the greased baking dish and place on top of the trivet. Seal the lid, select PRESSURE COOK mode for 25 minutes at High. Release the pressure quickly. Serve and enjoy!

Vanilla Quinoa Bowl

Ready in about: 13-15 minutes | **Serves:** 4 | **Per Serving:** Calories 186; Carbs 3g; Fat 3g; Protein 6g

INGREDIENTS

1 cup Quinoa
2 tbsp Maple Syrup
1 tsp Vanilla Extract
1 ½ cups Water
A pinch of Sea Salt
A bunch of fresh mint leaves, for garnish

DIRECTIONS

Put all ingredients in your pressure cooker. Stir to combine well. Seal the lid and turn clockwise to seal. Set to PRESSURE COOK mode and adjust the time to 12 minutes.

When ready, do a quick pressure release. Open the lid and fluff with a fork. Ladle to serving bowls and top with mint leaves for fresh taste optionally.

Crustless Three-Meat Quiche

Ready in about: 50 minutes | **Serves:** 4 | **Per Serving:** Calories 523; Carbs 6g; Fat 40g; Protein 32g

INGREDIENTS

6 Eggs, beaten
1 cup Ground Sausage, cooked
4 Bacon slices, cooked and crumbled
2 Green Onions, chopped
½ cup Milk

4 Ham Slices, diced
1 ½ cups Water
1 cup Cheddar Cheese, grated
A pinch of Salt and Black Pepper

DIRECTIONS

Lower a trivet and pour in the water. Make a sling with foil to remove the dish. In a bowl, combine the eggs, milk, salt, and pepper. Set aside.

Mix the sausage, cheese, bacon, ham, and onions in a baking dish and pour the egg mixture over. Place the baking dish inside the cooker.

Cover with aluminum foil, and close the lid. Turn clockwise to seal and cook on MEAT/STEW mode for 30 minutes. When it goes off, do a quick pressure release. Let cool before slicing it, and serve.

Chorizo and Kale Egg Casserole

Ready in about: 30 minutes | **Serves:** 4 | **Per serving:** Calories 426; Carbs 13g; Fat 30g; Protein 24g

INGREDIENTS

8 ounces Chorizo, cooked
1 tbsp Coconut Oil
6 Eggs
¾ cup Leeks, sliced
1 ½ cups Water

1 cup Kale, chopped
1 Sweet Potato, shredded
1 tsp Garlic, minced
1 tsp roughly chopped Parsley

DIRECTIONS

Place the veggies in a greased baking dish and set aside. Set to SAUTÉ mode and melt the coconut oil. Sauté garlic, kale, and leeks for 2 minutes, until fragrant.

Beat eggs in a small bowl, and pour them over the veggies. Stir in chorizo and potato. Pour the water in the pressure cooker and set a wire rack.

Lower the baking dish onto the rack. Cook on BEANS/CHILI for 25 minutes at High. Do a quick pressure release. Sprinkle with chopped parsley.

Cherry and Dark Chocolate Oatmeal

Ready in about: 15 minutes | **Serves:** 4 | **Per serving:** Calories 283; Carbs 54g; Fat 6g; Protein 5g

INGREDIENTS

3 ½ cups Water
⅛ cup Cane Sugar
1 cup Steel-Cut Oats

3 tbsp Dark Chocolate Chips
1 cup Frozen Cherries, pitted
A pinch of Sea Salt

DIRECTIONS

Put all ingredients, except the chocolate, in your pressure cooker. Stir well to combine, seal the lid, and set to PRESSURE COOK for 12 minutes. Do a quick pressure release, stir in chocolate chips, and serve.

Big-Sized Coconut Pancake

Ready in about: 55 minutes | **Serves:** 4 | **Per serving:** Calories 358; Carbs 39g; Fat 15g; Protein 16g

INGREDIENTS

1 cup Coconut Flour
1 tsp Coconut Extract
2 tbsp Honey
2 Eggs

1 ½ cups Coconut Milk
1 cup ground Almonds
½ tsp Baking Soda
Cooking spray, for greasing

DIRECTIONS

Whisk together eggs and milk, in a bowl. Stir the other ingredients gradually, while constantly whisking. Spray the inner pot of the pressure cooker with some cooking spray and pour the batter inside.

Cook on PRESSURE COOK for 20 minutes at High. Do a quick pressure release. Serve with castor sugar.

Crispy Bacon and Egg Burger

Ready in about: 15 minutes | **Serves:** 1 | **Per Serving:** Calories 368; Carbs 31g; Fat 13g; Protein 20g

INGREDIENTS

1 Bun
1 Egg
2 slices Bacon

1 tsp Olive Oil
1 tbsp Gouda Cheese, grated
1 cup Water

DIRECTIONS

Het oil on SAUTÉ, and cook the bacon until crispy, about 2-3 minutes per side. Remove to a paper towel and wipe out excess grease. Put a trivet and pour water in the cooker. Crumble the bacon in a ramekin, and crack the egg on top.

Sprinkle with Gouda cheese, cover with aluminum foil and place the ramekin on top of the trivet. Seal the lid. Cook for 15 minutes at High on PRESSURE COOK. When ready, do a quick pressure release.

Assemble the burger by cutting the bun in half and placing the mixture in the middle.

Tip: You can assemble in between 2 slices of bread and heat in a pan for a few minutes.

Zesty and Citrusy French Toast

Ready in about: 35 minutes | **Serves:** 4 | **Per serving:** Calories 455; Carbs 64 g; Fat 16 g; Protein 15 g

INGREDIENTS

Zest of 1 Orange
1 cup Water
¼ cup Sugar
2 Large Eggs
3 tbsp Butter, melted

1 ¼ cups Milk
½ tsp Vanilla Extract
½ loaf of Challah Bread, cut into pieces
A pinch of Sea Salt

DIRECTIONS

Whisk together all ingredients, except for the water and bread, in a large bowl. Dip the bread in the bowl and coat with the mixture. Arrange coated bread pieces in a baking pan that fits inside the cooker.

Add the trivet and pour the water in. Lower the baking pan onto the trivet. Close the lid and turn clockwise to seal. Adjust the time to 25 minutes on BEANS/CHILI mode at High pressure.

When ready, press CANCEL, and do a quick pressure release by turning the valve to "open" position.

Sweet Potato Tomato Frittata

Ready in about: 28 minutes | **Serves:** 4 | **Per serving:** Calories 189; Carbs 11g; Fat 11g; Protein 10g

INGREDIENTS

6 Large Eggs, beaten
1 Tomato, chopped
¼ cup Almond Milk
1 tbsp Tomato Paste
1 tbsp Olive Oil

2 tbsp Coconut Flour
1 ½ cups Water
5 tbsp Onion, chopped
1 tsp Garlic Clove, minced
4 ounces Sweet Potatoes, shredded

DIRECTIONS

Beat eggs, tomato, milk, and oil in a bowl until mixed. Add flour, onion, garlic, and potatoes and stir. Pour the egg mixture into a greased baking dish.

Add a trivet in the Pressure cooker and pour the water in. Lay the baking dish onto the trivet and select PRESSURE COOK mode. Adjust the time to 18 minutes at High pressure.

When ready, do a quick pressure release by turning the valve to "open" position.

Lemon and Chocolate Bread Pudding

Ready in about: 45 minutes | **Serves:** 4 | **Per serving:** Calories 467; Carbs 51g; Fat 14g; Protein 12g

INGREDIENTS

3 ½ cups Bread, cubed
¾ cup Heavy Cream
1 tsp Butter, melted
2 tbsp Lemon Juice
Zest of 1 Lemon
3 Eggs

3 ounces Chocolate, chopped
½ cup Milk
¼ cup plus 1 tbsp Sugar
2 cups Water
1 tsp Almond Extract
A pinch of Salt

DIRECTIONS

Beat the eggs along with ¼ cup sugar, in a bowl. Stir in cream, lemon juice, zest, extract, milk, and salt. Soak the bread for 5 minutes. Stir in the chocolate.

Pour the water in your pressure cooker and add a trivet. Lightly grease a baking dish with melted butter. Pour in the batter. Sprinkle the remaining sugar on top. Lower the baking dish on the trivet. Seal the lid and cook on PRESSURE COOK at High pressure for 18 minutes. Do a quick pressure release.

Desserts Recipes

Bonfire Lava Cake

Ready in about: 40 minutes | **Serves:** 8 | **Per serving:** Calories 461; Carbs 28g; Fat 24g; Protein 10g

INGREDIENTS

1 cup Butter
4 tbsp Milk
4 tsp Vanilla Extract
1 ½ cups Chocolate Chips
1 ½ cups Sugar

Powdered sugar to garnish
7 tbsp All-purpose Flour
5 Eggs
1 cup Water

DIRECTIONS

Grease the cake pan with cooking spray and set aside. Fit the trivet at the bottom of the pot, and pour in water.

In a heatproof bowl, add the butter and chocolate and melt them in the microwave for about 2 minutes. Stir in sugar. Add eggs, milk, and vanilla extract and stir again. Finally, add the flour and stir it until even and smooth.

Pour the batter into the greased cake pan and use spatula to level it. Place the pan on the trivet, inside the pot, seal the lid, and select MANUAL mode at High for 15 minutes.

Do a natural pressure release for 12 minutes, then a quick pressure release. Remove the trivet with the pan on it and place the pan on a flat surface. Put a plate over the pan and flip the cake over onto the plate.

Pour the powdered sugar in a fine sieve and sift over the cake. Cut the cake into 8 slices and serve immediately.

Strawberry Cottage Cheesecake

Ready in about: 35 minutes | **Serves:** 6 | **Per serving:** Calories 241; Carbs 8g; Fat 20g; Protein 9g

INGREDIENTS

10 oz Cream Cheese
¼ cup Sugar
½ cup Cottage Cheese
One Lemon, zested and juiced
2 Eggs, cracked into a bowl

1 tsp Lemon Extract
3 tbsp Sour Cream
1 ½ cups Water
10 Strawberries, halved to decorate

DIRECTIONS

Blend with electric mixer, the cream cheese, quarter cup of sugar, cottage cheese, lemon zest, lemon juice, and lemon extract, until smooth consistency is formed. Adjust the sweet taste to liking with more sugar.

Reduce the speed of the mixer and add the eggs. Fold in at low speed until fully incorporated. Make sure not to fold the eggs in high speed to prevent a cracked crust. Grease the spring form pan with cooking spray.

Spoon the mixture into the pan. Level the top with spatula and cover with foil. Fit the trivet in the pot, and pour the water in. Place the cake pan on the trivet, seal the lid and select MANUAL at High pressure for 15 minutes.

Meanwhile, mix the sour cream and one tablespoon of sugar. Set aside. Once the timer has gone off, do a natural pressure release for 10 minutes, then a quick pressure release to let out any extra steam, and open the lid.

Remove the trivet, place the spring form pan on a flat surface, and open. Use a spatula to spread the sour cream mixture on the warm cake. Refrigerate for 8 hours. Top with strawberries; slice into 6 pieces and serve firm.

Tiramisu Cheesecake

Ready in: 1 hour + chilling time | **Serves:** 12 | **Per serving:** Calories 426, Carbs 47g, Fat 23g, Protein 8g

INGREDIENTS

1 tbsp Kahlua Liquor
1 ½ cups Ladyfingers, crushed
1 tbsp Granulated Espresso
1 tbsp Butter, melted
16 ounces Cream Cheese, softened
8 ounces Mascarpone Cheese, softened

2 Eggs
2 tbsp Powdered Sugar
½ cup White Sugar
1 tbsp Cocoa Powder
1 tsp Vanilla Extract

DIRECTIONS

In a bowl beat the cream cheese, mascarpone, and white sugar. Gradually beat in the eggs, the powdered sugar and vanilla. Combine the first 4 ingredients, in another bowl.

Spray a springform pan with cooking spray. Press the ladyfinger crust at the bottom. Pour the filling over. Cover the pan with a paper towel and then close it with aluminum foil.

Pour 1 cup of water in your pressure cooker and lower the trivet. Place the pan inside and seal the lid. Select MEAT/STEW mode and set to 35 minutes at High pressure.

Wait for about 10 minutes before pressing Cancel and releasing the pressure quickly. Allow to cool completely before refrigerating the cheesecake for 4 hours.

Chocolate and Banana Squares

Ready in about: 25 minutes | **Serves:** 6 | **Per serving:** Calories 140; Carbs 14g; Fat 10g; Protein 3g

INGREDIENTS

½ cup Butter
3 Bananas
2 tbsp Cocoa Powder

1 ½ cups Water
Cooking spray, to grease

DIRECTIONS

Place the bananas and butter in a bowl and mash finely with a fork. Add the cocoa powder and stir until well combined. Grease a baking dish that fits into the pressure cooker.

Pour the banana and almond batter into the dish. Pour the water in the pressure cooker and lower the trivet. Place the baking dish on top of the trivet and seal the lid.

Select PRESSURE COOK mode, for 15 minutes at High pressure. When it goes off, do a quick release. Let cool for a few minutes before cutting into squares

Coconut Pear Delight

Ready in about: 15 minutes | **Serves:** 2 | **Per serving:** Calories 140; Carbs 18g; Fat 8g; Protein 2g

INGREDIENTS

¼ cup Flour
1 cup Coconut Milk

2 Large Pears, peeled and diced
¼ cup Shredded Coconut, unsweetened

DIRECTIONS

Combine all ingredients in your Pressure cooker. Seal the lid, select PRESSURE COOK and set the timer to 5 minutes at High pressure. When ready, do a quick pressure release. Divide the mixture between two bowls.

Fruity Cheesecake

Ready in about: 30 minutes | **Serves:** 6 | **Per serving:** Calories 498; Carbs 48g; Fat 28g; Protein 9g

INGREDIENTS

1 ½ cups Graham Cracker Crust
1 cup Raspberries
3 cups Cream Cheese
1 tbsp fresh Orange Juice
3 Eggs

½ stick Butter, melted
¾ cup Sugar
1 tsp Vanilla Paste
1 tsp finely grated Orange Zest
1 ½ cups Water

DIRECTIONS

Insert the tray into the pressure cooker, and add 1 ½ cups of water. Grease a spring form. Mix in graham cracker crust with sugar and butter, in a bowl. Press the mixture to form a crust at the bottom.

Blend the raspberries and cream cheese with an electric mixer. Crack in the eggs and keep mixing until well combined. Mix in the remaining ingredients, and give it a good stir.

Pour this mixture into the pan, and cover the pan with aluminium foil. Lay the spring form on the tray.

Select PRESSURE COOK mode and cook for 20 minutes at High pressure. Once the cooking is complete, do a quick pressure release. Refrigerate the cheesecake for at least 2 hours.

Cinnamon and Lemon Apples

Ready in about: 13 minutes | **Serves:** 2 | **Per serving:** Calories 144; Carbs 25g; Fat 5g; Protein 2g

INGREDIENTS

2 Apples, peeled and cut into wedges
½ cup Lemon Juice
½ tsp Cinnamon

1 tbsp Butter
1 cup Water

DIRECTIONS

Combine lemon juice and water in the pressure cooker. Place the apple wedges in the steaming basket and lower the basket into the cooker. Seal the lid, select the PRESSURE COOK for 3 minutes at High.

Release the pressure quickly. Open the lid and remove the steaming basket. Transfer the apple wedges to a bowl. Drizzle with butter and sprinkle with cinnamon.

Compote with Blueberries and Lemon

Ready in about: 10 minutes + chilling time | **Serves:** 4 | **Per serving:** Calories 220; Carbs 61g; Fat 0g; Protein 1g

INGREDIENTS

2 cups Frozen Blueberries
2 tbsp Arrowroot or Cornstarch
¾ cups Coconut Sugar

Juice of ½ Lemon
½ cup Water + 2 tbsp

DIRECTIONS

Place blueberries, lemon juice, 1/2 cup water, and coconut sugar in your cooker. Seal the lid, cook on STEAM mode for 3 minutes at High pressure. Once done, do a quick pressure.

Meanwhile, combine the arrowroot and water, in a bowl. Stir in the mixture into the blueberries and cook until the mixture thickens, lid off, on SAUTÉ. Transfer the compote to a bowl and let cool completely before refrigerating for 2 hours.

Full Coconut Cake

Ready in about: 55 minutes | **Serves:** 4 | **Per serving:** Calories 350; Carbs 47g; Fat 14g; Protein 8g

INGREDIENTS

3 Eggs, Yolks and Whites separated
¾ cup Coconut Flour
½ tsp Coconut Extract
1 ½ cups warm Coconut Milk

½ cup Coconut Sugar
2 tbsp Coconut Oil, melted
1 cup Water

DIRECTIONS

In a bowl, beat in the egg yolks along with the coconut sugar. In a separate bowl, beat the whites until soft form peaks. Stir in coconut extract and coconut oil. Gently fold in the coconut flour. Line a baking dish and pour the batter inside. Cover with aluminum foil.

Pour the water in your pressure cooker and add a wire rack. Lower the dish onto the rack. Seal the lid, set on MEAT/STEW, cook for 40 minutes at High pressure. Do a quick pressure release, and serve.

Very Berry Cream

Ready in about: 4 hours 10 minutes | **Serves:** 2 | **Per serving:** Calories 90; Carbs 11g; Fat 3g; Protein 1g

INGREDIENTS

½ cup Blueberries
½ cup Strawberries, chopped
½ cup Raspberries

1 cup Milk
¼ tsp Vanilla Extract

DIRECTIONS

Place all ingredients, except the vanilla extract, inside your pressure cooker. Seal the lid, select PRESSURE COOK mode and set the timer to 2 minutes at High pressure.

When it goes off, do a quick pressure release. Remove to a blender. Add vanilla extract and pulse until smooth. Divide between two serving glasses and cool for 4 hours before serving.

Peanut Butter Bars

Ready in about: 55 minutes | **Serves:** 6 | **Per serving:** Calories 561; Carbs 61g; Fat 18g; Protein 8g

INGREDIENTS

1 cup Flour
1 ½ cups Water
1 Egg
½ cup Peanut Butter, softened
½ cup Butter, softened

1 cup Oats
½ cup Sugar
½ tsp Baking Soda
½ tsp Salt
½ cup Brown Sugar

DIRECTIONS

Grease a springform pan and line it with parchment paper. Set aside. Beat together the eggs, peanut butter, butter, salt, white sugar, and brown sugar. Fold in the oats, flour, and baking soda.

Press the batter into the pan. Cover the pan with a paper towel and with a piece of foil. Pour the water into the pressure cooker and add a trivet. Lower the springform pan onto the trivet. Seal the lid.

Press MEAT/STEW mode, and cook for 35 minutes at High pressure. When ready, do a quick release. Wait for 15 minutes before inverting onto a plate and cutting into bars.

Milk Dumplings in Sweet Cardamom Sauce

Ready in about: 30 minutes | **Serves:** 20 | **Per serving:** Calories 134; Carbs 29g; Fat 2g; Protein 2g

INGREDIENTS

6 cups Water
2 ½ cups Sugar
3 tbsp Lime Juice

6 cups Milk
1 tsp ground Cardamom

DIRECTIONS

Bring to a boil the milk, on SAUTÉ, and stir in the lime juice. The solids should start to separate. Pour milk through a cheesecloth-lined colander. Drain as much liquid as you can. Place the paneer on a smooth surface. Form a ball and divide into 20 equal pieces.

Pour water and bring to a boil. Add sugar and cardamom and cook until dissolved. Shape the dumplings into balls, and place them in the syrup. Seal the lid and cook for 5 minutes at High.

Once done, do a quick pressure release. Let cool and refrigerate for at least 2 hours.

Black Currant Poached Peaches

Ready in about: 15 minutes | **Serves:** 4 | **Per serving:** Calories 140; Carbs 15g; Fat 1g; Protein 1g

INGREDIENTS

½ cup Black Currants
4 Peaches, peeled, pits removed

1 cup Freshly Squeezed Orange Juice
1 Cinnamon Stick

DIRECTIONS

Place black currants and orange juice in a blender. Blend until the mixture becomes smooth. Pour the mixture in your pressure cooker, and add the cinnamon stick.

Add the peaches to the steamer basket and then insert the basket into the pot. Seal the lid, select PRESSURE COOK mode, and set to 5 minutes at High pressure.

When done, do a quick pressure release. Serve the peaches drizzled with sauce, to enjoy!

Restaurant-Style Crème Brulee

Ready in: 30 min + 6h for cooling | **Serves:** 4 | **Per serving:** Calories 487; Carbs 23g; Fat 41g; Protein 5g

INGREDIENTS

3 cups Heavy Whipping Cream
6 tbsp Sugar
7 large Egg Yolks

2 tbsp Vanilla Extract
2 cups Water

DIRECTIONS

In a mixing bowl, whisk the yolks, vanilla, whipping cream, and half of the sugar, until well combined.

Pour the mixture into the ramekins and cover them with aluminium foil. Fit the trivet in the pot, and pour in the water. Lay 3 ramekins on the trivet and place the remaining ramekins to sit on the edges of the ramekins below.

Seal the lid and select MANUAL mode at High pressure for 8 minutes. Do a natural pressure release for 15 minutes, then a quick pressure release. With a napkin in hand, remove the ramekins onto a flat surface.

Then refrigerate for at least 6 hours. After refrigeration, remove the ramekins and remove the aluminium foil. Sprinkle the remaining sugar over and use a hand torch to brown the top of the crème brulee.

Citrus Cheesecake

Ready in about: 55 minutes | **Serves:** 8 | **Per serving:** Calories 353; Carbs 21g; Fat 27g; Protein 7g

INGREDIENTS

4 oz Graham Crackers
1 tsp ground Cinnamon

For the Filling:
1 lb Cream Cheese, room temperature
¾ cup granulated Sugar
¼ cup Sour Cream, room temperature
2 Eggs
1 tsp Vanilla Extract

3 tbsp Butter, melted
1 cup Water

1 tsp Lemon Zest
1 tbsp Lemon Juice
1 pinch Salt
1 cup Water

DIRECTIONS

Mix graham crackers and cinnamon in a blender and blitz until the mixture resembles wet sand. Add the butter and blend a few more times. Pour crumbs into the bottom of a baking dish in a single layer.

For the filling, beat sour cream, sugar, and cream cheese with an electric mixer until creamy and fluffy, for about 2-3 minutes. Add eggs, vanilla extract, lemon zest, lemon juice, and salt.

Beat the mixture until the color is solid, for about 1-2 minutes more. Stir in filling over crust in the baking dish. Pour the water into your pressure cooker and lower the trivet.

Place the baking dish on the trivet. Seal the lid, and set to CAKE mode for 40 minutes at High. Once ready, do a quick pressure release. Refrigerate for at least 2 hours or until set. Once the cake has set, carefully remove from the dish and transfer to a serving plate.

Almond Pear Wedges

Ready in about: 15 minutes | **Serves:** 3 | **Per serving:** Calories 240; Carbs 22g; Fat 17g; Protein 1g

INGREDIENTS

2 Large Pears, peeled and cut into wedges
3 tbsp Almond Butter

2 tbsp Olive Oil

DIRECTIONS

Pour 1 cup of water in the ´pressure cooker. Place the pear wedges in a steamer basket and then lower the basket at the bottom. Seal the lid, and cook for 2 minutes High pressure.

When the timer goes off, do a quick pressure release. Remove the basket, discard the water and wipe clean the cooker. Press the SAUTÉ and heat the oil. Add the pears and cook until browned. Top them with almond butter, to serve.

Creamy Almond and Apple Delight

Ready in about: 14 minutes | **Serves:** 4 | **Per serving:** Calories 60; Carbs 10g; Fat 1g; Protein 0

INGREDIENTS

3 Apples, peeled and diced
½ cup Almonds, chopped or slivered

½ cup Milk
¼ tsp Cinnamon

DIRECTIONS

Place all ingredients in the pressure cooker. Stir well to combine and seal the lid. Cook on PRESSURE COOK for 4 minutes at High. Release the pressure quickly. Divide the mixture among 4 serving bowls.

Pressure Cooked Cherry Pie

Ready in about: 45 minutes | **Serves:** 6 | **Per serving:** Calories 393; Carbs 69g; Fat 12g; Protein 2g

INGREDIENTS

1 9-inch double Pie Crust
2 cups Water
½ tsp Vanilla Extract
4 cups Cherries, pitted

¼ tsp Almond Extract
4 tbsp Quick Tapioca
1 cup Sugar
A pinch of Salt

DIRECTIONS

Pour water inside your cooker and add the trivet. Combine the cherries with tapioca, sugar, extracts, and salt, in a bowl. Place one pie crust at the bottom of a lined springform pan.

Spread the cherries mixture and top with the other crust. Lower the pan onto the trivet. Seal the lid, set to PRESSURE COOK mode for 18 minutes at High pressure. Once cooking is completed, do a quick pressure release. Let cool the pie on a cooling rack. Slice to serve.

Honeyed Butternut Squash Pie

Ready in about: 30 minutes | **Serves:** 4 | **Per serving:** Calories 172; Carbs 39g; Fat 2g; Protein 3g

INGREDIENTS

1 pound Butternut Squash, diced
1 Egg
¼ cup Honey
½ cup Milk

½ tsp Cinnamon
½ tbsp Cornstarch
1 cup Water
A pinch of Sea Salt

DIRECTIONS

Pour the water inside your pressure cooker and add a trivet. Lower the butternut squash onto the trivet. Seal the lid, and cook on PRESSURE COOK mode for 4 minutes at High pressure.

Meanwhile, whisk all remaining ingredients in a bowl. Do a quick pressure. Drain the squash and add it to the milk mixture. Pour the batter into a greased baking dish. Place in the cooker, and seal the lid.

Cook for 10 minutes at High pressure. Do a quick pressure release. Transfer pie to wire rack to cool.

Impossible Oatmeal Chocolate Cookies

Ready in about: 30 minutes | **Serves:** 2 | **Per serving:** Calories 412; Carbs 59g; Fat 20g; Protein 6g

INGREDIENTS

¼ cup Whole Wheat Flour
¼ cup Oats
1 tbsp Butter
2 tbsp Sugar
½ tsp Vanilla Extract

1 tbsp Honey
2 tbsp Milk
2 tsp Coconut Oil
¾ tsp Sea Salt
3 tbsp Chocolate Chips

DIRECTIONS

Mix all ingredients, in a bowl. Line a baking pan with parchment paper. Shape lemon-sized cookies out of the mixture, and flatten onto the lined pan. Pour 1 cup water, and add a trivet.

Lower the baking pan onto the rack. Seal the lid, set on POULTRY mode for 15 minutes at High pressure. When cooking is over, do a quick pressure. Cool for 15 minutes to serve.

Easiest Pressure Cooked Raspberry Curd

Ready in: 10 minutes + chilling time | **Serves:** 5 | **Per serving:** Calories 249; Carbs 48g; Fat 7g; Protein 2g

INGREDIENTS

12 ounces Raspberries
2 tbsp Butter
Juice of ½ Lemon

1 cup Sugar
2 Egg Yolks

DIRECTIONS

Add the raspberries, sugar, and lemon juice in your pressure cooker. Seal the lid and cook for 1 minute at High. Once ready, do a quick pressure release.

With a hand mixer, puree the raspberries and discard the seeds. Whisk the yolks in a bowl. Combine the yolks with the hot raspberry puree. Pour the mixture in your pressure cooker.

On SAUTÉ, cook for a minute, lid off. Stir in the butter and cook for a couple more minutes, until thick. Transfer to a container with a lid. Refrigerate for at least an hour before serving.

Homemade Chocolate Pudding

Ready in about: 20 minutes | **Serves:** 4 | **Per serving:** Calories 388; Carbs 33g; Fat 29g; Protein 11g

INGREDIENTS

Zest and Juice from ½ Lime
2 oz chocolate, coarsely chopped
¼ cup Sugar
2 tbsp Butter, softened
3 Eggs, separated into whites and yolks

¼ cup Cornstarch
1 cup Almond Milk
A pinch of Salt
½ tsp Ginger, caramelized
1 ½ cups of Water

DIRECTIONS

Combine together the sugar, cornstarch, salt, and softened butter, in a bowl. Mix in lime juice and grated lime zest. Add in the egg yolks, ginger, almond milk, and whisk to mix well.

Mix in egg whites. Pour this mixture into custard cups and cover with aluminium foil. Add 1 ½ cups of water to the pressure cooker. Place a trivet into the pressure cooker, and lower the cups onto the rack.

Select CAKE mode and cook for 25 minutes at High Pressure. Once the cooking is complete, do a quick pressure release. Carefully open the lid, and stir in the chocolate. Serve chilled.

Tutty Fruity Sauce

Ready in about: 15 minutes | **Serves:** 2 | **Per serving:** Calories 125; Carbs 16g; Fat 4g; Protein 1g

INGREDIENTS

1 cup Pineapple Chunks
1 cup Berry Mix
2 Apples, peeled and diced

¼ cup Almonds, chopped
¼ cup Fresh Orange Juice
1 tbsp Olive Oil

DIRECTIONS

Pour ½ cup of water, orange juice, and fruits, in the pressure cooker. Give it a good stir and seal the lid. Press PRESSURE COOK and set the timer to 5 minutes at High pressure.

When it goes off, release the pressure quickly. Blend the mixture with a hand blender and immediately stir in the coconut oil. Serve sprinkled with chopped almonds. Enjoy!

Chocolate Molten Lava Cake

Ready in about: 20 minutes | **Serves:** 4 | **Per serving:** Calories 413; Carbs 48g; Fat 23g; Protein 8g

INGREDIENTS

2 tbsp Butter, melted
1 cup Dark Chocolate, melted
6 tbsp Almond Flour
1 cup Water
1 tsp Vanilla
3 Eggs plus
1 Yolk, beaten
¾ cup Coconut Sugar

DIRECTIONS

Combine all ingredients, except the water, in a bowl. Grease four ramekins with cooking spray. Divide the filling between the ramekins. Pour the water in your Pressure cooker.

Place the ramekins on the trivet. Seal the lid and cook for 9 minutes at High pressure. When ready, do a quick pressure release. Serve immediately and enjoy.

Vanilla and Yogurt Light Cheesecake

Ready in: 70 minutes + chilling time | **Serves:** 8 | **Per serving:** Calories 280; Carbs 26g, Fat 9g, Protein 6g

INGREDIENTS

2 Eggs
¼ cup Sugar
1 ½ cups Yogurt
1 tsp Vanilla
4 ounces Cream Cheese, softened
1 ½ cups ground Graham Cracker Crumbs
4 tbsp Butter, melted
1 cup Water

DIRECTIONS

Mix the butter and cracker crumbs, and press the mixture onto the bottom of a springform pan. In a bowl, beat cream cheese with yogurt, vanilla, and sugar. Beat in the eggs one at a time. Spread the filling on top of the crust. Pour water in your cooker and add the trivet.

Lower the pan onto the trivet. Lock the lid, press MEAT/STEW for 35 minutes at High. Once cooking is completed, do a quick pressure release. Let cool and refrigerate for 6 hours.

Buttery Banana Bread

Ready in about: 45 minutes | **Serves:** 12 | **Per serving:** Calories 295; Carbs 48g; Fat 14g; Protein 5g

INGREDIENTS

3 ripe Bananas, mashed
1 ¼ cups Sugar
1 cup Milk
2 cups all-purpose Flour
1 tsp Baking Soda
1 tsp Baking Powder
1 tbsp Orange Juice
1 stick Butter, room temperature
A pinch of Salt
¼ tsp Cinnamon
½ tsp Pure Vanilla Extract

DIRECTIONS

In a bowl, mix together the flour, baking powder, baking soda, sugar, vanilla, and salt. Add in the bananas, cinnamon, and orange juice. Slowly stir in the butter and milk.

Give it a good stir until everything is well combined. Pour the batter into a medium-sized round pan.

Place the trivet at the bottom of the pressure cooker and fill with 2 cups of water. Place the pan on the trivet. Select PRESSURE COOK and cook for 40 minutes at High. Do a quick pressure release.

Berry-Vanilla Pudding Temptation

Ready in: 35 minutes + 6h for cooling | **Serves:** 4 | **Per serving:** Calories 183; Carbs 12g; Fat 14g; Protein 3g

INGREDIENTS

1 cup Heavy Cream
4 Egg Yolks
4 tbsp Water + 1 ½ cups Water
½ cup Milk

1 tsp Vanilla
½ cup Sugar
4 Raspberries
4 Blueberries

DIRECTIONS

Fit the trivet at the bottom of the pot, and pour one and a half cups of water. In a small pan set over low heat on a stove top, add 4 tablespoons for water and the sugar. Stir constantly until it dissolves. Turn off the heat.

Add milk, heavy cream, and vanilla. Stir it with a whisk until evenly combined. Crack the eggs into a bowl and add a tablespoon of the cream mixture. Whisk, and then very slowly, whisk in the remaining cream mixture.

Pour the mixture into the ramekins and place them on the trivet. Seal the lid and select MANUAL mode at High Pressure for 4 minutes. Once the timer has gone off, do a quick pressure release. With a napkin in hand, carefully remove the ramekins onto a flat surface. Let them cool for about 15 minutes and then refrigerate for 6 hours.

After 6 hours, remove from the fridge and garnish with raspberries and blueberries.

Peaches with Chocolate Biscuits

Ready in about: 20 minutes | **Serves:** 4 | **Per serving:** Calories 302; Carbs 39g; Fat 16g; Protein 7g

INGREDIENTS

4 small Peaches, halved lengthwise and pitted
8 dried Dates, chopped
4 tbsp Walnuts, chopped
1 cup Coarsely Crumbled Cookies

1 tsp Cinnamon Powder
¼ tsp grated nutmeg
¼ tsp ground Cloves

DIRECTIONS

Pour 2 cups of water into the pressure cooker and add a trivet. Arrange the peaches on a greased baking dish cut-side-up. To prepare the filling, mix all of the remaining ingredients.

Stuff the peaches with the mixture. Cover with aluminium foil and lower it onto the trivet.

Seal the lid, press PRESSURE COOK and cook for 15 minutes at High Pressure. Do a quick pressure release.

Hazelnut Chocolate Spread

Ready in about: 25 minutes | **Serves:** 16 | **Per serving:** Calories 166; Carbs 23g; Fat 10g; Protein 1g

INGREDIENTS

1 ¼ pounds Hazelnuts, halved
½ cup Cocoa Powder
½ cups icing Sugar, sifted
1 tsp Vanilla Extract

¼ tsp Cardamom, grated
¼ tsp Cinnamon powder
½ tsp grated Nutmeg
10 ounces Water

DIRECTIONS

Place the hazelnut in a blender and blend until you obtain a paste. Place in the cooker along with the remaining ingredients. Seal the lid, select RICE and cook for 15 minutes at High pressure.

Once the cooking is over, allow for a natural pressure release, for 10 minutes.

Apricots with Blueberry Sauce

Ready in about: 15 minutes | **Serves:** 4 | **Per serving:** Calories 205; Carbs 45g; Fat 2g; Protein 2g

INGREDIENTS

8 Apricots, pitted and halved
2 cups Blueberries
¼ cup Honey
1 ½ tbsp Cornstarch

½ Vanilla Bean, sliced lengthwise
¼ tsp ground Cardamom
½ Cinnamon stick
1 ¼ cups Water

DIRECTIONS

Add all ingredients, except for the honey and the cornstarch, to your pressure cooker. Seal the lid, select RICE mode and cook for 8 minutes at High pressure. Do a quick pressure release and open the lid.

Remove the apricots with a slotted spoon. Choose SAUTÉ, add the honey and cornstarch, then let simmer until the sauce thickens, for about 5 minutes.

Split up the apricots among serving plates and top with the blueberry sauce, to serve.

Coconut Crème Caramel

Ready in about: 20 minutes | **Serves:** 4 | **Per serving:** Calories 121; Carbs 17g; Fat 3g; Protein 3g

INGREDIENTS

2 Eggs
7 ounces Condensed Coconut Milk
½ cup Coconut Milk

1 ½ cups Water
½ tsp Vanilla
4 tbsp Caramel Syrup

DIRECTIONS

Divide the caramel syrup between 4 small ramekins. Pour water in the pressure cooker and add the trivet. In a bowl, beat the rest of the ingredients. Divide them between the ramekins. Cover them with aluminum foil and lower onto the trivet.

Seal the lid, and set on RICE mode for 15 minutes at High pressure. Once cooking is completed, do a quick pressure release. Let cool completely. To unmold the flan, insert a spatula along the ramekin' sides and flip onto a dish.

Hot Milk Chocolate Fondue

Ready in about: 5 minutes | **Serves:** 12 | **Per serving:** Calories 198; Carbs 12g; Fat 16g; Protein 3g

INGREDIENTS

10 ounces Milk Chocolate, chopped into small pieces
2 tsp Coconut Liqueur
8 ounces Heavy Whipping Cream

¼ tsp Cinnamon Powder
1 ½ cups Lukewarm Water
A pinch of Salt

DIRECTIONS

Melt the chocolate in a heat-proof recipient. Add the remaining ingredients, except for the liqueur. Transfer this recipient to the metal trivet. Pour 1 ½ cups of water into the cooker, and place a trivet inside.

Seal the lid, select PRESSURE COOK and cook for 5 minutes at High.

Once the cooking is complete, do a quick pressure release. Pull out the container with tongs. Mix in the coconut liqueur and serve right now with fresh fruits. Enjoy!

Delicious Stuffed Apples

Ready in about: 20 minutes | **Serves:** 6 | **Per serving:** Calories 152; 3g Fat; 21g Carbs; 2g Protein

INGREDIENTS

3 ½ pounds Apples, cored
½ cup dried Apricots, chopped
¼ cup Sugar
¼ cup Pecans, chopped
¼ cup Graham Cracker Crumbs

¼ tsp Cardamom
½ tsp grated Nutmeg
½ tsp ground Cinnamon
1 ¼ cups Red Wine

DIRECTIONS

Lay the apples at the bottom of your cooker, and pour in the red wine. Combine the other ingredients, except the crumbs. Seal the lid, and cook at High pressure for 15 minutes.

Once ready, do a quick pressure release. Top with graham cracker crumbs and serve!

Homemade Egg Custard

Ready in about: 20 minutes | **Serves:** 4 | **Per serving:** Calories 425; Carbs 48g; Fat 25g; Protein 11g

INGREDIENTS

1 Egg plus 2 Egg yolks
½ cup Sugar
½ cups Milk

2 cups Heavy Cream
½ tsp pure rum extract
2 cups Water

DIRECTIONS

Beat the egg and the egg yolks in a bowl. Gently add pure rum extract. Mix in the milk and heavy cream. Give it a good, and add the sugar. Pour this mixture into 4 ramekins.

Add 2 cups of water, insert the trivet, and lay the ramekins on the trivet. Select PRESSURE COOK and cook for 10 minutes at High. Do a quick pressure release. Wait a bit before removing from ramekins.

Almond Butter Bananas

Ready in about: 8 minutes | **Serve:** 1 | **Per serving:** Calories 310; Carbs 28g; Fat 23g; Protein 2g

INGREDIENTS

1 Banana, sliced
1 tbsp Coconut oil

2 tbsp Almond Butter
½ tsp Cinnamon

DIRECTIONS

Melt oil on SAUTÉ mode. Add banana slices and fry them for a couple of minutes, or until golden on both sides.

Top the fried bananas with almond butter and sprinkle with cinnamon.

Poached Pears with Orange and Cinnamon

Ready in about: 20 minutes | **Serves:** 4 | **Per serving:** Calories 170; Carbs 43g; Fat 1g; Protein 1g

INGREDIENTS

4 Pears cut in half
1 tsp powdered Ginger
1 tsp Nutmeg

1 cup Orange Juice
2 tsp Cinnamon
¼ cup Coconut Sugar

DIRECTIONS

Place the trivet at the bottom of the pressure cooker. Stir in the juice and spices. Lay the pears on the trivet. Seal the lid, cook on PRESSURE COOK for 7 minutes, at High pressure.

When ready, do a quick release. Remove pears onto a serving plate. Pour juice over to serve.

Crema Catalana

Ready in about: 20 minutes + 2h chilled | **Serves:** 4 | **Per serving:** Calories 420; Carbs 57g; Fat 13g; Protein 4g

INGREDIENTS

1 ¼ cups Water
½ tsp Vanilla Paste
1 ½ cups warm Heavy Cream

3 large-sized Egg yolks,
1 cup Sugar

DIRECTIONS

In a bowl, mix the vanilla, heavy cream, sugar and egg yolks. Fill 4 ramekins with this mixture and wrap with foil. Pour the water into the Pressure Cooker. Add the trivet and lay the ramekins on top.

Seal the lid, press PRESSURE COOK and cook for 10 minutes at High. Once the cooking is complete, do a quick pressure release. Refrigerate Crema Catalana for at least 2 hours.

Juicy Apricots with Walnuts and Goat Cheese

Ready in about: 10 minutes | **Serves:** 4 | **Per serving:** Calories 302; Carbs 31g; Fat 17g; Protein 11g

INGREDIENTS

1 pound Apricots, pitted and halved
½ cup Orange Juice
4 tbsp Honey
¾ cup Goat Cheese
½ cup Walnuts, chopped

¼ tsp grated Nutmeg
½ tsp ground Cinnamon
½ tsp Vanilla Extract
½ cup Water

DIRECTIONS

Add all ingredients, except for cheese and walnuts, to your pressure cooker. Select PRESSURE COOK mode and cook for 5 minutes at High pressure. Do a quick pressure release. Remove apricots to serving plates and top with cheese and walnuts, to enjoy.

Apple and Peach Compote

Ready in about: 2 hours 10 minutes | **Serves:** 4 | **Per serving:** Calories 120; Carbs 23g; Fat 1g; Protein 1g

INGREDIENTS

2 ½ cups Peach, chopped
2 cups Apples, diced
Juice of 1 Orange

2 tbsp Cornstarch
½ cup Water
¼ tsp Cinnamon

DIRECTIONS

Place the peaches, apples, water, and orange juice, in the pressure cooker. Stir to combine and seal the lid, Select PRESSURE COOK and set the timer to 3 minutes at High pressure.

Do a quick release. Press SAUTÉ and whisk in the cornstarch. Cook until the compote thickens, for about 5 minutes. When thickened, transfer to an airtight container, and refrigerate for at least 2 hours.

Made in the USA
Lexington, KY
01 February 2019